PASTA
& more!

Texts by Leonardo Castellucci,
Carla Bardi, and Mariapaola Dèttore

Photography by Marco Lanza

Alexandria, Virginia

TIME-LIFE IS A TRADEMARK OF TIME WARNER INC.
AND AFFILIATED COMPANIES

TIME-LIFE BOOKS
President and CEO   George Artandi

TIME-LIFE CUSTOM PUBLISHING
Vice President and Publisher   Neil Levin
Editor for Special Markets   Anna Burgard
Director of Acquisitions and Editorial Resources   Jennifer Pearce

TIME-LIFE is a trademark of Time Warner Inc. U.S.A.

Cip data available upon application
ISBN 0-7370-0071-6

This book was conceived, edited and designed by McRae Books Srl, Florence Italy.
Text: Leonardo Castellucci, Carla Bardi, Mariapaola Dèttore
Photography: Marco Lanza
Set Design: Cinzia Calamai, Rosalba Gioffrè, Sara Vignozzi
Design: Marco Nardi
Translation from the Italian: Anne McRae and Erika Paoli
Layout and cutouts: Ornella Fassio and Adriano Nardi
Editing: Alison Leach, Anne McRae, Lynn McRae,

Color separations: R.A.F. and Fotolito Toscana, Florence, Italy
Printed and bound in China

Cover design: WorkHorse Creative

CONTENTS

INTRODUCTION

Modern Italian cooking combines simplicity and the use of fresh, natural ingredients to create a mouthwatering array of tasty, easy-to-prepare dishes. Pasta and More *brings you over three hundred classic recipes drawn from the many regional traditions that make up Italian cuisine. From the hot, sun-baked regions of the south, such as Sicily and Calabria, come spicy or sweet and sour spaghetti dishes; from Rome, Tuscany, and Bologna in central Italy, come recipes for fresh and filled pasta, including tagliatelle, tortellini, and many others; while from the more temperate north we have included wonderful suggestions for steaming risottos and hearty vegetable soups. There are also a host of tempting recipes for appetizers, gnocchi, and polenta. Many recipes are introduced by snippets of Italian folklore or helpful hints, while others provide variations. Each dish is accompanied by a suggestion for the best Italian wine to serve. To complete the book, and to make it really useful, the last chapter explains how to make fresh pasta at home. As the Italians say —* Buon appetito!

Salsa al pomodoro
Simple tomato sauce

Oil-based tomato sauce goes well with all dried, hard wheat pasta, such as spaghetti, spaghettini, penne, bucatini, and fusilli. It is also good with spinach and whole wheat pasta.

Serves: 6-7 (1¼ lb/625 g of pasta); Preparation: 15 minutes; Cooking: 20 minutes; Level of difficulty: Simple

Put the garlic and oil in a large skillet (frying pan) and sauté over medium heat until the garlic is golden brown. § Add the basil and tomatoes. Season with salt and pepper, and simmer for about 15–20 minutes, or until the oil begins to separate from the tomato.

VARIATIONS
– Sauté 1 small onion, 1 carrot, 1 stalk celery, and 1 tablespoon parsley, all finely chopped, with the garlic.
– Add ½ teaspoon crushed chilies.
– Crumble 2 anchovy fillets into the sauce with the tomatoes.
– Add 1 tablespoon small salted capers.

■ INGREDIENTS

• 3 cloves garlic, minced
• 4 tablespoons extra-virgin olive oil
• 2 tablespoons torn fresh basil leaves
• 1½ lb/750 g peeled and chopped fresh or canned tomatoes
• salt and freshly ground black pepper

Salsa di pomodoro fresco
Fresh tomato sauce

A simple sauce to serve in summer when tomatoes are tasty and abundant. It goes well with spaghetti, penne, fusilli, and many other dried pastas.

Serves: 4-5 (1 lb/500 g of pasta); Preparation: 10 minutes; Level of difficulty: Simple

Combine the tomatoes, garlic, oil, and basil in a bowl and season with salt and pepper. Mix well. § Set aside for about 15 minutes before tossing with the cooked pasta.

■ INGREDIENTS

• 1 lb/500 g firm, ripe tomatoes, diced
• 1 clove garlic, finely chopped
• 4 tablespoons extra-virgin olive oil
• 12 fresh basil leaves, torn
• salt and freshly ground black pepper

Salsa di burro e pomodoro
Tomato and butter sauce

This sauce is delicious with all types of fresh pasta and gnocchi.

Serves: 4-5 (1 lb/500 g of pasta); Preparation: 10 minutes; Cooking: 30 minutes; Level of difficulty: Simple

Combine the garlic and onion in a skillet (frying pan) with the butter and oil. Sauté over medium heat until the onion is transparent. § Add the tomatoes and season with salt and pepper. Simmer over medium-low heat for about 25 minutes. Add the basil just before removing from heat.

VARIATION
– Stir 1 cup/8 oz/250 ml light (single) cream into the sauce after removing from heat for a *rosé* or pink sauce.

■ INGREDIENTS

• 1 clove garlic, finely chopped
• 1 onion, finely chopped
• ¼ cup/2 oz/60 g butter
• 1 tablespoon extra-virgin olive oil
• 12 oz/375 g peeled and chopped fresh or canned tomatoes
• 6 fresh basil leaves, torn
• salt and freshly ground black pepper

Right: Salsa al pomodoro

Ragù di carne alla bolognese
Bolognese meat sauce

The secret of a successful ragù lies in the cooking; it should be simmered over a low heat for at least 2½ hours. It can be made ahead and kept in the refrigerator for up to 3 days, or frozen. Ragù is very versatile and can be served with most dried pasta shapes, with fresh, long pasta, such as tagliatelle, with many filled pasta dishes, and with potato and spinach gnocchi.

Serves: 6-7 (1¼ lb/625 g of pasta); Preparation: 30 minutes; Cooking: 3 hours; Level of difficulty: Simple

Combine the pancetta, onion, celery, and carrot in a sauté pan with the butter and cook over medium heat until the onion is light gold in color. § Add the beef, pork, and sausage and cook until the mixture is all the same color. Add the clove, cinnamon, and pepper. Stir in the tomatoes and continue to cook over medium heat for 15 minutes. § Add the milk and season with salt. Turn the heat down to low and simmer for at least 2½ hours, stirring from time to time.

■ INGREDIENTS

- ½ cup/2 oz/60 g diced pancetta
- 1 medium onion, 1 stalk celery, 1 small carrot, all finely chopped
- ¼ cup/2 oz/60 g butter
- 8 oz/250 g ground beef
- 2 oz/60 g ground pork
- 2 oz/60 g Italian pork sausage, peeled and crumbled
- 1 freshly ground clove
- dash of cinnamon
- ¼ teaspoon freshly ground black pepper
- one 14-oz/450-g can peeled and chopped tomatoes
- 1 cup/8 fl oz/250 ml whole/full cream milk
- salt

Sugo di carne veloce
Quick meat sauce

Serves: 4-5 (1 lb/500 g of pasta); Preparation: 20 minutes; Cooking: 25 minutes; Level of difficulty: Simple

Soak the mushrooms in a bowl of tepid water for 20 minutes. Rinse well and chop coarsely. § Put the onion, garlic, pancetta, and oil in a skillet (frying pan) and sauté over medium heat until the onion is transparent. Add the sausage and sauté for 5 more minutes. § Add the tomatoes and mushrooms, season with salt and pepper, and simmer over medium-low heat for about 20 minutes, stirring frequently.

■ INGREDIENTS

- 1 oz/30 g dried porcini mushrooms
- 1 large onion, finely chopped
- 1 clove garlic, finely chopped
- ½ cup/2 oz/60 g diced pancetta
- 2 tablespoons extra-virgin olive oil
- 8 oz/250 g Italian pork sausage, peeled and crumbled
- one 14-oz/450-g can peeled and chopped tomatoes
- salt and freshly ground black pepper

Right: *Tortellini al ragù di carne alla bolognese*

Ragù al pomodoro
Tomato meat sauce

This tomato ragù goes very well with any pasta and it is also perfect for simple or baked polenta (prepared with alternating layers of béchamel and grated or flaked cheese).

Serves: 4-5 (1 lb/500 g of pasta); Preparation: 10 minutes; Cooking: 2 hours; Level of difficulty: Simple

Melt the butter in a heavy-bottomed saucepan until it bubbles. Add the pancetta, onion, carrot, and celery and sauté over low heat for 10 minutes, stirring often. § Add the pork and veal or beef and cook for 5 minutes more, mixing well. § Add half the wine and, when it has partially evaporated, add a third of the broth. § Simmer until the liquid has reduced, then add the tomato paste and a little more wine and broth. § After 10–15 minutes, add the tomatoes, salt and pepper. § Continue cooking over low heat, gradually stirring in the remaining wine and broth. When cooked, the sauce should be fairly thick. This will take about 2 hours in all.

■ INGREDIENTS

- ¼ cup/2 oz/60 g butter
- ½ cup/2 oz/60 g diced pancetta
- 1 small onion, 1 small carrot, 1 stalk celery, all finely chopped
- 8 oz/250 g ground veal or beef
- 3½ oz/100 g lean ground pork
- 1 cup/8 fl oz/250 ml dry red wine
- 1¼ cups/10 fl oz/300 ml *Beef broth (see recipe p. 14)*
- 1 tablespoon tomato paste
- 12 oz/375 g peeled and chopped fresh or canned tomatoes
- salt and freshly ground black pepper

Intingolo di fegatini
Chicken liver sauce

This sauce is very good with polenta and with all egg-based, fresh pasta. It can also be served on simple boiled rice. It is particularly good with Risotto bianco al parmigiano (see recipe p. 155).

Serves: 4-5 (1 lb/500 g of pasta); Preparation: 15 minutes; Cooking: 30 minutes; Level of difficulty: Simple

Heat the oil in a small skillet (frying pan) and sauté the onion, carrot, and celery over medium-low heat for 6–7 minutes. § Add the chicken livers and cook for 2–3 minutes. § Pour in the wine and after another 2–3 minutes, add the tomato paste diluted in ⅔ cup/5 fl oz/150 ml of water. Mix well, and add the peas. § Cook for another 15–20 minutes.

■ INGREDIENTS

- 6 tablespoons extra-virgin olive oil
- 1 large onion, 1 large carrot, 1 stalk celery, all finely chopped
- 8 chicken livers, cleaned and coarsely chopped
- 5 tablespoons dry red or white wine
- 1 tablespoon tomato paste
- ¾ cup/4 oz/125 g shelled peas
- salt and freshly ground white pepper

Salsa di burro e parmigiano
Butter and parmesan sauce

This simple sauce is perfect with all kinds of dried and fresh pasta.

Serves: 4-5 (1 lb/500 g of pasta); Preparation & Cooking: 5 minutes; Level of difficulty: Simple

Cook the pasta, drain well and treansfer to a heated serving dish. § Add half the parmesan until it melts creamily over the pasta. § Add the remaining cheese and the butter and toss until the butter has melted. Serve hot.

■ INGREDIENTS

- 1½ cups freshly grated parmesan cheese
- ¾ cup/6 oz/180 g butter

Right: *Ragù al pomodoro*

SUGO FINTO
False "meat" sauce

This light sauce is just as versatile as any meat sauce. Serve it hot with all pasta shapes. For an entirely vegetarian sauce, omit the pancetta and add 1 oz/30 g of dried porcini mushrooms.

Serves: 4-5 (1 lb/500 g of pasta); Preparation: 15 minutes; Cooking: 35 minutes; Level of difficulty: Simple

Put the pancetta, parsley, onion, carrots, celery, and garlic in a sauté pan with the oil and butter. Cook over medium-high heat for 5 minutes. § Add the tomatoes and season with salt and pepper. § Simmer over medium-low heat for about 25 minutes.

■ INGREDIENTS

- ½ cup/3 oz/90 g diced pancetta
- 1 cup/1 oz/30 g finely chopped parsley
- 1 large onion, 2 carrots, 2 stalks celery, 2 cloves garlic, all finely chopped
- 2 tablespoons extra-virgin olive oil
- ¼ cup/2 oz/60 g butter
- 2 large tomatoes, peeled and chopped
- salt and freshly ground black pepper

RAGÙ DI PESCE
Fish sauce

Many different sorts of fish will work in this sauce. Ask your fish vendor for fish that are suitable for making soup. Long, dried shapes, like spaghetti and spaghettini, are the classic choice of pasta. Short, dried pasta shapes, such as penne and maccheroni, are also a good match.

Serves: 4-5 (1 lb/500 g of pasta); Preparation: 15 minutes; Cooking: 50 minutes; Level of difficulty: Medium

Place the fish in a pot with abundant water and the rosemary and bring to a boil. Cook for 15 minutes over medium-low heat. Take the fish out, remove the skin and bones, and crumble the cooked meat. Strain the liquid and discard the rosemary leaves. § Sauté the onion and garlic in a large skillet (frying pan) with the oil until light gold in color. Add the fish meat and 3 cups/24 fl oz/750 ml of the broth in which it was cooked. Season with salt and pepper and simmer over low heat for about 30–35 minutes.

■ INGREDIENTS

- 1½ lb/750 g assorted fresh fish, such as hake, sea bass, sea bream, and red snapper, gutted
- 2 tablespoons fresh rosemary leaves
- 1 onion, finely chopped
- 1 clove garlic, finely chopped
- ½ cup/4 fl oz/125 ml extra-virgin olive oil
- salt and freshly ground black pepper

SALSA DI BURRO E SALVIA
Butter and sage sauce

The clean, fuzzy taste of fresh sage melted in the butter combines well with fresh pasta and gnocchi.

Serves: 4-5 (1 lb/500 g of pasta); Preparation: 5 minutes; Cooking: 5 minutes; Level of difficulty: Simple

Cook the butter and sage in a heavy-bottomed pan over very low heat until the butter turns light gold.

■ INGREDIENTS

- ½ cup/4 oz/125 g butter
- 10 fresh sage leaves

Right: *Maccheroni al ragù di pesce*

Pesto alla genouese
Genoese basil sauce

Pesto *comes from the Liguria region in northern Italy and is named for its capital city Genoa. Traditionally it is served with trenette, a local egg-based pasta similar to fettuccine. It is also good with dried pasta, particularly the long shapes (spaghetti, spaghettini, linguine), and is delicious with potato gnocchi or instead of meat sauce in lasagne.*

Serves: 4–5 (1 lb/500 g of pasta); Preparation: 10 minutes; Level of difficulty: Simple

Combine the basil, pine nuts, garlic, olive oil, and salt in a food processor and chop until smooth. Place the mixture in a large serving bowl and stir in the cheeses. § Add the water and butter and stir well.

VARIATION
– for a richer sauce, add 1 tablespoon fresh ricotta cheese just before serving.

■ INGREDIENTS

- 2 cups/2 oz/60 g fresh basil leaves
- 2 tablespoons pine nuts
- 1 clove garlic
- ½ cup/4 fl oz/125 ml extra-virgin olive oil
- salt
- 2 tablespoons freshly grated parmesan cheese
- 2 tablespoons freshly grated pecorino cheese
- 2 tablespoons of water from the pasta pot
- knob of butter for serving

Pesto toscano
Tuscan-style pesto

This recipe is an up-dated version of one said to have been developed by the chefs of the Medici family in Florence in the 16th century. It can be served with most long and short dried pasta shapes.

Serves: 4–5 (1 lb/500 g of pasta); Preparation: 10 minutes; Level of difficulty: Simple

Put the walnuts, basil, and garlic in a food processor and chop to a cream. Transfer to a mixing bowl. § Remove the crust from the bread roll and soak the inside in the broth. Squeeze well and add to the walnut mixture. Add salt to taste, lemon juice, and oil (you may need slightly more or slightly less oil depending on how much the walnuts absorb), and mix well.

■ INGREDIENTS

- 20 shelled walnuts
- 1 cup/1 oz/30 g fresh basil leaves
- 1 clove garlic
- 1 medium bread roll
- 1 cup/8 fl oz/250 ml *Beef broth* (see recipe p. 14)
- salt
- juice of 1 lemon
- 2 tablespoons extra-virgin olive oil

Salsa al burro e rosmarino
Butter and rosemary sauce

This sauce is particularly good with fresh and filled pasta.

Serves: 4–5 (1 lb/500 g of pasta); Preparation: 2 minutes; Cooking: 3–4 minutes; Level of difficulty: Simple

Combine the garlic, butter, and rosemary in a skillet (frying pan) over medium heat and cook for 3–4 minutes.

■ INGREDIENTS

- 2 cloves garlic, finely chopped
- ½ cup/4 oz/125 g butter
- 4 tablespoons finely chopped fresh rosemary leaves

Right: *Linguine al pesto*

INTINGOLO DI FUNGHI PORCINI
Italian mushroom sauce

Fresh porcini mushrooms are hard to find outside of Italy and France but are widely available in their dried form. If you can't get fresh porcini, combine a small amount of soaked, dried porcini with fresh white mushrooms. The dried porcini have such a strong musky taste they will flavor the dish almost as well as the fresh ones. Mushroom sauce is very good with fresh pasta (tagliolini, fettuccine, tagliatelle, pappardelle) and also with long dried pasta shapes (spaghetti, bucatini, etc.). Try replacing the meat sauce in Lasagne al forno *(see recipe p. 82) with 1 quantity of this sauce.*

Serves: 4-5 (1 lb/500 g of pasta); Preparation: 15 minutes + time to soak the mushrooms; Cooking: 30 minutes; Level of difficulty: Simple

If you are using dried porcini, soak them in 1 cup/8 fl oz/250 ml of warm water for about 20 minutes. Drain and squeeze out the excess water. Chop coarsely. § Put the garlic and rosemary in a large skillet (frying pan) with the butter and oil and sauté over medium heat for 4–5 minutes. Add the mushrooms and season with salt and pepper. Cover and cook over medium-low heat for about 20–25 minutes, or until the mushrooms are very tender.

■ INGREDIENTS

- 14 oz/450 g coarsely chopped fresh porcini mushrooms (or 12 oz/ 375 g fresh white mushrooms and 1 oz/ 30 g dried porcini)
- 2 cloves garlic, finely chopped
- sprig of fresh rosemary, finely chopped
- 2 tablespoons/1 oz/30 g butter
- 4 tablespoons extra-virgin olive oil
- salt and freshly ground black pepper

SUGO DI CIPOLLA
Onion sauce

If you like onions, this sauce is for you. Serve with fresh and dried pasta or on bread or toast.
Serves: 4; Preparation: 5 minutes; Cooking: 1¼ hours; Level of difficulty: Simple

Sauté the onions in the oil in a heavy-bottomed pan for 6–7 minutes. Add the pancetta and sauté for 5 minutes more. § Add the tomatoes and then the wine. Season with salt and pepper. Cover and cook over medium-low heat for about 1 hour, stirring from time to time.

■ INGREDIENTS

- 1¼ lb/625 g white onions, sliced
- 4 tablespoons extra-virgin olive oil
- ½ cup/3 oz/90 g diced pancetta
- 2 large tomatoes, diced
- ½ cup/4 fl oz/125 ml dry red wine
- salt and freshly ground black pepper

INTINGOLO DI NOCI
Walnut sauce

Walnut sauce is good with fresh pasta and potato gnocchi.
Serves: 4-5 (1 lb/500 g of pasta); Preparation: 20 minutes; Cooking: 15 minutes; Level of difficulty: Simple

Roast the pine nuts in the oven at 350°F/180°C/gas 4 for 5–10 minutes, or until they are golden in color. Take them out and leave to cool. § Shell the walnuts and combine in a food processor with the pine nuts, garlic, parsley, and oil. Chop finely. Season with salt.

■ INGREDIENTS

- 1 lb/500 g walnuts, in their shells
- ⅓ cup/1½ oz/45 g pine nuts
- 2 cloves garlic
- 1 cup/1 oz/30 g parsley
- ½ cup/4 fl oz/125 ml extra-virgin olive oil
- salt

Right: Tagliolini ai funghi porcini

BRODO DI CARNE
Beef broth

Homemade beef broth is used as the basis for many soups, to serve stuffed pasta such as tortellini and agnolotti, and to flavor a wide range of other pasta and risotto dishes. It can be made ahead of time and kept in the refrigerator for up to 3 days or frozen.

Makes: about 9 cups/3½ pints/2 liters; Preparation: 15 minutes; Cooking: 3 hours; Level of difficulty: Simple

Put the meat, vegetables, herbs, and salt and pepper to taste in a large pot with the water. Cover and bring to a boil over medium heat. Simmer over low heat for 3 hours. Occasionally, skim the scum off the top so that the broth will be light and fresh to taste. § Remove from heat and leave to cool. When the broth is cool, a layer of fat will form on the top. This should be skimmed off.

■ INGREDIENTS

- 2 lb/1 kg beef
- 2 lb/1 kg meat bones
- 1 carrot
- 1 onion
- 1 stalk celery
- 1 whole clove
- 1 bay leaf
- 1 clove garlic
- 5 sprigs parsley
- 1 leek
- 1 ripe tomato
- 2½ quarts/5 pints/3 liters water
- salt and black pepper

BRODO DI PESCE
Fish broth

Fish broth makes a delicious change from beef broth as the basis for minestrine.

Makes: about 5 cups/2 pints/1.2 liters; Preparation: 15 minutes; Cooking: 1¼ hours; Level of difficulty: Simple

Put the fish, vegetables, and herbs in a large pot with the water. Bring to a boil. § Cover and leave to simmer over low heat for an hour. Season with salt and simmer for 15 more minutes.

■ INGREDIENTS

- 1¼ lb/625 g assorted fresh fish, such as hake, sea bass, sea bream, and red snapper, cleaned and gutted
- 2 stalks celery
- 1 carrot
- 1 medium onion
- 2 cloves garlic
- 2 ripe tomatoes
- 1 tablespoon parsley
- 6½ cups/2½ pints/ 1.5 liters water
- salt

BRODO DI VERDURE
Vegetable broth

Vegetable broth is an essential ingredient in many soups and risotti. Vegetarians can use it in recipes that call for chicken or beef broth. For a completely fat-free broth, omit the butter and put all the ingredients together in the lightly salted water, and simmer for about an hour.

Makes 2½ quarts/5 pints/3 liters; Preparation: 15 minutes; Cooking: 1¼ hours; Level of difficulty: Simple

Melt the butter in a fairly large pot and add the vegetables. Cover and simmer over low heat for 10 minutes, stirring occasionally. § Add the parsley, peppercorns, cloves, and bay leaf. § Add about 4 quarts/8 pints/5 liters of cold water, season lightly with salt, and simmer for 1 hour over low heat, skimming off the foam occasionally. § Strain the broth, discarding the vegetables.

■ INGREDIENTS

- ¼ cup/2 oz/ 60 g butter
- 2 onions, 2 carrots, 1 leek, 2 celery stalks, with leaves, cut in 4 pieces
- 3 tomatoes, cut in half
- 6 sprigs parsley
- 8 black peppercorns
- 1 clove
- 1 bay leaf (optional)
- salt

Right:
Minestrina in brodo

BRODO DI POLLO
Chicken broth

■ INGREDIENTS

• 1 chicken, cleaned,
 weighing about
 4 lb/2 kg

• 2 celery stalks, with
 leaves, washed and
 broken into 3 pieces

• 2 medium carrots,
 scraped and cut in half

• 1 large onion, stuck with
 2 cloves (optional)

• 4 black peppercorns

• salt

The tastiest chicken broth is made with free-range chickens; unfortunately they are not easy to find nowadays. Soup chickens do still exist however, even if battery-raised. Once again, it pays to make a large amount of broth and freeze it in small quantities to be used as needed.

Makes about 2½ quarts/5 pints/3 liters; Preparation: 10 minutes; Cooking: 3 hours; Level of difficulty: Simple

Put the chicken, whole, in a very large pot. Add the celery, carrots, onion, and peppercorns. Cover with about 4 quarts/8 pints/5 liters of cold water and simmer for 3 hours over medium-low heat. The water should barely move. § Strain the broth, discarding the vegetables. The chicken can be served hot or cold with a favorite sauce, or in chicken aspic, or salad. § To remove the fat, in part or completely, let the broth cool, then refrigerate for about 2 hours. The fat will solidify on the top and can easily be lifted off.

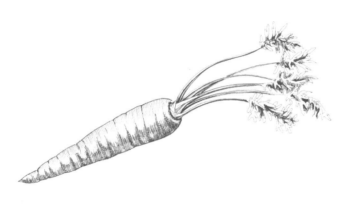

SALSA MAIONESE
Mayonnaise

■ INGREDIENTS

• 1 fresh egg yolk

• dash of salt

• ⅔ cup/5 fl oz/150 g
 extra-virgin olive oil

• freshly ground black
 pepper

• 1 tablespoon lemon juice
 (or white vinegar)

Serves 4; Preparation: 15-20 minutes; Level of difficulty: Medium

BY HAND: use a fork or hand whisk to beat the egg yolk in a bowl with the salt. § Add the oil a drop at a time at first, then in a steady drizzle, stirring all the time in the same direction. § When the mayonnaise begins to thicken, add, very gradually, the lemon juice (or vinegar), pepper, and a few more drops of oil until it is the right density. § If the mayonnaise curdles, start over again with another egg yolk and use the curdled mayonnaise in place of the oil.

IN THE BLENDER: use the same ingredients as above, except for the egg, which should be whole. § Place the egg, salt, pepper, 1–2 tablespoons of oil, and the lemon juice (or vinegar) in the blender and blend for a few seconds at maximum speed. § When the ingredients are well mixed, pour the remaining oil into the mixture very gradually. Blend until the right density is reached.

Right: *Brodo di pollo*

POLENTA
Basic polenta

■ INGREDIENTS

- 10 cups/4¼ pints/2.5 liters water
- 2 tablespoons coarse sea salt
- 3½ cups/14 oz/450 g coarse-grain yellow cornmeal

Serves 4; Preparation: 5 minutes; Cooking: 50-60 minutes; Level of difficulty: Medium

Bring the salted water to a boil in a heavy-bottomed pot large enough to hold 4 quarts/8 pints/5 liters. § Add the cornmeal gradually, stirring continuously and rapidly with a whisk so that no lumps form; polenta should always be perfectly smooth. § To cook, stir the polenta over high heat by moving a long, wooden spoon in a circular motion. At a certain point you'll notice that it begins to withdraw from the sides of the pot on which a thin crust is forming. § The polenta should be stirred almost continuously for the 50–60 minutes it takes to cook. § Quantities and method are the same when using an electric polenta cauldron. Stir the cornmeal into the boiling water gradually, then turn on the mixer. Leave for 50–60 minutes. § Serve hot or cold as suggested in the recipes.

CROSTINI DI POLENTA
Preparing polenta for crostini

■ INGREDIENTS

- 1 quantity basic polenta (see recipe above)
- 2 cups/16 fl oz/500 ml oil for frying

In Italy Crostini di polenta are usually made with leftover polenta prepared the day before. Prepare the polenta at least 12 hours before serving; it needs time to become firm before frying.

Serves 8-12; Preparation 5 minutes + 12 hours resting; Cooking: 50-60 minutes; Level of difficulty: Simple

Prepare the polenta. § Cut the polenta in ½-in (1-cm) slices. § Fry the polenta slices a few at a time in the hot oil for 6–8 minutes, or until golden brown on both sides. § Serve as they are or spread with a topping.

POLENTA BIANCA
White polenta

■ INGREDIENTS

- 10 cups/4¼ pints/2.5 liters water
- 2 tablespoons coarse sea salt
- 2¾ cups/12 oz/375 g white cornmeal

This polenta, typical of Veneto and Friuli in the northeast, is made with white cornmeal in exactly the same way as yellow cornmeal polenta.

Serves 4; Preparation: 5 minutes; Cooking: 50-60 minutes; Level of difficulty: Medium

Prepare the polenta as explained above. § When ready, spread out on a cutting board to a thickness of about 2 in (5 cm), cover with a damp cloth, and let cool. § Cut into slices about ½-in (1-cm) thick and roast on a charcoal grill or in a sizzling grill pan. § The slices can also be fried in oil or lard. § Serve hot or cold.

Right: *Polenta*

BRUSCHETTA ALLA ROMANA
Toasted bread with garlic, salt and oil

Bruschetta is a classic Roman appetizer, although many regions of Italy have similar dishes. It is difficult to recreate the authentic taste abroad because Roman bread is white, very compact, and unsalted. Choose bread that is not too fresh; yesterday's leftover loaf is best. Toast in the oven or under the broiler (or over a barbecue or open fire), rather than in the toaster. This will dry it out to just the right point.

Serves: 4; Preparation: 5 minutes; Cooking: 10 minutes; Level of difficulty: Simple

Toast the bread until golden brown on both sides. § Rub each slice with the garlic, sprinkle with salt and pepper, and drizzle with oil. § Serve hot.

■ INGREDIENTS

- 4 large, thick slices of white, unsalted bread
- 2 cloves garlic
- salt and freshly ground black pepper
- 4 tablespoons extra-virgin olive oil

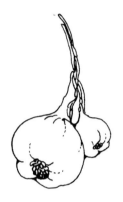

GNOCCHI DI PATATE
Potato gnocchi

Potato gnocchi are a simple mixture of boiled, mashed potatoes, eggs, and flour. The choice of potato is important. Don't use new potatoes or baking potatoes; the humble boiling potato is best. Potato gnocchi can be served with a wide variety of pasta sauces.

Serves: 6; Preparation: 20 minutes; Cooking: 35 minutes; Level of difficulty: Medium

Cook the potatoes in their skins in a pot of salted, boiling water until tender. Drain and peel while still hot. Mash until smooth. § Place in a bowl and add the eggs and most of the flour. Stir, adding more flour as required, until the mixture is soft and smooth, but just slightly sticky. The amount of flour will depend on how much the potatoes absorb, so don't add it all at once. § Dust a work surface with flour, take a piece of the dough and roll it into a long sausage about ¾ in (2 cm) in diameter. Cut into pieces about 1 in (2.5 cm) in length. Repeat until all the dough has been made into gnocchi. § Set a large pot of salted water to boil. The gnocchi should be cooked in batches. Lower the first batch (20–24 gnocchi) gently into the boiling water. After a few minutes they will rise to the top. Leave them to bob about for 1–2 minutes, then scoop them out with a slotted spoon. Place on a heated serving dish. Repeat until all the gnocchi are cooked.

■ INGREDIENTS

- 1½ lb/750 g boiling potatoes
- 2 eggs
- 2 cups/8 oz/250 g all-purpose/plain flour

Right:
A selection of common Italian breads, many of which can be used to make crostini or bruschette. Note the bruschetta in the foreground with garlic cloves on top.

BARCHETTE
Boat-shaped pastries

Barchette in Italian means "little boats" and refers to the shape of the molds traditionally used to prepare these little savory pastries. Freshly baked, they are delicious with all sorts of toppings and sauces. If you don't have boat-shaped molds on hand, use any small cake or other molds you have in the kitchen.

Serves: 4-6; Preparation: 15 minutes + 30 minutes resting; Cooking: 15 minutes; Level of difficulty: Simple

Sift the flour onto a clean work surface, and work the flour and butter together with your fingertips until the mixture is the same texture as a coarse meal. § Make a well in the center and add the water and salt. Mix until you have a rather soft dough. § Form a ball, wrap in waxed paper, and set aside in a cool place for 30 minutes. § Flour the work surface, then roll the dough out using a floured rolling pin to about ⅛-in (3-mm) thick. § Line the molds with the dough and prick the bottom with a fork. Cover with pieces of waxed paper and fill with dried beans. § Bake the *barchette* in a preheated oven at 350°F/180°C/gas 4 for 12–15 minutes. § Invert the molds, remove the waxed paper and beans, and set the *barchette* aside to cool. Use as indicated in the recipes (or invent new fillings).

■ INGREDIENTS

- 2 cups/8 oz/250 g all-purpose/plain flour
- ⅔ cup/5 oz/150 g butter
- 2–3 tablespoons cold water
- ½ teaspoon salt
- 3 cups/1 lb/500 g dried beans

SALSA BESCIAMELLA
Béchamel sauce

Béchamel sauce is used in many recipes. It is quick and easy to prepare.

Serves 4; Preparation: 5 minutes; Cooking: 7-8 minutes; Level of difficulty: Simple

Heat the milk in a saucepan until it is almost boiling. § In a heavy-bottomed saucepan, melt the butter with the flour over low heat, stirring rapidly with a wooden spoon. Cook for about 1 minute. § Remove from the heat and add half the hot milk, stirring constantly. Return to low heat and stir until the sauce starts to thicken. § Add the rest of the milk gradually and continue stirring until it comes to a boil. § Season with salt to taste and continue stirring until the béchamel is the right thickness. § If any lumps form, beat the sauce rapidly with a fork or whisk until they dissolve.

■ INGREDIENTS

- 2 cups/16 fl oz/500 ml milk
- ¼ cup/2 oz/60 g butter
- ½ cup/2 oz/60 g all-purpose/plain flour
- salt

Right:
Barchette

Dried Pasta

By dried pasta we mean store-bought pasta
made from hard-wheat flour and water.
It includes classics such as spaghetti,
penne, fusilli, and maccheroni.

Spaghettini con aglio olio e peperoncino
Spaghettini with garlic, oil, and chilies

The sauce is very quick to make and should be used immediately, so begin by cooking the spaghettini in a large pot of salted, boiling water.

Serves: 4-5; Preparation: 3 minutes; Cooking: 10 minutes; Level of difficulty: Simple

While the pasta is cooking, combine the oil, garlic, and chilies in a small skillet (frying pan) and cook over low heat until the garlic begins to change color. Remove from heat at once, taking care not to burn the garlic because it will give the sauce a bitter flavor. Add the parsley, if using, and salt to taste. § Drain the pasta when *al dente* and place in a heated serving dish. Pour the sauce over the pasta and toss vigorously. § Serve immediately.

■ INGREDIENTS

- ¾ cup/6 fl oz/180 ml extra-virgin olive oil
- 3 cloves garlic, finely chopped
- ½ teaspoon crushed chilies
- 2 tablespoons finely chopped parsley (optional)
- salt
- 1 lb/500 g spaghettini

Wine: a dry white (Trebbiano)

Spaghetti alla carbonara
Spaghetti with eggs and pancetta

La carbonara is a classic Roman sauce. According to some, it was first made during the last days of World War II as American troops advanced up the Italian peninsula bringing supplies of eggs and bacon which they asked the Italians to make into a sauce. Try replacing the pancetta with bacon and decide for yourself about the historical value of this theory!

Serves: 4-5; Preparation: 5 minutes; Cooking: 15 minutes; Level of difficulty: Simple

Chop the cloves of garlic in half. Combine the oil, garlic, and pancetta in a skillet (frying pan) and sauté over medium heat until the pancetta is golden brown but not crisp. Remove the skillet from the heat and take out the pieces of garlic. § In a mixing bowl lightly beat the eggs, parmesan, pecorino, and salt until smooth. Set aside. § Cook the spaghetti in a large pot of salted, boiling water until *al dente*. Drain and place in a large, heated serving dish. Add the egg mixture and toss. § Return the skillet with the pancetta to high heat for 1 minute. Pour the hot oil and pancetta over the pasta and egg, and toss vigorously. Grind a generous amount of black pepper over the top and serve immediately.

■ INGREDIENTS

- 3 whole cloves garlic
- 3 tablespoons extra-virgin olive oil
- 1 cup/6 oz/180 g diced pancetta
- 4 fresh eggs
- 3 tablespoons freshly grated parmesan cheese
- 3 tablespoons freshly grated pecorino cheese
- salt and freshly ground black pepper
- 1 lb/500 g spaghetti

Wine: a light, young red (Vino Novello)

Right:
Spaghetti alla carbonara

Bucatini con capperi e olive
Bucatini with capers and black olives

Serves: 4-5; Preparation: 10 minutes; Cooking: 15 minutes; Level of difficulty: Simple

Combine the oil, garlic, and parsley in a large sauté pan and cook over medium heat until the garlic starts to change color. § Stir the olives and capers into the sauce and cook over low heat for 2–3 minutes. § Cook the bucatini in a large pot of salted, boiling water until *al dente*. Drain and transfer to the sauté pan. § Toss with the capers and olives over medium-hot heat for 2 minutes. § Place in a heated serving dish and sprinkle with pecorino. § Serve hot.

■ INGREDIENTS

- 4 tablespoons extra-virgin olive oil
- 2 cloves garlic, finely chopped
- 3 tablespoons finely chopped parsley
- 1 cup/5 oz/150 g pitted and chopped black olives
- 3 tablespoons capers
- 6 tablespoons freshly grated pecorino cheese
- 1 lb/500 g bucatini pasta

Wine: a dry red (Nebbiolo)

Bucatini all'amatriciana
Bucatini with pancetta and spicy tomato sauce

Serves: 4-5; Preparation: 5 minutes; Cooking: 30 minutes; Level of difficulty: Simple

Sauté the pancetta in a skillet (frying pan) with the oil for 2–3 minutes. Add the onion and cook until it becomes transparent. § Stir in the tomatoes and chilies. Season with salt and cook over medium-low heat for about 20 minutes, or until the tomatoes have separated from the oil. § Cook the bucatini in a large pot of salted, boiling water until *al dente*. Drain well and transfer to a heated serving bowl. § Toss with the sauce and pecorino and serve immediately.

■ INGREDIENTS

- 1 cup/6 oz/180 g diced pancetta
- 2 tablespoons extra-virgin olive oil
- 1 onion, finely chopped
- two 14-oz/450-g cans chopped tomatoes
- ¾ teaspoon crushed chilies
- salt
- 8 tablespoons freshly grated pecorino cheese
- 1 lb/500 g bucatini pasta

Wine: a dry red (Refosco)

Spaghettini alla puttanesca
Spaghettini with spicy tomato sauce

This sauce is a specialty of the island of Ischia, off the coast of Naples in southern Italy.

Serves: 4-5; Preparation: 10 minutes; Cooking: 25-30 minutes; Level of difficulty: Simple

Sauté the garlic and chilies in a skillet (frying pan) with the oil over medium heat until the garlic begins to change color. Add the tomatoes, capers, and olives, and cook for 5 minutes. § Stir the anchovy fillets into the sauce. Season with salt and pepper and simmer over medium heat for 15–20 minutes, or until the oil and tomato begin to separate. § Cook the spaghettini in a large pot of salted, boiling water until *al dente*. Drain and transfer to a heated serving dish. Pour the sauce over the top and toss vigorously. Serve hot.

■ INGREDIENTS

- 2 cloves garlic, minced
- ½ teaspoon crushed chilies
- 4 tablespoons extra-virgin olive oil
- 1 lb/500 g peeled and chopped tomatoes
- 6 anchovy fillets, crumbled
- 1 cup/5 oz/150 g pitted and chopped black olives
- 2 tablespoons capers
- salt
- 1 lb/500 g spaghettini

Wine: a dry white (Vernaccia)

Right: *Bucatini all'amatriciana*

SPAGHETTI CON OLIVE
Spaghetti with tomato and black olive sauce

Serves: 4-5; Preparation: 10 minutes; Cooking: 20 minutes; Level of difficulty: Simple

Place the tomatoes in a heavy-bottomed saucepan. Add the garlic and simmer over a low heat for 15 minutes. § Add the oil, olives, oregano, and chilies and cook for 2 minutes more. Season with salt. § Cook the spaghetti in plenty of boiling salted water until *al dente*. § Drain and add to the tomato mixture. Toss briefly and serve.

■ INGREDIENTS

- 1 lb/500 g tomatoes, coarsely chopped
- 2 cloves garlic, finely chopped
- 5 tablespoons extra-virgin olive oil
- 1¼ cups/6 oz/180 g pitted and chopped black olives
- 2 teaspoons oregano
- ½ teaspoon crushed chilies
- salt to taste
- 1 lb/500 g spaghetti

■ INGREDIENTS

- 2 whole cloves garlic, slightly crushed
- ½ cup/4 fl oz/125 ml extra-virgin olive oil
- 10 anchovy fillets
- 1 tablespoon finely chopped parsley
- 1 lb/500 g peeled and chopped tomatoes
- salt
- 6 tablespoons fine dry breadcrumbs, toasted
- 1 lb/500 g spaghetti

Wine: a dry white (Alcamo)

■ INGREDIENTS

- 1 medium onion, finely chopped
- ¾ cup/6 oz/180 ml extra-virgin olive oil
- juice of 3 lemons
- salt and freshly ground black pepper
- 6 tablespoons freshly grated parmesan cheese
- 1 lb/500 g capelli d'angelo pasta

Wine: a dry white (Frascati)

■ INGREDIENTS

- 10 large ripe tomatoes
- 2 cloves garlic, minced
- 6 tablespoons extra-virgin olive oil
- juice of 1 lemon
- salt
- 5 oz/150 g mozzarella cheese, diced
- 8 fresh basil leaves, torn
- 1 lb/500 g penne rigate

Wine: a dry white (Pinot grigio)

Left: *Capelli d'angelo olio e limoni*

Spaghetti con pangrattato
Spaghetti with toasted breadcrumbs

Serves: 4–5; Preparation: 10 minutes; Cooking: 15 minutes; Level of difficulty: Simple

Sauté the garlic in the oil in a large skillet (frying pan) until it starts to color, then remove and discard. § Add the anchovies, crushing them with a fork so that they dissolve in the flavored oil. § Add the parsley and tomatoes. Simmer over low heat for 15–20 minutes. § Cook the pasta in plenty of boiling salted water until *al dente*. Drain, add to the sauce and toss briefly. § Transfer to a heated serving dish. Sprinkle with the toasted breadcrumbs and serve hot.

Capelli d'angelo olio e limone
Capelli d'angelo with oil and lemon sauce

Serves: 4–5; Preparation: 3 minutes; Cooking: 5 minutes; Level of difficulty: Simple

Combine the onion and oil in a large sauté pan. Cook over medium heat until the onion turns golden in color. § Cook the capelli d'angelo in a large pot of salted, boiling water until *al dente*. Drain well and transfer to the pan with the onion. Toss the pasta briefly with the onion over medium heat and transfer to a large, heated serving dish. Add the lemon juice, salt, pepper, and parmesan. Toss well and serve immediately.

Penne con salsa di pomodoro fresco
Penne with fresh tomatoes, garlic, and mozzarella cheese

Serves: 4–5; Preparation: 5 minutes; Cooking: 10 minutes; Level of difficulty: Simple

Peel the tomatoes with a swivel-bladed peeler. Chop them into bite-sized chunks and drain off any extra liquid. Place them in a serving bowl. Add the garlic, half of the oil, and the lemon juice. Season with salt. § Cook the penne in a large pot of salted, boiling water until *al dente*. Drain well and toss with the remaining oil. § Toss the pasta with the tomato sauce. Sprinkle with the mozzarella and basil and serve.

Fusilli tonno e origano
Fusilli with tuna and oregano

■ INGREDIENTS
- 2 cloves garlic, minced
- ½ cup/4 fl oz/125 ml extra-virgin olive oil
- 1 tablespoon oregano
- 1 cup/8 oz/250 g tuna packed in oil
- salt
- 1 lb/500 g fusilli pasta

Wine: a dry white (Pinot Bianco)

Serves: 4-5; Preparation: 5 minutes. Cooking: 15 minutes; Level of difficulty: Simple

Sauté the garlic in the oil for about 3 minutes. Add the oregano, stir, and after 3 minutes add the tuna. § Season with salt and cook for about 5 minutes (the tuna does not need to cook, but just blend in with the other flavors.) § Cook the fusilli in a large pot of salted, boiling water until *al dente*. Drain, toss with the sauce and serve at once.

Penne all'arrabbiata
Penne with "angry" tomato sauce

■ INGREDIENTS
- ¾ cup/2½ oz/75 g diced pancetta
- 4 cloves garlic, 1 celery stalk, 1 medium onion, all finely chopped
- ⅓ cup/2½ fl oz/75 ml extra-virgin olive oil
- 1½ lb/750 g peeled and chopped tomatoes
- 6 fresh basil leaves, torn
- 3 tablespoons finely chopped parsley
- ½ teaspoon crushed chilies
- salt and freshly ground black pepper
- 1 lb/500 g penne pasta

Wine: a dry red (Chianti)

Serves: 4-5; Preparation: 15 minutes; Cooking: 30 minutes; Level of difficulty: Simple

Put the pancetta, garlic, celery, and onion in a large sauté pan with the oil and cook until lightly browned. § Add the tomatoes, basil, parsley, and chilies. Season with salt and pepper. § Simmer over medium-low heat for about 20 minutes or until the tomatoes and oil begin to separate. § Cook the penne in a large pot of salted, boiling water until *al dente*. Drain and toss with the sauce in the pan over high heat for 2–3 minutes. Transfer to a heated serving dish and serve hot.

Penne strascicate
Penne Florentine-style

■ INGREDIENTS
- 1 quantity *Tomato meat sauce* (see recipe p. 6)
- salt
- 1 cup/5 oz/150 g freshly grated parmesan cheese
- 1 lb/500 g penne pasta

Wine: a young, dry red (Chianti dei Colli Fiorentini)

Serves: 4-5; Preparation: 5 minutes + 2 hours for the sauce; Cooking: 15 minutes; Level of difficulty: Simple

Prepare the meat sauce. § Bring a large saucepan of salted water to a boil and add the pasta. § Cook until just *al dente* but still with plenty of "bite". § Keep the meat sauce warm over a low heat, add the drained pasta, toss together and leave for 5 minutes so that the pasta is coated thoroughly with the sauce and has absorbed its flavors. § Turn off the heat, stir in the parmesan and serve at once.

Right:
Penne strascicate

■ INGREDIENTS

• ¾ cup/6 fl oz/180 ml
  whole/full cream milk

• 1 cup/8 oz/250 g very
  fresh ricotta cheese

• 1 tablespoon sugar

• 1 teaspoon cinnamon

• salt

• white pepper

• 1 lb/500 g penne pasta

Wine: a dry white (Verdicchio)

Penne con ricotta
Penne with ricotta cheese

This classic southern Italian recipe is very simple and relies on the quality and freshness of the ricotta. Buy it loose from a specialty store or a good Italian deli. It is also good with fresh pasta.

Serves: 4-5; Preparation: 5 minutes; Cooking: 10 minutes; Level of difficulty: Simple

Warm the milk and place in a bowl with the ricotta, sugar, cinnamon, and a dash of salt and white pepper. Mix with a fork to form a smooth, creamy sauce. § Cook the penne in a large pot of salted, boiling water until *al dente*. Drain well and place in a heated serving bowl. Toss with the sauce and serve.

Spaghetti allo scoglio
Spaghetti with seafood sauce

Serves: 4–5; Preparation: 25 minutes + 1 hour to soak the shellfish: Cooking 25 minutes;. Level of difficulty: Medium

Scrub the mussels and clams and soak them in cold water for 1 hour. § Clean the squid and cuttlefish as described on p. 38, chopping into rounds and leaving the tentacles whole. § Do not peel the shrimp tails. § Pour 3 tablespoons of the oil into a large skillet (frying pan), add the mussels and clams, and steam open over medium heat. This will take about 10 minutes. Discard any that have not opened. § Heat 6 tablespoons of the oil in a large nonstick skillet and sauté the garlic, parsley, and chilies for 2 minutes over medium heat, taking care not to brown. § Add the squid and cuttlefish. Season with salt and pepper, cook briefly, then moisten with the wine. § Cook for 12 minutes, then add the shrimp tails. § After 5 minutes add the clams and mussels (if preferred, extract the mollusks from their shells, leaving just a few in the shell to make the finished dish look more attractive). Mix well and cook for 2 minutes more. Turn off the heat, cover, and set aside. § Meanwhile, cook the spaghetti in a large pan of salted water until *al dente*. Drain, and add to the pan with the seafood sauce. Heat for 1–2 minutes over medium-high heat. § Transfer to a heated dish and serve immediately.

■ INGREDIENTS

- 10 oz/300 g each clams and mussels in shell
- 10 oz/300 g squid, cleaned and dried
- 10 oz/300 g cuttlefish
- 10 oz/300 g shrimp/ prawn tails, washed and dried
- ½ cup/4 fl oz/125 ml extra-virgin olive oil
- 2 cloves garlic, minced
- 3 tablespoons chopped parsley
- 1 teaspoon crushed chilies
- ½ cup/4 fl oz/125 ml dry white wine
- salt and pepper
- 1 lb/500 g spaghetti

Wine: a dry white (San Severo Bianco)

Rigatoni con gli zucchini
Rigatoni with zucchini

Serves: 4–5; Preparation: 10 minutes; Cooking: 25 minutes; Level of difficulty: Simple

Heat the butter and oil together in a skillet (frying pan). Cut the clove of garlic in half, add to the skillet, and sauté until it starts to change color. Remove the garlic pieces and add the zucchini. Sauté over a high heat until the zucchini begin to turn golden brown. § Turn the heat down, cover the pan with a lid, and simmer until the zucchini are tender. Season with salt and pepper. § Cook the rigatoni in a large pot of salted, boiling water until *al dente*. Drain and transfer to a heated serving dish. Add the zucchini, parsley, and parmesan, and toss well. Serve hot.

■ INGREDIENTS

- 3 tablespoons/1½ oz/45 g butter
- 3 tablespoons extra-virgin olive oil
- 2 cloves garlic
- 6 zucchini/courgettes, sliced into thin wheels
- salt and freshly ground black pepper
- 3 tablespoons finely chopped parsley
- 6 tablespoons freshly grated parmesan cheese
- 1 lb/500 g rigatoni pasta

Wine: a dry white (Orvieto Classico)

VARIATION
– Add ½ teaspoon crushed chilies for a spicy dish.

Right: Spaghetti allo scoglio

Linguine con le fave
Linguine with fava beans and fresh rosemary

If fresh fava beans are out of season, use 1-1¼ pounds/500-625 g of frozen ones. This sauce is also good with many short pastas, such as conchiglie, lumaconi, or rigatoni.

Serves: 4-5; Preparation: 15 minutes; Cooking: about 30 minutes; Level of difficulty: Simple

Pod the beans and set aside in a bowl of cold water. § Cut the clove of garlic in two and combine with the rosemary, half the butter, and the oil in a skillet (frying pan). Sauté until the garlic begins to change color. § Remove the garlic and rosemary, making sure that none of the leaves remain in the sauce. Lower heat to medium, add the onion, and sauté until transparent. § Drain the fava beans and add with the broth to the skillet. Season with salt and pepper. § Continue to cook over medium-low heat for about 20 minutes or until the beans are tender, stirring from time to time. § Cook the linguine in a large pot of salted, boiling water until *al dente*. Drain and place in a heated serving dish. Pour the sauce over the pasta and toss with the parmesan and the remaining butter until well mixed. Serve hot.

■ INGREDIENTS

- 3 lb/1.5 kg fava/broad beans in their pods
- 2 cloves garlic
- 3 sprigs fresh rosemary
- ¼ cup/2 oz/60 g butter
- 4 tablespoons extra-virgin olive oil
- 1 large onion, finely chopped
- 1½ cups/12 fl oz/375 ml *Beef broth* (see recipe p. 14)
- salt and freshly ground black pepper
- 6 tablespoons freshly grated parmesan cheese
- 1 lb/500 g linguine pasta

Wine: a light, dry white (Verdicchio)

Spaghetti alle vongole
Spaghetti with clams

Serves: 4-5; Preparation: 10 minutes + 1 hour to soak the clams; Cooking: 30 minutes; Level of difficulty: Simple

Scrub the clams thoroughly and soak in cold water for 1 hour. § Put 2 tablespoons of the oil in a large sauté pan and add the clams and white wine. Cook until all the clams are open. § Remove the clams, discarding any that have not opened, and set aside. Put the cooking liquid in a bowl and set aside. § Combine the remaining oil and garlic in the same pan and cook until the garlic begins to change color. § Add the tomatoes and cook over medium heat for about 5 minutes. § Pour in the clam liquid. Season with salt and pepper. Cook for 15 more minutes, or until the sauce has reduced. § Add the clams and parsley, and continue cooking for 2–3 minutes. § Cook the spaghetti in a large pot of salted, boiling water until *al dente*. Drain and transfer to the sauté pan with the sauce. Toss for 1–2 minutes over medium-high heat. Serve immediately.

■ INGREDIENTS

- 50 clams in shell
- 6 tablespoons extra-virgin olive oil
- 6 tablespoons dry white wine
- 3 cloves garlic, finely chopped
- 6 ripe tomatoes, peeled and chopped
- salt and freshly ground black pepper
- 2 tablespoons finely chopped parsley
- 1 lb/500 g spaghetti

Wine: a dry white (Tocai)

Right:
Linguine con le fave

■ INGREDIENTS

• ⅓ cup/2½ oz/75 g butter
• ¾ cup/6 oz/180 ml vodka
• juice of 1½ lemons
• 3 oz/90 g smoked salmon
• 3 teaspoons caviar (optional)
• 3 tablespoons light/single cream
• salt and freshly ground black pepper
• 1 lb/500 g farfalle pasta

Wine: a dry white (Soave)

FARFALLE AL SALMONE E VODKA

Farfalle with smoked salmon and vodka sauce

Serves: 4-5; Preparation: 5 minutes; Cooking: 15 minutes; Level of difficulty: Simple

Cook the butter, vodka, and lemon juice in a skillet (frying pan) over low heat until the vodka has evaporated. § Crumble the smoked salmon with a fork. Add the salmon and caviar (if using) to the pan. Cook over medium-low heat for 2–3 minutes. Add the cream and salt and pepper to taste. Remove from heat. § Cook the farfalle in a large pot of salted, boiling water until *al dente*. Drain well and transfer to the pan. Toss over medium heat and serve immediately.

Spaghetti con le seppie
Spaghetti with cuttlefish

■ INGREDIENTS

- 8 cuttlefish
- 2 onions, finely chopped
- 2 cloves garlic, finely chopped
- ½ cup/4 fl oz/125 ml extra-virgin olive oil
- 8 oz/250 g peeled and chopped canned tomatoes
- salt and freshly ground black pepper
- 1 lb/500 g spaghetti

Wine: a dry white (Pinot Grigio)

Serves: 4–5; Preparation: 20 minutes; Cooking: about 1 hour; Level of difficulty: Medium

Rinse the cuttlefish thoroughly in cold water. To clean, cut each cuttlefish lengthwise and remove the internal bone and the stomach. Take care not to break the internal ink sac. These can be added later, if liked. Set aside. § Cut the cuttlefish crosswise into thin half circles. § Combine the onion and garlic in a large sauté pan with the oil and cook over medium heat until they begin to change color. Add the cuttlefish and tomatoes. Season with salt and pepper. Turn the heat down low, cover, and simmer for about 45 minutes, or until the cuttlefish are tender. § Add the ink, if using, and stir over medium heat for 2–3 minutes. § Cook the spaghetti in a large pot of salted, boiling water until *al dente*. Drain well and transfer to a heated serving dish. Toss vigorously with the sauce and serve hot.

Penne alla polpa di granchio
Penne with crab meat

■ INGREDIENTS

- 12 fresh or frozen crab sticks
- ½ cup/4 fl oz/125 ml extra-virgin olive oil
- 2 small garlic cloves, minced
- 2 tablespoons chopped parsley
- 1 tablespoon orange rind, cut into julienne strips
- ⅓ cup/3 fl oz/90 ml cognac
- ½ cup/4 fl oz/125 ml orange juice
- salt and freshly ground black pepper
- ½ cup/4 fl oz/125 ml light/single cream
- 1 lb/500 g penne pasta

Wine: a dry white (Colli di Conegliano Bianco)

Serves: 4–5; Preparation: about 25 minutes; Cooking: 15 minutes;. Level of difficulty: Medium

Roughly chop the crab sticks. § Pour the oil into a large nonstick skillet (frying pan) and fry the garlic and parsley over medium-low heat for 1 minute. § Add the crab sticks and orange rind. Mix well and cook for 1 minute. Pour in the cognac and cook until it has evaporated. Add the orange juice. § Season with salt and a generous grinding of pepper. Cook until the the liquid has evaporated. § After about 10 minutes add the cream. § Cook the pasta in plenty of boiling salted water until *al dente*. Drain, and transfer the penne to the skillet and toss with the sauce for 1 minute. § Serve immediately.

Right:
Penne alla polpa di granchio

- 2 stalks celery heart, 2 tomatoes, sliced
- ¼ cup/2 fl oz/60 ml vinegar
- 1 cup/8 fl oz /250 ml extra-virgin olive oil
- salt
- 3 oz/90 g smoked salmon, thinly sliced
- 2 whole cloves garlic
- 6 tablespoons grated parmesan cheese
- 1 lb/500 g penne rigate

Wine: a dry white (Amelia Trebbiano)

- ½ cup/4 fl oz/125 ml extra-virgin olive oil
- 1 medium green, 1 medium yellow, and 1 medium red bell pepper/capsicum
- 1 large onion, finely chopped
- 2 cloves garlic, finely chopped
- 12 oz/375 g peeled and chopped ripe tomatoes
- 9 basil leaves, torn
- 3 tablespoons boiling water
- salt and freshly ground black pepper
- 3 tablespoons vinegar
- 6 anchovy fillets
- 1 lb/500 g penne rigate maccheroni

Wine: a dry red (Chianti Classico)

Left:

Penne al salmone

PENNE AL SALMONE
Penne with smoked salmon

This delicious dish is easy to prepare and convenient because it can be made in advance and eaten cold.

Serves: 4-5; Preparation: 10 minutes; Cooking: time to cook the pasta; Level of difficulty; Easy

Put the celery, tomatoes, vinegar, oil, salt, and smoked salmon in a large bowl. § Spear the garlic cloves with the tines of a fork and use it to stir the ingredients in the bowl. The garlic will flavor the mixture (take care that the cloves do not come off.) § Cook the penne in plenty of boiling salted water until *al dente*. Drain and transfer to the bowl. Add the parmesan and toss vigorously. § Serve hot or at room temperature.

MACCHERONI CON I PEPERONI
Maccheroni with bell peppers

Serves: 4-5; Preparation: 10 minutes; Cooking: 40 minutes; Level of difficulty: Simple

Cut the bell peppers in half lengthwise. Remove stalks, seeds and membrane, and cut crosswise into strips about ¼ in (6 mm) in width. § Combine oil, bell peppers, onion, and garlic in a large skillet (frying pan) and sauté until the garlic turns golden brown. Add the tomatoes, basil, and boiling water. Season with salt and pepper. Simmer over medium heat for 20–25 minutes or until the bell peppers are tender, stirring from time to time. § Stir in the vinegar and anchovies, and cook over high heat for 2–3 minutes until the vinegar evaporates. Remove from heat. § Cook the maccheroni in a large pot of salted, boiling water until *al dente*. Drain well and transfer to a heated serving dish. § Pour the sauce over the top and toss until well mixed. Serve hot.

VARIATION
– For a more filling, cold-weather dish, put the cooked pasta in a baking dish, pour the sauce over the top and mix well. Spread 7 oz/225 g of thinly sliced mozzarella cheese on top and bake in a preheated oven at 350°F/180°C/gas 4 for 10 minutes or until the mozzarella is golden.

Spaghetti al tonno
Spaghetti with tuna and tomato sauce

Serves: 4-5; Preparation: 10 minutes: Cooking: 15 minutes; Level of difficulty: Simple

Sauté the garlic and parsley in the oil over medium-low heat for 2 minutes. § Add the tomatoes, season with salt, and cook for 4–5 minutes. § Mix in the tuna, stir, and turn off the heat immediately. § Cook the spaghetti in a large pot of salted, boiling water until *al dente*. § Drain well and transfer to a heated serving dish. Toss vigorously with the sauce and serve hot.

■ INGREDIENTS

- 2 cloves garlic, minced
- 3 tablespoons finely chopped parsley
- ½ cup/4 fl oz/125 ml extra-virgin olive oil
- 6 small tomatoes, sliced
- salt
- 1 cup/8 oz/250 g tuna packed in oil, flaked
- 1 lb/500 g spaghetti

Wine: a dry white (Pinot Bianco)

Bucatoni con le cipolle
Bucatoni with onion sauce

Serves: 4-5; Preparation: 5 minutes; Cooking: 45 minutes; Level of difficulty: Simple

Sauté the onions in a sauté pan with the butter and oil over medium heat until they begin to change color. Add salt and pepper to taste. § Turn the heat down to low, cover, and simmer for about 40 minutes, or until the onions are very soft. § Uncover and add the wine. Turn the heat up to medium and stir while the wine evaporates. Remove from heat. § Break the thick bucatoni noodles in half and cook in a large pot of salted, boiling water until *al dente*. Drain well and transfer to a heated serving dish. § Pour the onion sauce over the top. Add the parsley and parmesan and toss vigorously. Serve hot.

■ INGREDIENTS

- 5 large onions, thinly sliced
- ¼ cup/2 oz/60 g butter
- 3 tablespoons extra-virgin olive oil
- salt and freshly ground black pepper
- ¾ cup/6 fl oz/180 ml dry white wine
- 3 tablespoons finely chopped parsley
- 8 tablespoons freshly grated parmesan cheese
- 1 lb/500 g bucatoni pasta

Wine: a dry white (Orvieto)

Spaghetti algli scampi
Spaghetti with saltwater crayfish

Serves: 4-5; Preparation: 20 minutes; Cooking: 15 minutes; Level of difficulty: Simple

Clean the saltwater crayfish, without removing the shells. Open them in half lengthwise and set aside in a small bowl. § Sauté the garlic and parsley in the oil for 2–3 minutes over a low heat. Increase the heat slightly and add the saltwater crayfish. Season with salt and mix well. § Add the wine, allow to evaporate, and cook for 8 minutes. Turn off the heat and cover the pan. § Cook the spaghetti in a large pot of salted, boiling water until *al dente*. § Drain well and return to the pan. Add the saltwater crayfish sauce and cook for 2 minutes over medium heat. § Transfer to a heated serving dish and serve.

■ INGREDIENTS

- 1 lb/500 g saltwater crayfish /Dublin Bay prawns
- 5 tablespoons extra-virgin olive oil
- 2 cloves garlic, minced
- 1 tablespoon chopped parsley
- salt
- ½ cup/4 fl oz/125 ml dry white wine
- 1 lb/500 g spaghetti

Wine: a dry white (Frascati)

Right: *Spaghetti al tonno*

■ INGREDIENTS

- 1¼ cups/7 oz/200 g
  fresh or frozen peas
- ¼ cup/2 oz/60 g butter
- 7 oz/200 g ham, diced
- 3 tablespoons light/single
  cream
- 2 tablespoons finely
  chopped parsley
- salt and freshly ground
  black pepper
- 4 tablespoons freshly
  grated parmesan cheese
- 1 lb/500 g farfalle pasta

Farfalle con piselli e prosciutto
Farfalle with peas and ham

Serves: 4–5; Preparation: 5 minutes; Cooking: 20 minutes; Level of difficulty: Simple

Boil the peas in salted water until half cooked. § Combine the peas, butter, and ham in a large skillet (frying pan). Cook over medium-low heat for 10 minutes. § Stir in half the cream and cook until the sauce thickens. § Add the parsley, and salt and pepper to taste. § Cook the farfalle in a large pot of salted, boiling water until *al dente*. Drain well and transfer to the skillet with the sauce. Add the remaining cream and parmesan. Toss well and serve hot.

Lumaconi all'ortolana
Lumaconi with vegetables

Serves: 4–5; Preparation: 10 minutes; Cooking: 35 minutes; Level of difficulty: Simple

Chop the onion coarsely. Peel the eggplant and dice it and the zucchini into bite-sized cubes. Remove the stalks and cores from the bell peppers and chop into ½-in (1-cm) square pieces. § Put the onion in a large sauté pan with the oil and cook over medium heat until it becomes transparent. Add the eggplant, bell peppers, and zucchini. Sauté the vegetables for 7–8 minutes. Add the tomatoes, crushed chilies, and salt to taste. Cook for 20 minutes. § Cook the lumaconi in a large pot of salted, boiling water until *al dente*. Drain and add to the sauté pan with the vegetables. Toss over high heat for 2–3 minutes until well mixed. Add the basil and parmesan. Transfer to a heated serving dish and serve hot.

■ INGREDIENTS

• 1 large onion
• 1 large eggplant/aubergine
• 2 large zucchini/courgettes
• 1 small green, 1 small yellow, and 1 small red bell pepper/capsicum
• ⅓ cup/2½ fl oz/80 ml extra-virgin olive oil
• two 14-oz/450-g cans of peeled and chopped tomatoes
• ½ teaspoon crushed chilies
• salt
• 8 basil leaves, torn
• 4 tablespoons freshly grated parmesan cheese
• 1 lb/500 g lumaconi pasta

Wine: a dry white (Bianco San Severo)

Bucatini al cavolfiore
Bucatini with cauliflower and raisins

Serves: 4–5; Preparation: 5 minutes; Cooking: 30 minutes; Level of difficulty: Simple

Boil the cauliflower in plenty of salted water until it is just tender. Drain, reserving the water. § Divide the cauliflower into small florets. Bring the water back to a boil and add the pasta. § Meanwhile, sauté the onion for 1–2 minutes in the oil in a large skillet (frying pan). § Add the anchovies, raisins, pine nuts, and saffron. Stir for 2–3 minutes, then add the cauliflower and continue cooking over very low heat, stirring occasionally. § When the pasta is cooked *al dente*, drain and add to the cauliflower mixture. § Combine carefully, then transfer to a heated serving dish. Sprinkle with a generous grinding of pepper. § Serve hot.

■ INGREDIENTS

• 1 small cauliflower
• salt
• 1 onion, thinly sliced
• 6 tablespoons extra-virgin olive oil
• 4 anchovy fillets
• 3 tablespoons seedless white raisins/sultanas
• 3 tablespoons pine nuts
• ¼ teaspoon saffron, dissolved in 3 tablespoons hot water
• freshly ground black pepper
• 1 lb/500 g bucatini pasta

Wine: a dry white (Alcamo)

VARIATION
– For a hearty winter dish, transfer the pasta and cauliflower mixture to a heated ovenproof dish and sprinkle with ½ cup/2 oz/60 g freshly grated pecorino cheese. Place in a preheated oven at 400°F/200°C/gas 6 for 10 minutes, or until the cheese topping has turned golden brown.

Right: Bucatini al cavolfiore

Malloreddus
Malloreddus with Italian sausages and pecorino cheese

Malloreddus ("little bulls"), or gnocchi sardi *as they are also known, are a specialty of the island of Sardinia. They are quite unlike the other dried pasta in this section, being made of bran flour and saffron. Malloreddus can be made fresh at home, but it is a difficult and time-consuming task and good commercial varieties are now available in specialty stores.*

Serves: 4–5; Preparation: 5 minutes; Cooking: 30 minutes; Level of difficulty: Simple

Combine the oil, sausages, onion, garlic, and basil in a skillet (frying pan) and sauté over medium heat until the onion turns golden brown. Add the tomatoes and salt and pepper to taste. Simmer for 15–20 minutes or until the sauce becomes thick. § Cook the malloreddus in a large pot of salted, boiling water until *al dente*. Drain well and transfer to a heated serving dish. Add the sauce and pecorino, and toss. Serve hot with lots of pecorino or parmesan on hand to sprinkle over each portion.

■ INGREDIENTS

- 3 tablespoons extra-virgin olive oil
- 9 oz/275 g Italian pork sausages, skinned and crumbled
- 1 large onion, finely chopped
- 3 cloves garlic, finely chopped
- 8 basil leaves, torn
- 1¾ lb/850 g fresh peeled and chopped tomatoes
- salt and freshly ground black pepper
- 6 tablespoons freshly grated pecorino cheese
- 1 lb/500 g malloreddus

Wine: a dry red (Cannonau)

Spaghetti alla Norma
Spaghetti with fried eggplant

Spaghetti alla Norma is a classic Sicilian dish. Debate rages about the origins of the name. Some say that it is named after Bellini's famous opera. Others maintain that it simply means la norma, *or something that happens often. It may also derive from the Catanese dialect, in which* norma *means "the very best."*

Serves: 4–5; Preparation: 1½ hours; Cooking: 40 minutes; Level of difficulty: Simple

Cut the eggplants into ¼-in (6-mm) thick slices, sprinkle with salt and place on a slanted cutting board, so that the bitter liquid they produce can run off. This will take about an hour. § Sauté the olive oil and garlic in a skillet (frying pan) over medium heat until the garlic turns gold. Add the tomatoes, basil, and salt and pepper to taste. Cook over medium-low heat for about 20 minutes, or until the oil and tomatoes begin to separate. § Run the eggplant under cold water and pat dry with paper towels. Put about 1¼ in (3 cm) of vegetable oil in a large skillet. When the oil is very hot, add as many slices of eggplant as will fit without overlapping. Fry to golden brown on both sides and drain on paper towels. When all the eggplant is fried, chop into large squares. § Cook the spaghetti in a large pot of salted, boiling water until *al dente*. Drain well and transfer to a heated serving dish. § Toss with the tomato sauce and fried eggplant. Sprinkle with the pecorino and serve hot.

■ INGREDIENTS

- 3 large eggplants/aubergines
- salt and freshly ground black pepper
- 3 tablespoons extra-virgin olive oil
- 3 cloves garlic, finely chopped
- 1½ lb/750 g peeled and chopped tomatoes
- 2 tablespoons basil, torn
- vegetable oil for frying
- 2 oz/60 g crumbled pecorino or salted ricotta cheese
- 1 lb/500 g spaghetti

Wine: a dry rosé (Cirò Superiore)

Right:
Spaghetti alla Norma

Bavette con fagiolini e pesto
Bavette with green beans, potatoes, and basil sauce

If you order pasta with pesto sauce in its hometown of Genoa, it will almost certainly be served with potatoes and green beans.

Serves: 4-5; Preparation: 15 minutes; Cooking: 25 minutes; Level of difficulty: Simple

Cook the vegetables in a large pot of salted, boiling water until tender. Take them out with a slotted spoon and use the same water to cook the pasta. § While the pasta is cooking, prepare the pesto. Add 2 tablespoons of boiling water from the pasta pot to make the pesto slightly more liquid. § When the pasta is cooked *al dente*, drain and transfer to a heated serving dish. Toss with the pesto, butter, and vegetables. Sprinkle with the cheeses, and serve hot.

■ INGREDIENTS

- 3 cups/1½ oz/750 g green beans, cut into lengths
- 3 medium new potatoes, peeled and diced
- 1 quantity *Genoese basil sauce* (see recipe p. 10)
- ¼ cup/2 oz/60 g butter
- 2 tablespoons freshly grated pecorino cheese
- 2 tablespoons freshly grated parmesan cheese
- 1 lb/500 g bavette pasta

Wine: a dry white (Vermentino)

Orecchiette con le bietole
Orecchiette with chard

For slightly different but equally delicious dishes, replace the Swiss chard with the same quantity of florets and diced stalks of green broccoli or cauliflower, or shredded savoy cabbage.

Serves: 4-5; Preparation: 10 minutes; Cooking: 15 minutes; Level of difficulty: Simple

Cook the chard in a pot of salted, boiling water (3–4 minutes for frozen, 8–10 minutes for fresh). Drain well and squeeze out any extra moisture. Chop finely. § Combine the garlic and anchovies in a large sauté pan with the oil. Sauté until the garlic turns gold. Add the chard. Season with salt and pepper. § Cook the orecchiette in a large pot of salted, boiling water until *al dente*. Drain well and transfer to the sauté pan with the sauce. Toss for 1–2 minutes over medium-high heat. Sprinkle with the pecorino and serve hot.

■ INGREDIENTS

- 1 lb/500 g fresh or 12 oz/375 g frozen Swiss chard/silverbeet
- 3 cloves garlic, finely chopped
- 8 tablespoons extra-virgin olive oil
- 2 anchovy fillets, crumbled
- 1 teaspoon crushed chilies
- salt and freshly ground black pepper
- freshly grated pecorino
- 1 lb/500 g orecchiette pasta

Wine: a dry red (Cirò)

Spaghetti di spinaci piccanti
Spicy spinach spaghetti

Serves: 4-5; Preparation: 15 minutes + 35 minutes for the sauce; Cooking: 12 minutes; Level of difficulty: Simple

Prepare the tomato sauce, stirring in the chilies just before it is ready. § Cook the spaghetti in a large pot of salted, boiling water until *al dente*. Drain well and transfer to the pan with the sauce. Toss for 1–2 minutes over medium-high heat. § Serve hot.

■ INGREDIENTS

- 1 quantity *Simple tomato sauce* (see recipe p. 2)
- 1 teapoon crushed chilis
- 1 lb/500 g spinach spaghetti

Wine: a dry red (Chianti)

Right: *Orecchiette con le bietole*

■ INGREDIENTS

- 1½ lb/750 g fresh asparagus
- ¼ cup/2 oz/ 60 g butter
- 8 oz/250 g ham, cut into thin strips
- 1 cup/8 fl oz/250 ml light/single cream
- 8 tablespoons freshly grated parmesan cheese
- salt and freshly ground black pepper
- 1 lb/500 g penne pasta

Wine: a dry white (Soave)

PENNE CON GLI ASPARAGI
Penne with asparagus

Serves: 4-5; Preparation: 10 minutes; Cooking: 15 minutes; Level of difficulty: Simple

Cook the asparagus in a pot of salted, boiling water until the tips are tender. Drain and remove the hard parts from each stalk. § Melt the butter in a saucepan with the ham. Cook for 2–3 minutes. Add the asparagus tips and cream, and stir gently over medium heat for 3–4 minutes, or until the cream thickens. Season with salt and pepper. § Cook the penne in a large pot of salted, boiling water until *al dente*. Drain and place in a heated serving dish. Add the sauce and toss well. Sprinkle with the parmesan and serve hot.

FUSILLI LUNGHI AI PORRI
Fusilli lunghi with leeks

■ INGREDIENTS

- 10 leeks
- 2 tablespoons/1 oz/30 g butter
- 6 tablespoons extra-virgin olive oil
- 1 onion, finely chopped
- 2 cloves garlic, finely chopped
- ⅔ cup/4 oz/125 g diced pancetta
- 1¼ cups/10 fl oz/300 ml boiling water
- salt and black pepper
- 2 egg yolks
- dash of sugar
- 4 tablespoons freshly grated pecorino cheese
- 1 lb/500 g fusilli lunghi

Wine: a light, dry red (Lambrusco)

Serves: 4-5; Preparation: 10 minutes; Cooking: 40 minutes; Level of difficulty: Simple

Prepare the leeks by discarding two layers of outer leaves and cutting off almost all the green part. Slice in thin wheels. Set aside. § Combine the butter, oil, onion, and garlic in a skillet (frying pan) and sauté over medium heat until the onion turns golden in color. Add the pancetta and stir until it browns. § Add the leeks and boiling water and simmer over low heat until the leeks are very tender. Season with salt and pepper. § Add the egg yolk and sugar, and stir vigorously. Remove from heat. § Cook the fusilli in a large pot of salted, boiling water until *al dente*. Drain well and transfer to a heated serving dish. Toss with the sauce and sprinkle with pecorino. Serve hot.

SPAGHETTI ALLA CARRETTIERA CLASSICA
Spaghetti with onion, garlic, and breadcrumbs

■ INGREDIENTS

- 1 large onion, finely chopped
- 2 cloves garlic, finely chopped
- 2 tablespoons finely chopped parsley
- 6 tablespoons extra-virgin olive oil
- 1 teaspoon oregano
- salt and freshly ground black pepper
- 3 tablespoons breadcrumbs
- 1 lb/500 g spaghetti

Wine: a dry white (Velletri)

This is a classic Roman recipe. It is said to have been the favorite dish of the carrettieri *(cart-drivers) who transported the Castelli Romani wine from the Alban Hills into Rome. There are many variations on the basic recipe given here. We have suggested the common tomato one below.*

Serves: 4-5; Preparation: 10 minutes; Cooking: 15 minutes; Level of difficulty: Simple

Sauté the onion, garlic, and parsley in a skillet (frying pan) with the oil, oregano, salt, and pepper to taste over medium heat until the onion and garlic turn golden in color. Remove from heat. § Toast the breadcrumbs in the oven and mix with a few drops of oil. § Cook the spaghetti in a large pot of salted, boiling water until *al dente*. Drain well and transfer to a heated serving dish. Toss with the sauce and breadcrumbs. Serve hot.

SPAGHETTI ALLA CARRETTIERA ROSSA
Spaghetti with onion, garlic, tomato, and bread crumbs

Serves: 4-5; Preparation: 10 minutes; Cooking: 15 minutes; Level of difficulty: Simple

Proceed as above, but add 6 medium peeled tomatoes and ¾ teaspoon crushed chilies to the onion and garlic mixture after it has changed color. § Cook over medium heat for 10–15 minutes until the tomatoes have reduced.

Left:
Fusilli lunghi ai porri

Insalata di ruote con le verdure
Ruote salad with vegetables

■ INGREDIENTS

- 6 tablespoons extra-virgin olive oil
- 1 large eggplant/aubergine
- 1 large yellow and 1 large red bell pepper/ capsicum
- 2 scallions/shallots
- 2½ tablespoons capers
- 1 teaspoon dried oregano
- 2 tablespoons finely chopped parsley
- 3 tablespoons freshly grated pecorino cheese
- salt and freshly ground black pepper
- 1 lb/500 g plain, whole wheat or colored ruote pasta

Wine: a dry white (Frascati)

Serves: 4-5; Preparation: 15 minutes; Cooking 15 minutes; Level of difficulty: Simple

Cook the ruote in a large pot of salted, boiling water until *al dente*. Drain thoroughly. Transfer to a large salad bowl and toss vigorously with half the oil. Set aside to cool. § Cut the stalk and hard base off the eggplant and peel. Cut crosswise into slices about ½ in (1 cm) thick. Place the slices under the broiler (grill) and cook for about 10 minutes, or until tender. Dice the cooked slices in ¾-in (2-cm) squares. § Quarter the bell peppers lengthwise and slice each quarter into thin strips. § Slice the white, bottom part of the scallion very finely. § When the pasta is completely cool, combine with the remaining oil, capers, oregano, parsley, eggplant, bell peppers, and pecorino and toss well. Sprinkle with salt and pepper and serve.

Insalata di fusilli con pomodori, aglio e mozzarella
Fusilli salad with tomato, garlic, and mozzarella cheese

■ INGREDIENTS

- salt and freshly ground black pepper
- 4 tablespoons extra-virgin olive oil
- 4 large ripe tomatoes
- 2 cloves garlic, minced
- 2 tablespoons finely chopped parsley
- 12 oz/375 g mozzarella cheese
- 6 fresh basil leaves
- 1 lb/500 g plain, whole wheat, or colored fusilli pasta

Wine: a dry white (Colonna)

Serves: 4-5; Preparation: 10 minutes; Cooking 10 minutes; Level of difficulty: Simple

Cook the fusilli in a large pot of salted, boiling water until *al dente*. Drain well. Transfer to a large salad bowl and toss vigorously with half the oil. Set aside to cool. § Cut the tomatoes into bite-size pieces and add to the pasta. Combine the garlic and parsley with the remainder of the oil and salt, and add to the salad bowl. Leave to cool completely. § Just before serving, dice the mozzarella into ½-in (1-cm) cubes on a cutting board. Slant the board slightly so that the extra liquid runs off. Sprinkle over the top of the salad with the torn basil leaves and freshly ground black pepper. Serve cool.

VARIATION
– Add 1 tablespoon of mustard to the oil for a sharper flavor.

Right:
Insalata di ruote con le verdure
and *Insalata di fusilli con pomodori*

■ INGREDIENTS

- salt
- 4 tablespoons extra-virgin olive oil
- 4 hard-cooked/hard-boiled eggs
- 3 large ripe tomatoes
- 7 oz/200 g tuna, preserved in oil
- 2 scallions/shallots
- 4 tablespoons mayonnaise
- 2 tablespoons finely chopped parsley
- 1 lb/500 g conchiglie pasta

Insalata di conchiglie splendida

Conchiglie with eggs, tomato, tuna, onion, and mayonnaise

Serves: 4-5; Preparation: 5 minutes; Cooking 12 minutes; Level of difficulty: Simple

Cook the conchiglie in a large pot of salted, boiling water until *al dente*. Drain very thoroughly. Transfer to a large salad bowl and toss well with half the oil. Set aside to cool. § Peel the eggs and cut into quarters lengthwise. Dice the tomatoes into bite-sized cubes. Break the tuna up by lightly pressing with a fork. Slice the white, bottom part of the scallion thinly. § When the pasta is cool, add the eggs, tomatoes, tuna, parsley, remaining oil, and mayonnaise. Sprinkle with salt, toss thoroughly, and serve.

Fresh and Filled Pasta

Fresh pasta, such as tagliatelle and fettucine, is made
of eggs and soft-wheat flour. Filled pasta is made
by wrapping small quantities of meat or vegetable
stuffing in fresh pasta. For the recipes in this chapter,
either make your own pasta (see pp. 292–295)
or buy it freshly made.

Tagliolini con carciofi
Tagliolini with artichoke and egg sauce

Serves: 4-5; Preparation: 5 minutes + time to make the pasta; Cooking: 25 minutes; Level of difficulty: Medium

Prepare the pasta. § Clean the artichokes as described on p. 210, slicing them thinly lengthwise. § Sauté the onion in the oil in a flameproof casserole until it is tender but not browned. § Add the artichokes and season with salt and pepper. Stir over a moderate heat for 2–3 minutes. § Pour in the water, cover and cook for about 20 minutes, or until very tender but not mushy. § Cook the tagliolini in plenty of salted, boiling water until they are cooked *al dente*. § Break the eggs into a deep, heated serving dish, beat with a fork and add 5 tablespoons of the cheese. § Drain the pasta and mix with the egg mixture, then stir in the artichokes. § Sprinkle with the remaining cheese and serve hot.

■ INGREDIENTS

- 8 baby artichokes
- 3 tablespoons finely chopped onion
- 5 tablespoons extra-virgin olive oil
- salt and freshly ground black pepper
- ½ cup/4 fl oz/125 ml water
- 3 fresh large eggs
- 7 tablespoons freshly grated pecorino cheese
- 1 lb/500 g tagliolini (see recipe pp. 292–294)

Wine: a dry white (Pinot Grigio)

Tagliolini al mascarpone
Tagliolini with mascarpone cheese sauce

Serves: 4-5; Preparation: 5 minutes + time to make the pasta; Cooking: 5 minutes; Level of difficulty: Medium

Prepare the pasta. § Warm the mascarpone in a saucepan. Remove from heat and stir in the egg yolks. Season with salt. § Cook the tagliolini in a large pot of salted, boiling water until *al dente*. Drain and toss with the sauce. Sprinkle with the parmesan and freshly ground black pepper. Serve hot.

■ INGREDIENTS

- 1 cup/3½ oz/100 g fresh mascarpone cheese
- 2 egg yolks
- salt and black pepper
- 8 tablespoons freshly grated parmesan cheese
- 1 lb/500 g tagliolini (see recipe pp. 292–294)

Wine: a dry white (Verdicchio)

Tagliatelle alle vongole con panna
Tagliatelle with clams and cream

Serves: 4-5; Preparation: 10 minutes + time to make the pasta + 1 hour to soak the clams; Cooking: 15 minutes; Level of difficulty: Medium

Prepare the pasta. § Scrub the clams and soak in cold water for 1 hour. § Put the clams in a large sauté pan, cover, and place over high heat until they open. Discard any that do not open. Remove from the pan and set aside with their juice. § Sauté the garlic in the same pan over medium heat with the oil, chilies, and bay leaves. When the garlic begins to change color, add the clams and their cooking juices, cream, tomatoes, and salt. Simmer over medium heat for 5–10 minutes, or until the sauce has reduced. § Cook the tagliatelle in a large pot of salted, boiling water until *al dente*. Drain well and transfer to the sauté pan with the clams. Toss quickly over medium-high heat and serve.

■ INGREDIENTS

- 2 lb/1 kg clams in shell
- 2 cloves garlic, minced
- 3 tablespoons extra-virgin olive oil
- ½ teaspoon crushed chilies
- 3 bay leaves
- ¾ cup/6 fl oz/180 ml light/single cream
- 3 large tomatoes, chopped
- salt
- 1 lb/500 g tagliatelle (see recipe pp. 292–294)

Wine: a dry white (Pinot Bianco)

Right: *Tagliolini con carciofi*

Pappardelle sulla lepre
Pappardelle with wild hare sauce

*This is a classic Tuscan dish. Traditionally the recipe calls for wild hare,
but if this is hard to find use the same amount of rabbit in its place.*

Serves: 4-5; Preparation: 20 minutes + time to make the pasta; Cooking: 2½ hours; Level of difficulty: Medium

Prepare the pasta. § Sauté the parsley, rosemary, onion, carrot, and celery with the oil in a heavy-bottomed pan over medium heat. When the onion and garlic begin to change color, add the hare meat and cook for 15–20 minutes or until the meat is well browned, stirring frequently. Add the wine and stir until it has evaporated. § Add the boiling water, milk, and tomato paste. Season with salt and pepper. Simmer over low heat for about 1½ hours. § Add the hare liver and, if necessary, more water. Cook for 30 more minutes, or until the hare is very tender. § Cook the pappardelle in a large pot of salted, boiling water until *al dente*. Drain well and place in a heated serving dish. Toss with the sauce and sprinkle with parmesan. Serve hot.

■ INGREDIENTS

- 3 tablespoons parsley, 1½ tablespoons fresh rosemary, 1 large onion, 1 large carrot, 1 stalk celery, all finely chopped
- ¾ cup/6 fl oz/180 ml extra-virgin olive oil
- 1¼ lb/625 g boneless wild hare meat, with liver, coarsely chopped
- 3 cups/24 fl oz/750 ml red wine
- 4 cups/1¾ pints/1 liter water
- ½ cup/4 fl oz/125 ml milk
- 2 tablespoons tomato paste
- salt and freshly ground black pepper
- 4 tablespoons freshly grated parmesan cheese
- 1 lb/500 g pappardelle (see recipe pp. 292–294)

Wine: a dry red (Chianti)

Tagliatelle al prosciutto
Tagliatelle with prosciutto

Serves: 4-5; Preparation: 5 minutes + time to make the pasta; Cooking: 12 minutes; Level of difficulty: Medium

Prepare the pasta. § Sauté the onion and fat from the prosciutto with the butter in a skillet (frying pan) until the onion begins to change color. Add the prosciutto and sauté for 2–3 minutes. Add the wine and simmer until it evaporates. Season with salt and pepper. § Cook the tagliatelle in a large pot of salted boiling water until *al dente*. Drain well and place in a heated serving dish. Pour the sauce over the top and toss vigorously. Sprinkle with parmesan and serve hot.

■ INGREDIENTS

- 1 medium onion, finely chopped
- 8 oz/250 g prosciutto, diced in ½-in/1-cm cubes
- ⅓ cup/2½ oz/75 g butter
- ¾ cup/6 fl oz/180 ml dry white wine
- salt and freshly ground black pepper
- 4 tablespoons freshly grated parmesan cheese
- 1 lb/500 g tagliatelle (see recipe pp. 292–294)

Wine: a rosé (Rosato di Carmignano)

Right: *Pappardelle sulla lepre*

INGREDIENTS

- 1 cup/6 oz/180 g diced pancetta
- ¼ cup/2 oz/60 g butter
- 2 cloves garlic, finely chopped
- salt and freshly ground black pepper
- 8 tablespoons freshly grated parmesan cheese
- 1 lb/500 g tagliatelle (see recipe pp. 292–294)

TAGLIATELLE ALLA PANCETTA
Tagliatelle with crispy-fried pancetta

Serves: 4-5; Preparation: 5 minutes + time to make the pasta; Cooking: 12 minutes; Level of difficulty: Medium

Prepare the pasta. § Sauté the pancetta, butter, and garlic over medium heat in a large skillet (frying pan) until the pancetta is crisp. § Cook the tagliatelle in a large pot of salted boiling water until *al dente*. Drain well and transfer to the skillet with the pancetta. Toss quickly over medium heat. § Sprinkle with the parmesan and season with pepper. Serve hot.

Paglia e fieno semplice
Paglia e fieno with cream and truffles

Two types of fettuccine, the plain yellow egg variety, and the green spinach variety, are often served together. This colorful mixture is called paglia e fieno, *which means "straw and hay."*

Serves: 4-5; Preparation: 5 minutes + time to make the pasta; Cooking: 10 minutes; Level of difficulty: Medium

Prepare the pasta. § Melt the butter in a heavy-bottomed pan and the white truffle. Leave to cook for 1 minute over low heat, then add the cream. Season with salt and pepper. Simmer for 4–5 minutes or until the cream reduces. § Cook the paglia e fieno in a large pot of salted, boiling water until *al dente*. Drain well and add to the pan with the truffle sauce. § Sprinkle with the parmesan and toss well over medium heat for 1–2 minutes. Serve hot.

■ INGREDIENTS

- ¼ cup/2 oz/60 g butter
- 1 white truffle, in shavings
- ¾ cup/6 fl oz/180 ml light/single cream
- salt and freshly ground black pepper
- 6 tablespoons freshly grated parmesan cheese
- 1 lb/500 g paglia e fieno (see recipe pp. 292–294)

Wine: a dry white (Pinot Bianco)

Paglia e fieno alla toscana
Tuscan-style paglia e fieno

Serves: 4-5; Preparation: 30 minutes + time to make the pasta; Cooking: 45 minutes; Level of difficulty: Medium

Prepare the pasta. § Place the pancetta, prosciutto, onion, celery, and carrot in a sauté pan with half the butter and sauté over medium heat until the onion is transparent. Add the tomatoes, mushrooms, nutmeg, and salt and pepper to taste. Cook over medium heat for 15 minutes. § Add the wine and, when it has all evaporated, the peas. Simmer over medium-low heat until the peas and mushrooms are tender, stirring in the meat broth as needed to keep the sauce liquid. § Cook the paglia e fieno together in a large pot of salted, boiling water until *al dente*. Drain well and transfer to a heated serving dish. Toss vigorously with the remaining butter. § Place the pasta, sauce, and parmesan separately on the table so that everyone can help themselves to as much cheese and sauce as they like.

■ INGREDIENTS

- ⅔ cup/4 oz/125 g diced pancetta
- ½ cup/2 oz/60 g diced prosciutto
- 1 large onion, 1 stalk celery, 1 large carrot, all finely chopped
- ¼ cup/2 oz/60 g butter
- 1¼ lb/625 g peeled and chopped tomatoes
- 12 oz/375 g mushrooms
- dash of nutmeg
- salt and black pepper
- ¾ cup/6 fl oz/180 ml dry white wine
- 3 cups/14 oz/450 g fresh or frozen peas
- ¾ cup/6 fl oz/180 ml *Beef broth* (see recipe p. 14)
- ¾ cup/3 oz/90 g freshly grated parmesan cheese
- 1 lb/500 g paglia e fieno (see recipe pp. 292–294)

Wine: a dry red (Chianti)

Right:
Paglia e fieno alla toscana

Tagliolini al curry
Tagliolini with curry sauce

■ INGREDIENTS

- 1 quantity *Béchamel sauce*
  (see recipe p. 22)
- 1 cup/8 fl oz/250 ml
  heavy/double cream
- 2 tablespoons fresh curry
  powder
- salt and black pepper
- 1 tablespoon/½ oz/15 g butter
- 8 tablespoons freshly
  grated parmesan cheese
- 1 lb/500 g tagliolini
  (see recipe pp. 292–294)

Serves: 4-5; Preparation: 10 minutes + time to make the pasta; Cooking: 15 minutes; Level of difficulty: Simple

Prepare the pasta and the béchamel sauce. § Stir the cream and curry powder into the béchamel and cook for 2–3 more minutes. Season with salt and pepper. § Cook the tagliolini in a large pot of salted, boiling water until *al dente*. Drain well and transfer to a heated serving dish. § Toss with the butter and the curry sauce. Sprinkle with parmesan and serve immediately.

■ INGREDIENTS

- 1¼ cups/7 oz/200 g fresh
  or frozen peas
- 3 oz/90 g gorgonzola
  cheese
- 1⅓ cup/10 fl oz/300 ml
  light/single cream
- salt and freshly ground
  black pepper
- 2 tablespoons finely
  chopped parsley
- 8 tablespoons freshly
  grated parmesan cheese
- 1 lb/500 g spinach
  tagliatelle (see recipe pp.
  292–294)

Wine: a light, dry white (Soave)

■ INGREDIENTS

- 4 cloves garlic, finely
  chopped
- ⅓ cup/3 fl oz/90 ml
  extra-virgin olive oil
- 1 lb/500 g ground lamb
- 5 oz/150 g ground lean pork
- 2 bay leaves
- 1½ lb/750 g peeled and
  chopped tomatoes
- 8 fresh basil leaves
- 1 teaspoon marjoram
- salt and freshly ground
  black pepper
- freshly grated pecorino
  cheese
- 1 lb/500 g maltagliati
  (see recipe pp. 292–294)

*Wine: a dry red
(Rosso di Montalcino)*

Left: *Tagliatelle verdi primaverili*

TAGLIATELLE VERDI PRIMAVERILI
Spinach tagliatelle with fresh cream, peas, and gorgonzola cheese

Serves: 4-5; Preparation: 10 minutes + time to make the pasta; Cooking: 15 minutes; Level of difficulty: Medium

Prepare the pasta. § Cook the peas in a pot of salted, boiling water. Drain well and set aside. § Place the gorgonzola, diced into ½-in (1-cm) squares, in a large heavy-bottomed pan over low heat. Stir the cheese until it melts. § Stir in the cream. Add the peas and salt and pepper to taste. § Cook the pasta in a large pot of salted, boiling water until *al dente*. Drain well and transfer to the pan containing the sauce. § Add the parsley and parmesan. Toss well and serve hot.

MALTAGLIATI AL RAGÙ DI AGNELLO
Maltagliati with lamb sauce

Maltagliati *(literally "badly cut") are usually served in broth, with minestrone, or pasta soups, but they are sometimes prepared with sauces. In some Italian dialects this pasta is known as* spruzzamusi, *or* bagnanasi, *words which are difficult to translate but which mean that you are likely to get broth or sauce on your nose, cheeks, and chin.*

Serves: 4-5; Preparation: 15 minutes + time to make the pasta; Cooking: 1¼ hours; Level of difficulty: Medium

Prepare the pasta. § Sauté the garlic with the oil in a heavy-bottomed pan over a medium heat until the garlic turns light gold in color. Add the lamb, pork, and bay leaf and sauté for 8–10 minutes. § Add the tomatoes, basil, and marjoram. Season with salt and pepper, and simmer over low heat for 1 hour. § Cook the maltagliati in a large pot of salted, boiling water until *al dente*. Drain, transfer to a heated serving dish, and toss with the sauce. § Serve hot, with lots of pecorino for sprinkling over each portion.

Tagliatelle alla frantoiana
Tagliatelle with olives and mushrooms

Serves: 4–5; Preparation: 10 minutes + time to make the pasta; Cooking: 25 minutes; Level of difficulty: Medium

Prepare the pasta. § Combine the garlic and parsley in a skillet (frying pan) with the oil and sauté until the garlic begins to change color. Add the mushrooms and cook until the water they produce has evaporated. § Add the olives, mint, salt, pepper, and boiling water. Simmer for 5 minutes. § Cook the tagliatelle in a large pot of salted, boiling water until *al dente*. Drain and transfer to a heated serving dish. Toss vigorously with the sauce and serve at once.

Fettuccine alla romagnola
Fettuccine with simple butter and tomato sauce

Serves: 4–5; Preparation: 5 minutes + time to make the pasta; Cooking: 35 minutes; Level of difficulty: Medium

Prepare the pasta. § Sauté the garlic and parsley with the butter in a skillet (frying pan). When the garlic begins to change color, add the tomatoes and season with salt and pepper. Simmer over medium-low heat for about 30 minutes. § Cook the fettuccine in a large pot of salted, boiling water until *al dente*. Drain well and transfer to a heated serving dish. § Toss vigorously with the tomato sauce and basil. Serve hot.

Tagliatelle verdi con burro e rosmarino
Spinach tagliatelle with butter and fresh rosemary sauce

Serves: 4–5; Preparation: 5 minutes + time to make the pasta; Cooking: 10 minutes; Level of difficulty: Medium

Prepare the pasta and the sauce. § Cook the pasta in a large pot of salted, boiling water until *al dente*. Drain well and transfer to a heated serving dish. § Pour the sauce over the top, toss well, and serve at once.

■ INGREDIENTS

- 2 cloves garlic, finely chopped
- 3 tablespoons finely chopped parsley
- ½ cup/4 fl oz/125 ml extra-virgin olive oil
- 4 cups/12 oz/375 g coarsely chopped mushrooms
- 1 cup/5 oz/150 g coarsely chopped black olives
- 8 mint leaves, torn
- salt and freshly ground black pepper
- ⅓ cup/3 fl oz/90 ml boiling water
- 1 lb/500 g tagliatelle (see recipe pp. 292–294)

Wine: a dry, sparkling red (Lambrusco)

■ INGREDIENTS

- 3 cloves garlic, finely chopped
- 3 tablespoons finely chopped parsley
- ½ cup/4 oz/125 g butter
- 2 lb/1 kg chopped tomatoes
- salt and freshly ground black pepper
- 8 fresh basil leaves, torn
- 1 lb/500 g fettuccine (see recipe pp. 292–294)

Wine: a rosé (Castel del Monte)

■ INGREDIENTS

- 1 quantity *Butter and rosemary sauce* (see recipe p. 10)
- 1 lb/500 g spinach tagliatelle (see recipe pp. 292–294)

Wine: a dry white (Verdicchio)

Right: *Fettuccine alla romagnola*

Tagliatelle al sugo d'anatra
Tagliatelle with duck sauce

Serves: 4–5; Preparation: 20 minutes + time to make the pasta; Cooking: 2½ hours; Level of difficulty: Medium

Prepare the pasta. § Wash the duck and pat it dry with paper towels. Sprinkle with the oil, salt, pepper, rosemary, sage, and bay leaf, and roast in a preheated oven for about 1 hour. Turn the duck and baste it with the white wine while it is cooking. Remove from the oven and set aside. § Sauté the garlic, onion, carrot, and celery in the gravy from the roast duck until the onion is transparent. Add the tomato paste and water. Season with salt and pepper. Simmer over medium-low heat for 15 minutes. § Bone the duck and chop the meat coarsely. Add to the pan with the vegetables and cook for 45 more minutes, adding water if necessary. § Cook the tagliatelle in a large pot of salted, boiling water until *al dente*. Drain well and transfer to a heated serving bowl. Pour the sauce over the top and sprinkle with the parmesan. Toss well, and serve hot.

■ INGREDIENTS

- 1 duck, cleaned and gutted, weighing about 2 lb/1 kg
- 3 tablespoons extra-virgin olive oil
- salt and freshly ground black pepper
- sprigs of fresh rosemary and sage
- 1 bay leaf
- 1 cup/8 fl oz/250 ml dry white wine
- 2 cloves garlic, 1 medium onion, 1 carrot, 1 stalk celery, all finely chopped
- 4 tablespoons tomato paste, dissolved in 1 cup/ 8 fl oz/250 ml water
- 6 tablespoons freshly grated parmesan cheese
- 1 lb/500 g tagliatelle (see recipe pp. 292–294)

Wine: a dry red (Sangiovese)

Tagliatelle al rosmarino
Tagliatelle in butter and rosemary sauce

This recipe comes from Piedmont in northern Italy. In another traditional Piedmontese recipe, the tagliatelle are served with the cooking juices left in the pan after roasting beef, pork, or poultry, and sprinkled with a little freshly grated parmesan.

Serves: 4–5; Preparation: 30 minutes + time to make the pasta; Cooking: 3 minutes; Level of difficulty: Medium

Prepare the pasta. § Cook the tagliatelle in a large pot of boiling salted water for 2–3 minutes. § Drain well, transfer to a heated serving dish and sprinkle with the parmesan. § Prepare the sauce. Drizzle over the tagliatelle and toss gently. § Top with slivers of fresh truffle, if using, and serve hot.

■ INGREDIENTS

- 1 lb/500 g tagliatelle (see recipe pp. 292–294)
- 3 tablespoons freshly grated parmesan cheese
- 1 quantity *Butter and rosemary sauce* (see recipe p. 10)
- wafer thin slices of fresh white truffle (optional)

Wine: a young dry red (Roero)

Right: Fettuccine all'Alfredo

INGREDIENTS

- ⅓ cup/2½ oz/75 g butter
- 1¼ cups/10 fl oz/300 ml heavy/double cream
- 8 tablespoons freshly grated parmesan cheese
- dash of nutmeg
- salt and freshly ground black pepper
- 1 lb/500 g tagliatelle (see recipe pp. 292–294)

Fettuccine all'Alfredo
Fettuccine with butter and cream sauce

Serves: 4–5; Preparation: 5 minutes + time to make the pasta; Cooking: 10 minutes; Level of difficulty: Medium

Place the butter and cream in a heavy-bottomed pan and cook over high heat for 2 minutes. Remove from heat. § Cook the fettuccine in a large pot of salted, boiling water until *al dente*. Drain well and transfer to the pan with the cream. Add the parmesan, nutmeg, salt and pepper to taste, and place over medium-low heat for 1 minute, tossing the pasta constantly. § Serve immediately.

Agnolotti con burro e salvia
Agnolotti with butter and sage sauce

Serves: 4-5; Preparation: 2 hours + time to make the pasta; Cooking: 3–5 minutes; Level of difficulty: Medium

Prepare the pasta dough. § Melt the butter for the filling in a saucepan and add the meat juices, cabbage, leek, and sausage meat. Cook for 5–6 minutes, stirring frequently and moistening, if necessary, with a little water. § Leave to cool before grinding twice together with the roast meat. § Place the finely ground mixture in a mixing bowl and add the egg, parmesan, nutmeg, salt, and pepper. Mix thoroughly, then set aside. § Prepare the agnolotti as shown on p. 295. § Spread the agnolotti out in a single layer on a lightly floured clean cloth and leave to dry in a cool place for at least 2 hours. § Cook the agnolotti in plenty of boiling salted water for 3–5 minutes. § Drain thoroughly and transfer to a heated serving dish. § Heat the butter and sage until golden brown and drizzle over the agnolotti. Sprinkle with the parmesan and serve.

Agnolotti con sugo di carne
Agnolotti with meat sauce

Serves: 4-5; Preparation: 30 minutes + time to make the pasta and the meat sauce; Cooking: 15 minutes; Level of difficulty: Medium

Make the pasta dough. § Prepare the agnolotti filling as explained above. § Prepare the agnolotti as shown on p. 295. § Prepare the meat sauce. § Cook the agnolotti in a large pot of salted, boiling water until the pasta round the sealed edges is *al dente*. Remove from the water using a slotted spoon and place on a heated serving dish. § Cover with the hot meat sauce. Sprinkle with the parmesan and, if using, shavings of white truffle. Serve hot.

■ INGREDIENTS

PASTA: see recipe pp. 292–295
FILLING

- 2 tablespoons/1 oz/30 g butter
- 3 tablespoons cooking juices from roast meat
- ½ cup/3 oz/90 g finely chopped savoy cabbage
- white part of a small leek, finely chopped
- ½ cup/2 oz/60 g Italian sausage meat
- ½ cup/6 oz/180 g each, lean roast beef and pork
- 1 egg
- 2 tablespoons freshly grated parmesan cheese
- freshly grated nutmeg
- salt and freshly ground white pepper

- 1 quantity *Butter and sage sauce* (see recipe p. 8)
- 4 tablespoons freshly grated parmesan cheese

Wine: a light, dry red (Grignolino)

■ INGREDIENTS

PASTA: see recipe pp. 292–295
FILLING: see above

- 1 quantity *Bolognese* or *Quick meat sauce* (see recipes p. 4)
- 4 tablespoons freshly grated parmesan cheese
- white truffle (optional)

Wine: a dry red (Dolcetto)

Right: *Agnolotti con burro e salvia*

RAVIOLI SEMPLICI AL BURRO
Ravioli with Italian sausage filling in butter and sage sauce

Serves: 4–5; Preparation: 20 minutes + time to make the pasta; Cooking: 10 minutes; Level of difficulty: Medium

Make the pasta dough. § Cook the spinach and chard in a pot of salted water until tender (3–4 minutes if frozen, 8–10 minutes if fresh). Squeeze out excess moisture and chop finely. § Mix the sausages, ricotta, eggs, parmesan, and marjoram with the spinach and chard in a mixing bowl. Combine thoroughly and season with salt. § Prepare the ravioli as shown on p. 295. § Cook in a large pot of salted, boiling water until the sealed edges of the ravioli are *al dente*. Drain and transfer to a heated serving dish. While the ravioli are cooking, prepare the sauce. § Pour the sauce over the ravioli and sprinkle with extra grated parmesan.

> VARIATION
> – *Ravioli semplici* are also very good with meat sauces (see recipes p. 4) or *Tomato and butter sauce* (see recipe p. 2).

■ INGREDIENTS

PASTA: see recipe pp. 292–295
FILLING
- 8 oz/250 g fresh or 5 oz/ 150 g frozen spinach
- 1¼ lbs/625 g fresh or 12 oz/375 g frozen Swiss chard/silverbeet
- 8 oz/250 g Italian pork sausages, skinned and crumbled
- 1 cup/8 oz/250 g fresh ricotta cheese
- 2 eggs
- 4 tablespoons freshly grated parmesan cheese
- 1 teaspoon fresh marjoram
- salt
- 1 quantity *Butter and sage sauce* (see recipe p. 8)

Wine: a dry red (Freisa)

RAVIOLI VERDI AL POMODORO
Spinach ravioli with ricotta cheese filling in tomato sauce

Serves: 4–5; Preparation: 30 minutes + time to make the pasta and the sauce; Cooking: 10 minutes; Level of difficulty: Medium

Make the spinach pasta dough. § Place the ricotta in a mixing bowl. Add the parsley, basil, eggs, nutmeg, and salt to taste. Combine the ingredients thoroughly and set aside. § Prepare the tomato and butter sauce. § Prepare the ravioli as shown on p. 295. § Cook in a large pot of salted, boiling water until the sealed edges of the ravioli are *al dente*. Drain well and transfer to a heated serving dish. § Pour the hot tomato sauce over the ravioli and toss gently. Sprinkle with the parmesan and serve hot.

■ INGREDIENTS

PASTA: see recipe pp. 292–295
FILLING
- 1 cup/8 oz/250 g fresh ricotta cheese
- 4 cups/4 oz/125 g parsley and 5 cups/5 oz/150 g fresh basil, finely chopped
- 2 eggs
- ¼ teaspoon nutmeg
- salt
- 4 tablespoons freshly grated parmesan cheese
- 1 quantity *Tomato and butter sauce* (see recipe p. 2)

Right: *Ravioli semplici al burro*

■ INGREDIENTS

PASTA: see recipe pp. 292–295

FILLING

- 1¾ cups/14 oz/450 g
  fresh ricotta cheese
- 2 eggs
- ¼ teaspoon nutmeg
- 4 tablespoons freshly
  grated parmesan cheese
- salt
- 1 quantity *Butter and sage
  sauce* (see recipe p. 8)

Wine: a dry white (Frascati)

RAVIOLI DI RICOTTA AL BURRO E SALVIA
Ravioli with ricotta filling in butter and sage sauce

Serves: 4-5; Preparation: 10 minutes + time to make the pasta; Cooking: 10 minutes; Level of difficulty: Medium

Make the pasta dough. § Place the ricotta in a mixing bowl and add eggs, nutmeg, parmesan, and salt to taste. Combine thoroughly. § Prepare the ravioli as shown on p. 295. § Cook the ravioli in a large pot of salted, boiling water until the pasta around the sealed edges is *al dente*. Drain well and transfer to a heated serving dish. § Cover with the sage sauce and extra grated parmesan. Toss gently and serve hot.

■ INGREDIENTS

- ½ quantity *Beef broth* (see recipe p. 14)

PASTA: see recipe pp. 292–295
FILLING

- ¼ cup/2 oz/ 60 g butter
- 4 oz/125 g lean pork (tenderloin), chopped into small pieces
- 4 oz/125 g mortadella
- 3 oz/90 g prosciutto
- 1¾ cups/7 oz/200 g freshly grated parmesan cheese
- 1 egg
- freshly grated nutmeg
- salt and freshly ground black pepper

Wine: a dry, lightly sparkling red (Lambrusco)

TORTELLINI IN BRODO
Tortellini in meat broth

Serves: 4-5; Preparation: 1 hour + time to make the pasta and the broth; Cooking: 2–3 minutes; Level of difficulty: Medium

Prepare the broth. § Make the pasta dough. § Shape the dough into a ball and set aside to rest for about 1 hour, wrapped in saran wrap (cling film). § Melt the butter in a skillet (frying pan) and gently fry the pork. § When cooked, grind it finely with the mortadella and prosciutto. § Transfer the meat mixture to a bowl and add the egg, parmesan, nutmeg, salt, and pepper. Mix well. § Using this mixture, prepare the tortellini as shown on p. 295. § Add the tortellini to the boiling broth and simmer for 2–3 minutes. Make sure that the broth is not boiling too fast, as the tortellini may come apart during cooking. § Serve in fairly deep soup dishes, allowing about 1 tablespoonful of stock for each tortellino.

■ INGREDIENTS

PASTA: see recipe pp. 292–295
FILLING: see recipe above
SAUCE

- 2 cups/10 oz/300 g fresh or frozen peas
- 14 oz/450 g coarsely chopped mushrooms
- 2 cloves garlic, minced
- 3 tablespoons finely chopped parsley
- 4 tablespoons extra-virgin olive oil
- two 14-oz/450-g cans peeled and chopped tomatoes
- salt and freshly ground black pepper

Wine: a dry red (Sangiovese)

Left: *Tortellini in brodo*

TORTELLINI ALLA BOSCAIOLA
Tortellini with woodsmen-style sauce

Serves: 4-5; Preparation: 25 minutes + time to make the pasta; Cooking: 35 minutes; Level of difficulty: Medium

Make the pasta dough. § Make the tortellini filling and set aside. § Cook the peas in boiling water. Drain and set aside. § Put the mushrooms, garlic, and parsley in a large sauté pan with the oil and cook for 5 minutes, or until the water the mushrooms produce has evaporated. Add the tomatoes and simmer for about 20 minutes. Add the cooked peas and salt and pepper to taste. Cook for 3–4 more minutes. § While the sauce is cooking, prepare the tortellini as shown on p. 295. § Cook in a large pot of salted, boiling water until sealed pasta edges are *al dente*. Drain well and transfer to the sauté pan. Toss gently and serve hot.

Ravioli di pesce con salsa di verdure
Ravioli with fish filling in vegetable sauce

Serves: 4-5; Preparation: 1 hour + time to make the pasta; Cooking: 15 minutes; Level of difficulty: Complicated

Make the pasta dough. § Melt the butter in a skillet (frying pan). Add the fish fillets and cook over medium heat for 5 minutes, or until tender. Chop the cooked fish very finely with a knife or in a food processor. § Cook the Swiss chard in a pot of salted water until tender (3–4 minutes if frozen, 8–10 minutes if fresh). Squeeze out excess moisture and chop finely. § Combine the fish and chard in a bowl with the ricotta, eggs, parmesan, and nutmeg. Add salt to taste and mix well. § Prepare the ravioli as shown on p. 295. Set aside. § Put the mushrooms in a small bowl of warm water and leave for 10 minutes. § Remove from the water and chop finely. Combine the vegetables with the butter in the pan used to cook the fish, add the tomatoes and 1 cup/8 fl oz/250 ml of water, and cook over medium-low heat for 20 minutes. Add salt to taste. § Roast the pine nuts in the oven and chop finely in a food processor. Add to the tomato sauce. § Cook the ravioli in a large pot of salted, boiling water until the sealed edges of the pasta are *al dente*. Drain well and transfer to a heated serving dish. § Pour the sauce over the top, sprinkle with parmesan, and serve immediately.

■ INGREDIENTS

PASTA: see recipe pp. 292–295
FILLING
• ¼ cup/2 oz/60 g butter
• 14 oz/450 g bass fillets
• 12 oz/375 g fresh or 7 oz/200 g frozen Swiss chard/silverbeet
• ¼ cup/2 oz/60 g fresh ricotta cheese
• 2 eggs
• 6 tablespoons freshly grated parmesan cheese
• ¼ teaspoon nutmeg
• salt
SAUCE
• 2½ tablespoons dried mushrooms
• 1 stalk celery, 1 medium onion, 1 tablespoon parsley, all finely chopped
• ½ cup/4 oz/125 g butter
• 4 ripe tomatoes, chopped
• salt
• 3 tablespoons pine nuts
• 8 tablespoons freshly grated parmesan cheese
Wine: a dry white (Cinque Terre)

Tortelli con le biete
Tortelli with Swiss chard filling in butter and parmesan sauce

Serves: 4-5; Preparation: 45 minutes + time to make the pasta; Cooking: 10-15 minutes; Level of difficulty: Medium

Make the pasta dough. § Cook the chard in a pot of salted water until tender (3–4 minutes if frozen, 8–10 minutes if fresh). Drain well and squeeze out any extra moisture. Chop finely and place in a mixing bowl. Add the ricotta, mascarpone, parmesan, eggs, and nutmeg. Mix thoroughly and add salt to taste. § Prepare the tortelli as shown on p. 295. § Cook the tortelli in a large pot of salted, boiling water until the sealed edges of the pasta are *al dente*. Drain well and transfer to a heated serving dish. Cover with the sauce, toss gently, and serve immediately.

■ INGREDIENTS

PASTA: see recipe pp. 292–295
FILLING
• 1 lb/500 g fresh or 11 oz/375 g frozen Swiss chard/silverbeet
• 1 cup/8 oz/250 g fresh ricotta cheese
• ⅔ cup/5 oz/150 g mascarpone cheese
• 6 tablespoons freshly grated parmesan cheese
• 2 eggs
• ¼ teaspoon nutmeg
• salt
• 1 quantity *Butter and parmesan sauce* (see recipe p. 6)
Wine: a dry red (Brachetto d'Acqui)

Right: *Tortelli con le biete*

Ravioli alle zucchine

Ravioli with zucchini filling in butter and rosemary sauce

Serves: 4-5; Preparation: 30 minutes + time to make the pasta; Cooking: 10 minutes; Level of difficulty: Medium

Make the pasta dough. § Cook the zucchini in a pot of salted, boiling water until tender. Drain, transfer to a bowl, and mash finely with a fork. Add the amaretti, ricotta, three-quarters of the parmesan, and nutmeg. Season with salt. Mix well to form a thick cream. If the filling is too liquid, add dry bread crumbs; if it is too thick add a little milk. § Prepare the ravioli as shown on p. 295. § Cook in a large pot of salted, boiling water until the sealed edges of the pasta are *al dente*. Drain well and transfer to a heated serving dish. § While the pasta is cooking, prepare the sauce. Place the garlic in a small saucepan with the butter and rosemary and cook for 3–4 minutes over medium heat, stirring frequently. § Pour the sauce over the ravioli, sprinkle with the parmesan, and serve.

■ INGREDIENTS

PASTA: see recipe pp. 292–295
FILLING

• 2 medium zucchini/
  courgettes
• ¾ cup/2½ oz/75 g
  crushed amaretti cookies
• ⅔ cup/5 oz/150 g fresh
  ricotta cheese
• 1 cup/4 oz/125 g grated
  parmesan cheese
• ¼ teaspoon nutmeg
• salt
• 1 quantity *Butter and rosemary
  sauce* (see recipe p. 10)

*Wine: a dry white
(Pinot Bianco)*

Rotolo ripieno

Stuffed pasta roll

Serves: 4-5; Preparation: 1 hour + time to make the pasta; Cooking: 1½ hours; Level of difficulty: Medium

Make the pasta dough. Roll it out to a thin, rectangular sheet measuring 12 x 16 in (30 x 40 cm). Cover with a clean cloth. § Wash the spinach and cook until tender. Squeeze out excess moisture and chop coarsely. § Sauté the spinach in 2 tablespoons/1 oz/30 g of butter and stir in 1 tablespoon of parmesan. § Sauté the mushrooms in 2 tablespoons/1 oz/30 g of butter for 4–5 minutes. § Poach the chicken livers in a little water, drain and chop finely. § Melt 1 tablespoon/½ oz/15 g of butter in a saucepan and fry the sausage meat over a low heat with the chopped chicken livers and ground veal. Season with salt and cook for 10 minutes, moistening with a little water if necessary. § Spread this mixture over the sheet of pasta dough, stopping just short of the edges. Cover with with an even layer of spinach. § Roll up lengthwise to form a long sausage. § Wrap tightly in a piece of cheesecloth and tie the gathered ends of the cloth with string. § Place the roll in boiling water in an oval casserole dish and simmer for 50 minutes. § Remove from the water and set aside to cool a little before untying and removing the cloth. § Slice and serve sprinkled with the remaining butter and parmesan.

■ INGREDIENTS

PASTA: see recipe pp. 292–295
FILLING

• 2 lb/1 kg spinach leaves
• 7 oz/200 g butter
• scant 1 cup/3½ oz/100 g
  freshly grated parmesan
  cheese
• 7 oz/200 g fresh
  mushrooms, thinly sliced
• scant 1 cup/7 oz/200 g
  trimmed chicken livers
• scant ½ cup/3½ oz/100 g
  fresh Italian sausage
  meat
• scant 1 cup/7 oz/200 g
  finely ground lean veal
• salt to taste

Wine: a dry red (Sangiovese)

Right: *Rotolo ripieno*

PASTA: see recipe pp. 292–295

• 1 quantity *Bolognese* or *Quick meat sauce* (see recipes p. 4)

FILLING

• 1¼ lb/625 g potatoes
• 1 medium onion
• ¼ cup/2 oz/125 g butter
• 6 tablespoons freshly grated parmesan cheese
• 3 eggs
• ¼ teaspoon nutmeg
• freshly ground black pepper

TORTELLI DI PATATE AL RAGÙ
Tortelli with potato filling in meat sauce

Serves: 4-5; Preparation: 40 minutes + time to make the pasta and meat sauce; Cooking: 10-15 minutes; Level of difficulty: Medium

Make the pasta dough. § Prepare the meat sauce. § Use the ingredients listed to prepare the potato tortelli as explained on p. 78. § Make the tortelli as shown on p. 295. § Cook the tortelli in a large pot of salted, boiling water until the sealed edges of the pasta are *al dente*. Drain well and transfer to a heated serving dish. § Spoon the meat sauce over the tortelli. Sprinkle with parmesan and serve.

Tortelli di patate al burro e salvia
Tortelli with potato filling in butter and sage sauce

Serves: 4-5; Preparation: 40 minutes + time to make the pasta; Cooking: 10-15 minutes; Level of difficulty: Medium

Make the pasta dough. § Peel the potatoes and cook them in salted, boiling water. § Put the onion and butter in a large sauté pan and cook until the onion begins to change color. § Mash the potatoes in a mixing bowl and add the onion, half the parmesan, the eggs, nutmeg and a dash of pepper. Mix thoroughly and set aside to cool. § Prepare the tortelli as shown on p. 295. § Cook the tortelli in a large pot of salted, boiling water until the sealed edges of the pasta are *al dente*. Drain well and transfer to a heated serving dish. § Make the butter and sage sauce and pour over the tortelli. Sprinkle with parmesan and serve hot.

■ INGREDIENTS

PASTA: see recipe pp. 292–295
FILLING
- 1¼ lb/625 g potatoes
- 1 medium onion
- ¼ cup/2 oz/125 g butter
- 6 tablespoons freshly grated parmesan cheese
- 3 eggs
- ¼ teaspoon nutmeg
- freshly ground black pepper
- 1 quantity *Butter and sage sauce* (see recipe p. 8)

Wine: a light, young dry white (Riesling dell'Oltrepò Pavese)

Tortelloni valdostani
Tortelloni with veal, spinach, and rosemary filling in cheese sauce

*Tortelloni are the same shape as tortellini only larger.
This dish comes from the Val d'Aosta, near the French border in northern Italy.*

Serves: 4-6; Preparation: 1½ hours + time to make the pasta; Cooking: 5-8 minutes; Level of difficulty: Medium

Make the pasta dough. § Place the rosemary in a sauté pan with the butter and sauté for 2–3 minutes. Add the veal and white wine, and simmer over medium-low heat. When the veal is tender, remove from the pan and chop finely with a knife or in a food processor. § Cook the spinach in a pot of salted water until tender (3–4 minutes if frozen, 8–10 minutes if fresh). Squeeze out excess moisture and chop finely. § Combine the veal and spinach in a bowl and add the eggs, parmesan, and nutmeg. Season with salt and pepper. Mix well with a fork and set aside for 1 hour. § Prepare the tortelloni as shown on p. 295. § Cook the tortelloni in a large pot of salted, boiling water until the sealed edges of the pasta are *al dente*. Drain well and transfer to a heated serving dish. § While the pasta is cooking, prepare the sauce. Combine the cheese, butter, and nutmeg in a small saucepan over very low heat until the cheese is melted. Pour over the tortelloni and serve hot.

■ INGREDIENTS

PASTA: see recipe pp. 292–295
FILLING
- 1 tablespoon finely chopped fresh rosemary
- ¼ cup/2 oz/60 g butter
- 10 oz/300 g lean veal
- 2 tablespoons dry white wine
- 8 oz/250 g fresh or 5 oz/150 g frozen spinach
- 1 egg and 1 egg yolk
- 4 tablespoons freshly grated parmesan cheese
- dash of nutmeg
- salt and freshly ground black pepper
SAUCE
- 7 oz/200 g fontina cheese
- ¼ cup/2 oz/60 g butter
- ½ teaspoon nutmeg

Right: Tortelloni valdostani

Baked Pasta

Baked pasta dishes are hearty fare, well-suited to cold winter evenings. Lasagna is the classic baked pasta dish, but there are many others. Most baked dishes are based on precooked pasta combined with béchamel, tomato, or meat sauces, sprinkled with tasty parmesan cheese which forms a golden crust in the oven.

RIGATONI GIGANTI FARCITI
Rigatoni giganti filled with meat sauce

Serves: 4; Preparation: 35 minutes + time to make the sauce; Cooking: 15 minutes; Level of difficulty: Medium

Prepare the meat sauce. § Cook the rigatoni in a large pot of salted, boiling water for half the cooking time indicated on the package. Drain well and place on dry dishcloths. § Sauté the mushrooms and half the butter over medium-low heat for 10 minutes, or until the mushrooms are tender. § Combine the mushrooms with the beef, half the meat sauce, the egg, flour, and wine in a heavy-bottomed pan. Mix well. Add all but 1 tablespoon of the tomato and water mixture. Season with salt and pepper. Cover, and cook over medium-low heat for about 15 minutes, stirring frequently. Remove from heat. § Fill a piping bag with the mixture and stuff the rigatoni. § Grease an ovenproof dish with butter and place the filled rigatoni in it. Mix the remaining tomato mixture and meat sauce together and pour over the top. Sprinkle with the parmesan and dot with the remaining butter. § Bake in a preheated oven at 350° F/180 °C/gas 4 for 15 minutes or until a golden crust has formed on top.

■ INGREDIENTS
- 1 quantity *Bolognese* or *Quick meat sauce* (see recipes p. 4)
- 1¼ cups/3½ oz/100 g chopped mushrooms
- ¼ cup/2 oz/60 g butter
- 10 oz/300 g ground beef
- 1 egg
- ½ tablespoon all-purpose/plain flour
- 4 tablespoons dry white wine
- 1 tablespoon tomato paste, dissolved in 1 cup /8 fl oz/250 ml hot water
- salt and freshly ground black pepper
- 8 tablespoons freshly grated parmesan cheese
- 14 oz/450 g rigatoni giganti

Wine: a dry red (Chianti)

LASAGNE AL FORNO
Lasagne with Bolognese meat sauce

Serves: 4-6; Preparation: 30 minutes + time to make the pasta and the sauce; Cooking: 20 minutes; Level of difficulty: Complicated

Prepare the meat sauce. § Make the pasta dough and prepare the lasagne. § Cook the lasagne 4–5 sheets at a time in a large pot of salted, boiling water for about 1½ minutes. Remove with a slotted spoon, plunge into a bowl of cold water to stop the cooking process. Remove quickly, and rinse gently under cold running water. Lay the sheets out separately on dry dishcloths and pat dry. § Prepare the béchamel and combine with the meat sauce. § Smear the bottom of a large oval baking dish with butter to stop the lasagne from sticking. Line with a single layer of cooked lasagne sheets. Cover with a thin layer of meat and béchamel sauce. Sprinkle with grated parmesan, then add another layer of lasagne. Repeat until there are at least 6 layers. Leave enough sauce to spread a thin layer on top. Sprinkle with parmesan and add knobs of butter. § Bake in a preheated oven at 400°F/200°C/gas 6 for 15–20 minutes, until a crust has formed on the top. Serve hot.

■ INGREDIENTS
- 1 quantity *Bolognese meat sauce* (see recipe p. 4)
- 1 lb/500 g spinach lasagne (see recipe pp. 292–294)
- 2 knobs butter
- 1 cup/4 oz/125 g freshly grated parmesan cheese
- 1 quantity *Béchamel sauce* (see recipe p. 22)

Wine: a dry red (Sangiovese)

Right: Lasagne al forno

Fusilli con mozzarella e pomodoro
Fusilli with tomatoes and mozzarella cheese

Serves: 4; Preparation: 30 minutes; Cooking: 30 minutes; Level of difficulty: Simple

Combine the garlic, parsley, and basil with the oil in a skillet (frying pan) and cook over medium heat until the garlic begins to change color. Add the tomatoes and chilies. Season with salt and pepper. Stir well and simmer over low heat for about 20 minutes, or until sauce has reduced. § Cook the fusilli in a large pot of salted, boiling water for half the time recommended on the package. Drain thoroughly and combine with the tomato sauce. Transfer the mixture to a greased baking dish and arrange the mozzarella over the top. Sprinkle with the pecorino. § Bake in a preheated oven at 350°F/180°C/gas 4 for about 30 minutes, or until the cheese is lightly browned.

Cannelloni di ricotta e spinaci
Cannelloni with ricotta and spinach filling in tomato and béchamel sauce

Serves: 4-6; Preparation: 40 minutes; Cooking: 20 minutes; Level of difficulty: Medium

Prepare the tomato sauce. § Cook the spinach in a pot of salted water until tender (3–4 minutes if frozen, 8–10 minutes if fresh). Drain, squeeze out excess moisture and chop finely. § Put half the butter in a skillet (frying pan) with the spinach. Season with salt and pepper. Cook briefly over high heat until the spinach has absorbed the flavor of the butter. § Transfer to a bowl and mix well with the ricotta, half the parmesan and the eggs. § Prepare the béchamel. § Cook the cannelloni in a large pot of salted, boiling water until half-cooked (about 5 minutes). Drain, and pass the colander with the pasta under cold running water. Dry the cannelloni with paper towels and stuff with the ricotta and spinach. § Line the bottom of an ovenproof dish with a layer of béchamel and place the cannelloni in a single layer on it. Cover with alternate spoonfuls of béchamel and tomato sauce. Sprinkle with the remaining parmesan and dot with butter. § Cook at 400°F/200°C/gas 6 for about 20 minutes or until a golden crust has formed on the top. Serve hot.

VARIATION
– Replace the tomato sauce with 1 quantity of *Bolognese* or *Quick meat sauce* (see recipes p. 4).

■ INGREDIENTS

- 2 cloves garlic, minced
- 2 tablespoons finely chopped parsley
- 8 fresh basil leaves, torn
- ⅓ cup/3 fl oz/90 ml extra-virgin olive oil
- two 14-oz/450-g cans chopped tomatoes
- ½ teaspoon crushed chilies
- salt and freshly ground black pepper
- 5 oz/150 g mozzarella cheese, thinly sliced
- 6 tablespoons freshly grated pecorino cheese
- 14 oz/450 g fusilli pasta

Wine: a dry red (Oltrepò Pavese)

■ INGREDIENTS

SAUCE
- ½ quantity *Tomato and butter sauce* (see recipe p. 2)
- 1 quantity *Béchamel sauce* (see recipe p. 22)

FILLING
- 1 lb/500 g fresh or 11 oz/300 g frozen spinach
- ¼ cup/2 oz/60 g butter
- 10 oz/300 g fresh ricotta cheese
- ¾ cup/3 oz/90 g freshly grated parmesan cheese
- 2 eggs
- salt and freshly ground black pepper
- 12 store-bought cannelloni (spinach or plain)

Wine: a light, dry red (Vino Novello)

Left:
Cannelloni di ricotta e spinaci

■ INGREDIENTS

- 1 quantity *Genoese basil sauce:* (see recipe p. 10)
- 1 lb/500 g spinach lasagne sheets (see recipe pp. 292–294)
- 2 knobs butter
- 1 cup/4 oz/125 g freshly grated parmesan cheese
- 1 quantity *Béchamel sauce* (see recipe p. 22)

Wine: a dry red (Sangiovese)

Lasagne verde al pesto

Spinach lasagne with basil sauce

This is the perfect recipe for vegetarians who don't want to give up the pleasures of this delicious Bolognese dish. For a mushroom version, replace the basil sauce with mushroom sauce (see recipe p. 12) and proceed in the same way.

Serves: 4-5; Preparation: 30 minutes + time to make the pasta and the sauce; Cooking: 20 minutes; Level of difficulty: Complicated

Prepare the basil sauce. § Make the pasta dough and prepare the lasagne. § Continue in exactly the same way as for *Lasagne with Bolognese meat sauce* (see instructions p. 82).

Penne gratinate al forno
Baked penne rigate

Serves: 4; Preparation: 30 minutes; Cooking: 30 minutes; Level of difficulty: Simple

Sauté the parsley, onion, and garlic with the oil in a skillet (frying pan) until lightly browned. Add the tomatoes and simmer over low heat for 25 minutes. § Cook the penne in a large pot of salted, boiling water for half the time shown on the package. Drain well. § Place a layer of pasta in a greased baking dish. Cover with a layer of pancetta, tomato mixture, and both cheeses. Repeat layers until the dish is full, reserving a little of both cheeses to sprinkle on top. They will turn golden brown in the oven. Bake in a preheated oven at 350°F/180/gas 4 for 30 minutes and serve piping hot.

Maccheroni incaciati
Maccheroni baked with veal, salami, eggs, mozzarella cheese, and vegetables

Serves: 4-6; Preparation: 1½ hours; Cooking 20 minutes; Level of difficulty: Simple

Cut the eggplants in ¼-in (6-mm) slices. To take away the harsh taste, sprinkle each slice with salt and place in a large bowl. Cover, and set aside for an hour. § Put the slices on a cutting board and remove the peel with a knife. Rinse under cold running water and pat dry with paper towels. § Dust the slices with flour. Heat the vegetable oil in a large skillet (frying pan) until very hot and add the eggplant. Sauté until golden brown on both sides. Remove from the pan and place on a platter covered with paper towels. § Grease a deep-sided ovenproof dish with a little oil and line the bottom with slices of fried eggplant. § Cook the garlic in a large sauté pan with the olive oil until it begins to change color. Add the tomatoes, veal, salami, peas, and basil and simmer over medium-low heat for about 30 minutes, stirring occasionally with a wooden spoon. Add the chopped chicken livers and cook for 5 more minutes. § Cook the maccheroni in a large pot of salted, boiling water for half the cooking time indicated on the package. Drain well. § Mix with the sauce, eggs, and any remaining eggplant slices. Pour into the baking dish with the eggplant. Cover with the sliced mozzarella and grated pecorino. Bake in a preheated oven at 400°F/200°C/gas 6 for about 20 minutes, or until a golden crust has formed on top. Serve hot in the baking dish.

■ INGREDIENTS

- 4 tablespoons parsley, 1 large onion, 2 cloves garlic, all finely chopped
- ¼ cup/2 fl oz/60 ml extra-virgin olive oil
- 1½ lb/750 g peeled and chopped fresh tomatoes
- salt and freshly ground black pepper
- 1½ cups/5 oz/150 g diced pancetta
- 8 oz/250 g diced mozzarella cheese
- 1 cup/4 oz/125 g freshly grated pecorino cheese
- 14 oz/450 g penne pasta

Wine: a dry red (Valpolicella)

■ INGREDIENTS

- 2 medium eggplants/ aubergines
- salt and black pepper
- 4 tablespoons all-purpose/plain flour
- vegetable oil for frying
- 1 clove garlic, chopped
- 4 tablespoons extra-virgin olive oil
- 14 oz/450 g tomatoes
- 3½ oz/100 g coarsely chopped veal
- ⅔ cup/3 oz/90 g diced salami
- 3½ oz/100 g peas
- 4 basil leaves, torn
- 3½ oz/100 g coarsely chopped chicken livers
- 2 hard-cooked/hard-boiled eggs, cut in quarters
- 1¼ cups/5 oz/150 g mozzarella cheese
- 4 tablespoons freshly grated pecorino cheese
- 14 oz /450 g maccheroni

Right: *Penne gratinate al forno*

Timballo di maccheroni alla ferrarese
Maccheroni with meat sauce, béchamel, and truffles baked in pastry casing

Serves: 4-6; Preparation: 30 minutes + time to make sauces; Cooking: 30 minutes; Level of difficulty: Complicated

Prepare the meat and béchamel sauces. § Prepare the pastry dough. § Cook the maccheroni in a large pot of salted, boiling water for half the time indicated on the package. Drain well and mix with half the meat sauce. § Grease an ovenproof baking dish with butter and sprinkle with finely ground breadcrumbs. Roll the dough out to about ⅛ in (3 mm) thick and line the baking dish. Line the bottom with a layer of béchamel, then cover with pasta and meat sauce. Sprinkle with fine shavings of truffle. Repeat until all the ingredients are in the baking dish. The last layer should be of béchamel. Sprinkle with the parmesan. § Bake in a preheated oven at 350°F/180°C/gas 4 for about 30 minutes. Serve hot.

■ INGREDIENTS

- 1 quantity *Bolognese meat sauce* (see recipe p. 4)
- 1 quantity *Béchamel sauce* (see recipe p. 22)
- 1 quantity plain pastry (see recipe for *Timballo di gnocchi* p. 98)
- 2 tablespoons/1 oz/30 g butter
- 2 tablespoons breadcrumbs
- 1 whole white truffle
- 1 cup/4 oz/125 g freshly grated parmesan cheese
- 1 lb/500 g maccheroni

Wine: a dry red (Barbaresco)

Strudel di spinaci al forno
Baked spinach and ricotta roll

Serves: 4-6; Preparation: 1 hour + time to make the pasta; Cooking: 45 minutes; Level of difficulty: Complicated

Make the pasta dough. § Cook the spinach in a pot of salted water until tender (3–4 minutes if frozen, 8–10 minutes if fresh). Drain, squeeze out excess moisture and chop finely. § Put the spinach in a bowl and add the ricotta, first measure of parmesan, and nutmeg. Combine thoroughly and season with salt. § Lightly flour a table top or flat work surface and roll the pasta dough out until it is very thin. Cut the dough into a 12 x 16-in (30 x 40-cm) rectangle. § Spread the spinach and ricotta mixture evenly over the top and roll it up. Seal the ends by squeezing the dough together. Wrap the roll tightly in cheesecloth, tying the ends with string. § Bring a large pot of salted water to a boil. The pot should be wide enough so that the roll can lie flat. Immerse the roll carefully into the boiling water and simmer for about 20 minutes. Remove from the pot and set aside. § While the roll is cooking, prepare the béchamel sauce. § Unwrap the spinach roll and cut into slices about ½ in (1 cm) thick. Cover the bottom of an ovenproof dish with the béchamel and top with slices of spinach roll. Sprinkle with the second measure of parmesan and bake in a preheated oven at 350°F/180°C/gas 4 for about 15 minutes, or until a golden crust forms on top. Serve hot.

■ INGREDIENTS

- 1 lb/500 g pasta (see recipe pp. 292–294)

FILLING

- 1¾ lb/875 g fresh or 1 lb/500 g frozen spinach
- 1 cup/8 oz/250 g fresh ricotta cheese
- 3 tablespoons freshly grated parmesan cheese
- ¼ teaspoon nutmeg
- salt
- 1 quantity *Béchamel sauce* (see recipe p. 22)
- 1 cup/4 oz/125 g freshly grated parmesan cheese

Wine: a dry red (Collio Merlot)

Right:
Strudel di spinaci al forno

Pasticcio di maltagliati al prosciutto
Baked maltagliati with ham, cream, and eggs

Serves: 4; Preparation: 15 minutes; Cooking: 1 hour; Level of difficulty: Medium

Melt the butter in a saucepan over low heat. Add the egg yolks, ham, and parsley, and stir with a wooden spoon for 2–3 minutes. Add the nutmeg and season with salt and pepper. Remove from heat. § Whip the cream until stiff. In a separate bowl, beat the egg whites until stiff. Gently stir the whipped cream into the egg whites and add to the butter mixture. § Cook the pasta in a large pot of salted, boiling water for half the recommended time. Drain well and place on dry dishcloths. § Grease an ovenproof dish with butter and place the pasta in it. Cover with the egg, cream, and ham mixture. Sprinkle with the parmesan cheese. Bake in a preheated oven at 350°F/180°C/gas 4 for about 50 minutes. Serve in the ovenproof dish.

VARIATION
– Replace the cream and egg whites with 1 quantity of *Béchamel sauce* (see recipe p. 22).

Pomodori ripieni di pasta
Baked tomatoes with pasta filling

Choose firm, red tomatoes with their stalks still attached for this tasty, baked tomato dish. The tomatoes can be served hot straight from the oven or left to cool and served as a cold entrée.

Serves: 4; Preparation: 20 minutes; Cooking: 40 minutes; Level of difficulty: Simple

Rinse the tomatoes and dry well. Cut the top off each tomato (with its stalk) and set aside. Hollow out the insides of the bottom parts with a teaspoon. Put the pulp in a bowl. § Place a basil leaf in the bottom of each hollow shell. § Cook the pasta in a medium pot of salted, boiling water for half the time indicated on the package. Drain well. § Combine the pasta with the tomato mixture. Add the parsley and 2 tablespoons of the oil. Season with salt and pepper. § Stuff the hollow tomatoes with the mixture. § Grease an ovenproof dish with the remaining oil and carefully place the tomatoes on it. Cover with the tomato tops. § Bake for about 40 minutes in a preheated oven at 350°F/180°C/gas 4. Serve either hot or cold.

*Left:
Pomodori ripieni di pasta*

Gnocchi

The most common type of gnocchi are the white
potato ones, made with mashed potatoes and flour.
But there are also spinach gnocchi, ricotta gnocchi,
baked semolina gnocchi, and fried gnocchi.

Gnocchi di patate al gorgonzola
Potato gnocchi with gorgonzola cheese sauce

Serves: 6; Preparation: 10 minutes + time to make the gnocchi; Cooking: 10 minutes; Level of difficulty: Medium

Prepare the potato gnocchi. § Put the gorgozola and butter in a heavy-bottomed pan. Place over low heat and stir gently with a wooden spoon until the cheese and butter have melted. Add the cream and cook over low heat for 3–4 minutes, or until the cream has reduced and the sauce is thick and creamy. Season with salt and pepper. § Cook the gnocchi, following the instructions on p. 20. Drain well and transfer to a heated serving dish. § Pour the gorgonzola sauce over the gnocchi, sprinkle with the parmesan and serve immediately.

■ INGREDIENTS

- 1 quantity *Potato gnocchi* (see recipe p. 20)

SAUCE

- 6 oz/200 g gorgonzola cheese
- ⅓ cup/2½ oz/75 g butter
- 1¼ cups/10 oz/300 ml fresh light/single cream
- salt and freshly ground black pepper
- 8 tablespoons freshly grated parmesan cheese

Wine: a dry white
(Corvo di Salaparuta)

Gnocchi di patate e spinaci al burro e salvia
Potato and spinach gnocchi in butter and sage sauce

Serves: 6; Preparation: 20 minutes; Cooking: 50 minutes; Level of difficulty: Medium

Cook the potatoes in their skins in a pot of salted, boiling water for 20 minutes, or until tender. Drain and peel while hot. § Cook the spinach in a pot of salted water until tender (3–4 minutes if frozen, 8–10 minutes if fresh). Drain and squeeze out excess moisture. § Purée the potatoes and spinach together in a food mill. Place the mixture on a flat work surface. Work the eggs and flour in gradually. Add the nutmeg. Season with salt and pepper. Knead the mixture until smooth. § To prepare and cook the gnocchi, follow the instructions for potato gnocchi on p. 20. § When the gnocchi are cooked, quickly prepare the butter and sage sauce. Pour over the gnocchi and toss gently. Sprinkle with parmesan and serve hot.

■ INGREDIENTS

- 1 lb/500 g boiling potatoes
- 1 lb/500 g fresh or 11 oz/ 300 g frozen spinach
- 2 eggs
- ⅔ cup/2½ oz/75 g all-purpose/plain flour
- ¼ cup/2 oz/60 g butter
- dash of nutmeg
- salt and freshly ground black pepper
- 2 tablespoons freshly grated parmesan cheese
- 1 quantity *Butter and sage sauce* (see recipe p. 8)

Wine: a dry red
(Rosso di Montalcino)

VARIATION
– These gnocchi make a delicious winter dish when baked. When they are cooked, drain well and place them in an ovenproof baking dish. Pour the melted butter and sage sauce over the top (or replace with 1 quantity *Basic tomato sauce*–see recipe p. 2). Sprinkle with ½ cup/2 oz/60 g freshly grated parmesan and bake in a preheated oven at 350°F/180°C/gas 4 for about 15 minutes, or until the topping is golden brown.

Right:
Gnocchi di patate al gorgonzola

■ INGREDIENTS

- 1 quantity *Potato gnocchi* (see recipe p. 20)
- ½ quantity *Béchamel sauce* (see recipe p. 22)
- 8 oz/250 g coarsely chopped fontina cheese
- 5 oz/150 g coarsely chopped gorgonzola cheese
- 5 oz/150 g mascarpone cheese
- 1 cup/4 oz/125 g freshly grated parmesan cheese
- salt and freshly ground black pepper

Gnocchi di patate ai quattro formaggi
Potato gnocchi with four-cheese sauce

Serves: 6; Preparation: 20 minutes + time to make the gnocchi; Cooking: 30 minutes; Level of difficulty: Medium

Prepare the potato gnocchi. § Prepare the béchamel sauce. Add the four cheeses and stir over low heat until they have melted and the sauce is smooth and creamy. Season with salt and pepper. § Cook the gnocchi in a large pot of salted, boiling water following the instructions on p. 20. When all the gnocchi are cooked and laid out on a heated serving dish, pour the cheese sauce over the top and toss gently. Serve hot.

Malfatti di parmigiano e spinaci
Parmesan and spinach gnocchi

Malfatti in Italian means "badly made" and refers to the fact that these little dumplings are similar to the stuffing used for ravioli. They are badly made because they lack their pasta wrappings. In Tuscany they are sometimes called Strozzaprete, or "priest chokers," although the origin of this name remains obscure.

Serves 6; Preparation: 20 minutes; Cooking: 20 minutes; Level of difficulty: Medium

Cook the spinach in a pot of salted, boiling water until tender (3–4 minutes if frozen, 8–10 minutes if fresh). Drain well and squeeze out excess moisture. Chop finely. § Mix the spinach with the ricotta, eggs, parmesan (reserving 2 tablespoons), and nutmeg. Season with salt and pepper. § Mold the mixture into walnut-sized balls. § Bring a large pot of salted water to a boil, add the dumplings, and cook until they rise to the surface. § Remove with a slotted spoon and place in a serving dish. § Prepare the sauce and pour over the dumplings. Sprinkle with the remaining parmesan and serve hot.

■ INGREDIENTS

- 1½ lb/750 g fresh or 1 lb /500 g frozen spinach
- 5 oz/150 g ricotta cheese
- 1 egg and 1 yolk
- 1 cup/4 oz/125 g freshly grated parmesan cheese
- dash of nutmeg
- salt and freshly ground black pepper
- 1 quantity *Butter and sage sauce* (see recipe p. 8) or 1 quantity *Butter and parmesan sauce* (see recipe p. 6)

Wine: a young, dry red (Vino Novello)

Gnocchi di spinaci e ricotta al pomodoro
Spinach and ricotta gnocchi in tomato and butter sauce

Serves: 6; Preparation: 45 minutes; Cooking: 25 minutes; Level of difficulty: Medium

Prepare the tomato and butter sauce. § Put the onion in a saucepan with the butter and sauté over medium heat until it turns golden brown. Remove the onion with a fork, leaving as much butter as possible in the pan. § Cook the spinach in a pot of salted water until tender (3–4 minutes if frozen, 8–10 minutes if fresh). Drain and squeeze out excess moisture. Chop finely. § Add the spinach to the pan with the butter. Sauté over medium-low heat for 10 minutes. Remove from heat and set aside. § When the spinach is cool, put it in a bowl with the ricotta, eggs, nutmeg, and all but 4 tablespoons of parmesan. Season with salt and pepper and mix well. Stir in the flour gradually until the dough is firm. § Lightly dust your hands with flour and roll pieces of dough into walnut-size balls. Place the gnocchi on a lightly floured platter. § Cook the gnocchi following the instructions on p. 20 for potato gnocchi. § Toss the gnocchi gently in the tomato sauce. Sprinkle with the remaining parmesan and serve hot.

■ INGREDIENTS

- 1 quantity *Tomato and butter sauce* (see recipe p. 2)
- 1 small onion, sliced in thin rings
- ¼ cup /2 oz/60 g butter
- 1½ lb/750 g fresh or 1 lb /500 g frozen spinach
- 7 oz/200 g fresh ricotta cheese
- 3 eggs
- dash of nutmeg
- 1½ cups/5 oz/150 g freshly grated parmesan cheese
- salt and freshly ground black pepper
- 2½ cups/10 oz/300 g all-purpose/plain flour

Wine: a dry red (Lambrusco)

Right:
Malfatti di parmigiano e spinaci

TIMBALLO DI GNOCCHI

Potato gnocchi in béchamel sauce baked in a pastry casing

■ INGREDIENTS

• 1 quantity *Potato gnocchi* (see recipe p. 20)

PASTRY

• 2 cups/8 oz/250 g all-purpose/plain flour

• ½ cup/4 oz/125 g butter

• 2 egg yolks

• finely grated rind of 1 lemon

• salt

• 1 quantity *Béchamel sauce* (see recipe p. 22)

• 8 tablespoons freshly grated parmesan cheese

• ¼ cup/2 oz/60 g butter

*Wine: a dry red
(Chianti delle Colline Pisane)*

Serves: 6; Preparation: 1 hour; Cooking: 1 hour; Level of difficulty: Complicated

Sift the flour into a mixing bowl with the eggs, lemon rind, and salt. Add the butter and mix well. When the dough is moist and firm but not sticky, roll it into a ball, cover with cling film, and place in the fridge for an hour. § Roll the dough out until it is about ⅜ in (9 mm) thick. Grease the bottom and sides of a baking dish with butter and line with the dough. Prick well with a fork so that it doesn't swell while in the oven. § Bake in a preheated oven at 400 °F/200 °C/gas 6 for about 20 minutes, or until the pastry is golden brown. § Prepare and cook the potato gnocchi. § Prepare the béchamel sauce. § Put the cooked gnocchi in the béchamel and mix gently. Transfer to the baking dish with the pastry. Sprinkle with the parmesan cheese. Return to the oven and bake for 10 minutes more. § Remove from the oven and slip the pastry casing containing the gnocchi out of the baking dish. Serve hot.

GNOCCHI DI LATTE

Fried gnocchi

■ INGREDIENTS

• 1 egg and 5 egg yolks

• 1 tablespoon sugar

• ¾ cup/3½ oz/100 g potato flour

• 2 cups/16 fl oz/500 ml milk

• ⅔ cup/5 oz/150 g butter

• ¼ teaspoon nutmeg

• ¼ teaspoon cinnamon

• salt

• 4 tablespoons all-purpose/plain flour

• 6 tablespoons breadcrumbs

• 8 tablespoons freshly grated parmesan cheese

Wine: a dry red (Collio Merlot)

Serves: 4-6; Preparation: 50 minutes; Cooking: 40 minutes; Level of difficulty: Medium

Beat the egg yolks in a bowl with the sugar until smooth. § Place the potato flour in a heavy-bottomed pan. Stir the milk in gradually. Add the egg mixture, 2 tablespoons/1 oz/30 g of the butter, nutmeg, cinnamon, and salt. Mix well with a wooden spoon. § Place the pan over medium heat and, stirring continually, bring to a boil. Boil for 10 minutes, stirring all the time. Remove from heat. § Turn the gnocchi batter out onto a flat work surface. Using a spatula dipped in cold water, spread it out to a thickness of about ½ in (1 cm) and leave to cool for 30 minutes. § Cut the batter into ½-in (1-cm) cubes. Beat the remaining egg in a bowl with a fork. Dust the gnocchi with flour, drop them into the beaten egg, then roll them in breadcrumbs. § Fry the gnocchi in the remaining butter until they are golden brown. Place on a heated serving dish, sprinkle with parmesan and serve.

Right: *Timballo di gnocchi* and *Gnocchi di latte*

Gnocchi alla romana
Baked semolina gnocchi

■ INGREDIENTS

• 5 cups/2 pints/1.2 liters milk
• ½ cup/4 oz/125 g butter
• 1¾ cups/10 oz/300 g semolina
• 4 egg yolks
• 1 teaspoon salt
• 8 tablespoons freshly grated parmesan cheese
• 8 tablespoons freshly grated gruyère cheese

Wine: a medium red
(Merlot di Aprilia)

Serves: 6; Preparation: 25 minutes; Cooking: 45 minutes; Level of difficulty: Medium

Put the milk and 2 tablespoons/1 oz/30 g of the butter in a heavy-bottomed pan and bring to a boil. Add the semolina very gradually just as the milk is beginning to boil. Stirring continually, cook over low heat for 15–20 minutes, or until the mixture is thick and no longer sticks to the sides of the pan. § Remove from heat and leave to cool for 2–3 minutes. Add the egg yolks, salt, 2 tablespoons of the parmesan and 2 tablespoons of the gruyère and mix well. § Wet a flat work surface with cold water and turn the gnocchi batter out onto it. Using a spatula dipped in cold water, spread it out to a thickness of about ½ in (1 cm). Leave the batter to cool to room temperature. § Use a cookie cutter or small glass with a diameter of about 1½–2 in (3–5 cm) to cut the gnocchi into round disks. § Grease a baking dish with butter and place a row of gnocchi at one end. Lean the next row of gnocchi on the bottoms of the first, roof-tile fashion. Repeat until the baking dish is full. § Melt the remaining butter and pour over the gnocchi. Sprinkle with the remaining parmesan and gruyère. § Bake in a preheated oven at 400°F/200°C/gas 6 for about 20 minutes, or until a golden crust forms on top. Serve hot.

Gnocchi alla bava
Baked potato gnocchi

■ INGREDIENTS

• 1 quantity *Potato gnocchi* (see recipe p. 20)

SAUCE
• 8 oz/250 g fontina cheese, sliced thinly
• ½ cup/4 oz/60 g butter
• 8 tablespoons freshly grated parmesan cheese

Wine: a dry red
(Barbaresco)

Right:
Gnocchi alla romana

Serves: 6; Preparation: 25 minutes; Cooking: 40 minutes; Level of difficulty: Medium

Prepare and cook the potato gnocchi. Place them in a greased baking dish and cover with the sliced fontina. Dot with butter and sprinkle with the parmesan. § Bake in a preheated oven at 430° F/230°C/gas 7 for about 10 minutes, or until a golden crust has formed. Serve hot.

VARIATIONS
— Melt half the butter with a clove of finely chopped garlic and pour over the gnocchi before adding the cheese.
— Spinach and ricotta gnocchi can also be baked in the same way (see recipe p. 96).

Soups

Soups are more typical of the northern and central regions of Italy. They range from simple broths and delicate creams, to rustic minestrone and other hearty soups, often prepared with bread, rice, or pasta.

Minestrone alla milanese
Milanese-style minestrone

Traditional Milanese minestrone contains cotenna and rice rather than pasta. If you can't find cotenna, double the quantity of pancetta. If you can't get fresh beans for this and other recipes in this chapter, use presoaked dried beans in their place.

Serves 4; Preparation: 30 minutes; Cooking: 2 hours; Level of difficulty: Simple

Put the cotenna (scraped and cut in ¼-in/6-mm strips), pancetta, garlic, onion, celery, parsley, sage, rosemary, potatoes, carrots, zucchini, tomatoes, and beans in a large pot. Add 2½ quarts/5 pints/3 liters boiling water, cover and simmer over low heat for at least 1¼ hours. § Chop the cabbage in ¾-in (2-cm) strips and add with the peas. Cook for another 25 minutes. § Season with salt and pepper and add the rice. § The minestrone will be cooked in about 20 minutes. § Serve with the parmesan passed separately.

> VARIATIONS
> – Add 2 leaves of finely chopped sage.
> – If you want a simple but very special vegetable soup, omit the rice.

■ INGREDIENTS

- 5 oz/150 g cotenna
- ½ cup/3 oz/90 g diced pancetta
- 1 clove garlic, minced
- 1 onion, coarsely chopped
- 2 celery stalks, sliced
- 1 tablespoon coarsely chopped parsley
- dash of finely chopped fresh rosemary leaves
- 1 potato, 2 carrots, 2 zucchini/courgettes, 2 tomatoes, diced
- 1 cup/5 oz/150 g fresh red kidney beans
- ½ cup/3 oz/90 g shelled peas
- ½ small savoy cabbage
- ¾ cup/5 oz/150 g short-grain rice
- salt and black pepper
- 4 tablespoons freshly grated parmesan cheese

Wine: a light, dry red (Riviera del Garda Bresciano - Chiaretto)

Minestrone di Asti
Asti-style minestrone

Serves 4; Preparation: 20 minutes; Cooking: 1¼ hours; Level of difficulty: Simple

Put the beans in a large pot, and cover with cold water to about 2 in (5 cm) above the top of the beans. § Cover and simmer over low heat for about 30 minutes. § Cut the cabbage in ¼-in (6-mm) thick strips, discarding the core. § Add the cabbage, potatoes, carrots, and celery to the pot, stir, and cook for 30 minutes more. § If needed, add a little boiling water, although the soup should be quite thick. § Add the rice and, after 15 minutes, the lard, garlic, parsley, and basil. Stir well. § Taste for salt and pepper. § Turn off the heat and let the minestrone stand for a few minutes while the rice finishes cooking. § Serve with the parmesan passed separately.

■ INGREDIENTS

- 1½ cups/8 oz/250 g fresh red kidney beans
- ½ small savoy cabbage
- 2 medium potatoes, 2 small carrots, diced
- 2 celery stalks, sliced
- 1 cup/7 oz/200 g short-grain rice
- ½ cup/3½ oz/100 g lard
- 1 clove garlic, minced
- 2 tablespoons parsley, finely chopped
- salt and black pepper
- 4 tablespoons freshly grated parmesan cheese

Wine: a dry red (Dolcetto d'Asti)

Right: *Minestrone alla milanese*

Zuppa alla pavese
Pavia soup

Serves 4; Preparation: 10 minutes; Cooking: 5 minutes; Level of difficulty: Simple

Fry the bread in the butter until crisp and golden brown on both sides. § Place two slices in each preheated, individual soup bowl. § Break one or two eggs carefully over the slices, making sure the yolks remain whole. Sprinkle with cheese and dust with pepper. Pour the boiling broth into each plate, being careful not to pour it directly onto the eggs. § Serve after a minute.

■ INGREDIENTS

- 8 thick slices dense grain, home-style bread
- ¼ cup/2 oz/60 g butter
- 4–8 fresh eggs
- 4 tablespoons of freshly grated parmesan cheese
- freshly ground black pepper
- 5 cups/2 pints/1.2 liters *Beef broth* (see recipe p. 14)

Wine: a dry white (Pinot Bianco)

Minestra di riso e prezzemolo
Rice and parsley soup

Serves 4; Preparation: 5 minutes; Cooking: 20 minutes; Level of difficulty: Simple

Bring the broth to a boil and add the rice. § Simmer for about 15 minutes. § Just before removing from the heat, add the parsley and butter. § Taste for salt, sprinkle with the parmesan, and serve immediately.

■ INGREDIENTS

- 6½ cups/2½ pints/1.5 liters *Beef broth* (see recipe p. 14)
- 1 cup/7 oz/200 g short-grain rice
- 1 tablespoon finely chopped parsley
- 1 tablespoon/½ oz/15 g butter
- salt
- 4 tablespoons freshly grated parmesan cheese

Passatelli
Cheese dumpling soup

Serves 4-5; Preparation: 25 minutes + 30 minutes' resting for the dumplings; Cooking: 5 minutes; Level of difficulty: Simple

Mix the parmesan with the breadcrumbs and eggs in a mixing bowl. § Soften the butter in a small saucepan and combine with the breadcrumbs. § Add the nutmeg, lemon rind, and salt and set aside for 30 minutes. § Press the mixture through a food mill, fitted with the disk with the largest holes, to produce short, cylindrical dumplings, about 1½ in (4 cm) long. Cut them off with the tip of a sharp knife as they are squeezed out of the mill. § Let the little worm-shaped dumplings fall directly into a saucepan of boiling broth and simmer until they bob up to the surface. § Turn off the heat. Leave to stand for a few minutes and then serve.

■ INGREDIENTS

- 1 cup/4 oz/125 g freshly grated parmesan cheese
- 1¼ cups/5 oz/150 g very fine dry breadcrumbs
- 3 eggs
- 1 tablespoon/½ oz/15 g butter
- freshly grated nutmeg
- grated peel of 1 lemon
- salt
- 6½ cups/2½ pints/1.5 liters *Beef broth* (see recipe p. 14)

Wine: a dry white (Chardonnay)

Right: *Minestra di riso e prezzemolo*

■ INGREDIENTS

- 1 carrot, 1 medium turnip, 1 zucchini/courgette, 1 large potato, diced
- 1 leek (white part only), 2 small celery hearts, sliced
- 1 medium onion, 1 oz/ 30 g spinach, coarsely chopped
- 1 tablespoon finely chopped parsley
- ½ cup/3 oz/90 g diced smoked pancetta (bacon)
- 9 cups/3½ pints/2 liters boiling *Beef broth* (see recipe p. 14)
- 1 cup/7 oz/200 g brown barley
- salt and freshly ground black pepper
- 4 tablespoons extra-virgin olive oil

Wine: a dry rosè (Casteller)

■ INGREDIENTS

- ¼ cup/2 oz/60 g butter
- 1 medium potato, diced
- 2 small leeks (white part only), sliced
- 3 cups/5 oz/150 g spinach, coarsely chopped
- 6½ cups/2½ pints/1.5 liters boiling *Beef broth* (see recipe p. 14)
- ¾ cup/5 oz/150 g short-grain rice
- salt
- 4 tablespoons freshly grated parmesan cheese

Wine: a dry white (Tocai di Lison)

Left: Orzetto alla Trentina

ORZETTO ALLA TRENTINA
Trento-style barley soup

Some versions of this delicious soup use pearl barley. I prefer to use unrefined brown barley, which differs in flavor and consistency. If you are unable to find it, use pearl barley. It will take about 30 minutes less to cook.

Serves 4; Preparation: 30 minutes; Cooking: 1½ hours; Level of difficulty: Simple

Put all the vegetables and the pancetta in a large pot. § Add the broth and when it begins to boil, add the barley (previously rinsed by putting it in a colander and passing it under the cold water faucet). Cover the pot, and simmer for 1½ hours, stirring occasionally. § Season with salt and pepper, and add the oil. Alternatively, pass the oil separately to be added at table.

MINESTRA DI RISO E VERDURE
Rice and vegetable soup

This is just one of the many light and tasty soups in Milanese cuisine. They are usually served for the evening meal.

Serves 4; Preparation: 20 minutes; Cooking: 30 minutes; Level of difficulty: Simple

Melt the butter in a saucepan over low heat and add the potato, leeks, and spinach. Sauté for a couple of minutes, stirring continuously. § Add the broth and simmer, covered, for 10 or more minutes. § Add the rice and stir. § The rice will be cooked in about 15 minutes. Taste for salt and sprinkle with the parmesan.

VARIATION
– Use the same quantity of Swiss chard/silverbeet instead of spinach.

RISO E LATTE
Rice and milk

Serves 4; Preparation: 5 minutes; Cooking: 35 minutes; Level of difficulty: Simple

Put the milk and water in a saucepan with ½ teaspoon salt and bring to a boil over high heat. § Add the rice and stir. Reduce the heat and cook for 25 minutes. The amount of cooking time depends on the quality of the rice, so taste it after about 25 minutes to see if it is ready. It should be *al dente* (slightly firm, but cooked). Add more salt if necessary. § Turn off the heat and add the butter. § Cover and let the soup stand for a few minutes. Serve hot with a bowl of parmesan passed separately to sprinkle over the soup.

■ INGREDIENTS

- 9 cups/3½ pints/2 liters whole/full cream milk
- 1 cup/8 fl oz/250 ml water
- salt
- 1½ cups/7 oz/200 g short-grain rice
- 1 tablespoon/½ oz/15 g butter
- grated parmesan cheese

Wine: a dry white (Gambellara)

CREMA DI ASPARAGI
Cream of asparagus soup

Serves 4; Preparation: 10 minutes; Cooking: 20-25 minutes; Level of difficulty: Simple

Trim the tough white parts off the asparagus and discard. § Melt half the butter in a heavy-bottomed pan and add the flour, stirring all the time. § Pour in the milk and then the broth. § Bring to a boil and add the asparagus. Season with salt and pepper. § Cook for about 15–20 minutes, or until the mixture is dense. § Press the mixture through a strainer or food mill and return to heat. § Mix the egg yolks, the remaining butter (softened), the parmesan, and cream together in a bowl. § Pour this mixture into the asparagus and stir until the cream is well mixed and dense. § Serve hot.

■ INGREDIENTS

- 2 lb/1 kg asparagus
- ¼ cup/2 oz/60 g butter
- 1 cup/4 oz/125 g all-purpose/plain flour
- 2 cups/16 fl oz/500 ml milk
- 2 cups/16 fl oz/500 ml *Beef broth* (see recipe p. 14)
- salt and white pepper
- 3 egg yolks
- ¾ cup/3 oz/90 g freshly grated parmesan cheese
- ½ cup/4 fl oz/125 ml light/single cream

Wine: a dry white (Breganze Vespaiolo)

CREMA DI PISELLI
Cream of pea soup

Serves 4; Preparation: 10 minutes; Cooking: 20-25 minutes; Level of difficulty: Simple

Melt the butter in a saucepan over low heat. Add the onion and sauté until it is soft and translucent. § Stir in the peas and cook for 2 minutes. § Add two-thirds of the boiling broth and cook for 20 minutes. § In the meantime, make the béchamel and set aside. § When the peas are cooked, press them through a strainer, or use a blender to make them into a smooth, fairly liquid purée. § Incorporate the béchamel sauce and mix thoroughly. If the soup seems too dense, add some of the remaining broth. Taste for salt. § Return the pan to the heat for 2–3 minutes until the soup is hot enough to be served.

■ INGREDIENTS

- 2 tablespoons/1 oz/30 g butter
- 1 onion, finely chopped
- 3 cups/14 oz/450 g shelled fresh peas
- 5 cups/2 pints/1.2 liters *Beef broth* (see recipe p. 14)
- ½ quantity béchamel sauce (see recipe p. 22)
- salt

Wine: a dry white (Pinot Grigio)

Right: *Crema di piselli*

- 1 large celery plant
- juice of 1 lemon
- salt and freshly ground
  black pepper
- 1 tablespoon/½ oz/15 g
  butter
- 1 tablespoon white wine
- 1 tablespoon parsley and
  1 clove garlic, finely chopped
- 1 cup/8 fl oz/250 ml *Vegetable
  broth* (see recipe p. 14)

Wine: a dry white (Frascati)

CREMA DI SEDANO
Cream of celery soup

Serves 4; Preparation: 15 minutes; Cooking: 20 minutes; Level of difficulty: Simple

Clean the celery and remove any tough outer stalks and stringy fibers. Chop coarsely and soak in a bowl of water with the lemon juice for 10 minutes. § Cook the celery in a pot of salted, boiling water for 5 minutes. Drain well. § Transfer to a heavy-bottomed pan and add the butter, wine, parsley, garlic, salt and pepper. Cook until the wine evaporates. § Add the broth and simmer for 10–15 minutes more. § Purée in a food mill. Return to the heat for 2–3 minutes. § Serve hot.

ZUPPA DI LENTICCHIE
Lentil soup

The amount of cooking time will vary depending on the age and quality of the lentils used.
If they are not soft after 50 minutes, add a little boiling water and continue cooking until they are.

Serves 4; Preparation: 10 minutes + 3 hours for soaking lentils; Cooking: 50 minutes; Level of difficulty: Simple

Put the lentils in a bowl and add cold water to cover by about 1¼ in (3 cm) Let soak for 3 hours. § Drain the lentils and place in a saucepan with the onion, carrots, celery, bay leaf, and garlic. Add enough cold water to cover to about 2 in (5 cm) above the level of the lentils. § Cover and cook over low heat for about 45 minutes. § Discard the bay leaf, add the sage and rosemary, and continue cooking, still covered and over low heat, for another 5–10 minutes or so. § At this point the lentils should be very soft and will begin to disintegrate. Add salt and pepper to taste, drizzle with the oil, and serve hot.

> VARIATION
> – To make cream of lentil soup, press the cooked lentils through a strainer, or purée in a processor or with an electric hand mixer. Sprinkle with 1 tablespoon of finely chopped parsley just before serving.

■ INGREDIENTS

- 1½ cups/10 oz/300 g dry lentils
- 1 medium onion, finely chopped
- 2 small carrots, diced
- 2 celery stalks, thinly sliced
- 1 bay leaf
- 2 cloves garlic, whole or finely chopped (optional)
- 3 fresh sage leaves, finely chopped
- 2 tablespoons finely chopped fresh rosemary
- salt and freshly ground white or black pepper
- 4 tablespoons extra-virgin olive oil

Wine: a dry white
(Verdicchio dei Castelli di Jesi)

ZUPPA DI BROCCOLO ROMANESCO
Green Roman cauliflower soup

This type of cauliflower is a beautiful emerald green and the florets are pointed rather than rounded as in white cauliflower. It is typical of Latium, the region around Rome. If you can't find it in your local market, use green sprouting broccoli in its place.

Serves 4; Preparation: 10 minutes; Cooking: 10 minutes; Level of difficulty: Simple

Separate the florets from the core of the cauliflower, keeping the tender inner leaves. Rinse thoroughly and place in a pot of salted, boiling water. Cook for about 8–10 minutes. § In the meantime, toast the bread, rub the slices with the garlic, and place them in individual soup bowls. When the cauliflower is cooked, pour several tablespoons of the cooking water over each slice. § Arrange the florets and leaves, well drained, on the toasted bread. Drizzle with the oil and lemon juice, and add salt and pepper to taste. Serve hot.

■ INGREDIENTS

- 1 green Roman cauliflower, weighing about 2 lb/1 kg
- 4 thick slices dense grain, home-style bread
- 1 large clove garlic
- 6 tablespoons extra-virgin olive oil
- 1 tablespoon lemon juice
- salt and freshly ground white or black pepper

Wine: a flavorful white (Marino)

Right:
Zuppa di lenticchie

■ INGREDIENTS

- 2 lb/1 kg yellow squash (hubbard or pumpkin) peeled and cut in pieces
- 10 oz/300 g each of carrots and leeks, diced
- 3 small celery stalks, from the heart, cut in pieces
- 5 cups/2 pints/1.2 liters Beef broth (see recipe p. 14)
- ½ cup/4 fl oz/125 ml light/single cream
- salt and white pepper
- 6 tablespoons freshly grated parmesan cheese

Wine: a light red (Bardolino)

■ INGREDIENTS

- 6½ cups/2½ pints/1.5 liters Beef broth (see recipe p. 14)
- ½ cup/3 oz/90 g coarse-grain semolina
- salt
- 2 tablespoons/1 oz/30 g butter
- freshly grated parmesan cheese

Wine: a light white (Colli Euganei Bianco)

■ INGREDIENTS

- 1 lb/500 g fresh spinach
- 3 eggs
- salt and pepper
- dash of nutmeg
- ¾ cup/3 oz/90 g freshly grated parmesan cheese
- 5 cups/2 pints/1.2 liters Beef broth (see recipe p. 14)

Left: *Crema di zucca*

CREMA DI ZUCCA
Cream of squash

Serves 4; Preparation: 30 minutes; Cooking: 30 minutes; Level of difficulty: Simple

Put all the vegetables in a pot and add the boiling broth, reserving a cup. Cover and simmer for 25 minutes, stirring occasionally. If necessary, add more broth. § Press through a strainer or use a blender to obtain a smooth, not too liquid purée. § Set over medium heat for 1–2 minutes. § Stir in the cream and add salt and pepper. § Let stand for a minute, sprinkle with the parmesan, and serve.

SEMOLINO IN BRODO
Semolina in beef broth

Serves 4; Preparation: 5 minutes; Cooking: 20 minutes; Level of difficulty: Simple

Sift the semolina slowly into the boiling broth, stirring with a wire whisk so no lumps will form. § Simmer for 20 minutes, stirring occasionally. § Taste for salt. § One minute before serving, add the butter and stir one last time. § Serve with a bowl of freshly grated parmesan passed separately.

ZUPPA DI SPINACI
Spinach soup

Serves 4; Preparation: 15 minutes; Cooking: 20 minutes; Level of difficulty: Simple

Cook the spinach for 8–10 minutes in a little salted water. § Chop finely and combine with the eggs, salt, pepper, nutmeg and parmesan in a bowl. § Add to a saucepan with the boiling broth and cook, stirring all the time for 1 minute. § Remove from the heat, cover, and set aside for 4–5 minutes. The egg will form a thick layer on top. § Serve hot with croutons or bread lightly fried in butter and garlic.

Zuppa di farro e verdure
Spelt and vegetable soup

Spelt has been grown in Italy for thousands of years. It has become popular again in recent years as healthier, wholefood eating habits have gained popularity. Look for it in specialty stores, or replace it with equal quantities of pearl barley.

Serves 4; Preparation: 20 minutes; Cooking: 1¾ hours; Level of difficulty: Simple

Put the beans in a saucepan with the sage and enough cold water to cover by 2 in (5 cm). Cover, and simmer for 45 minutes. § Discard the sage. Press half the beans through a strainer (or use a blender), with as much of the cooking water as needed to make a fairly dense cream. Then add the rest of the beans. § When only 20 minutes of the spelt's soaking time remain, combine the pancetta, leek, celery, carrot, Swiss chard, chilies, and garlic in a saucepan. § Add the broth, bring to a boil, and cook over medium heat for 15 minutes. § Add the spelt and half the oil and continue cooking for 20 minutes. § Add the beans and cook for another 20 minutes. § Season with salt, pepper, and a dash of nutmeg, if liked. § Drizzle with the remaining oil just before serving. § Serve hot.

Passatelli
Cheese Dumpling Soup

This hearty and healthy soup will be even tastier if made the day before serving.

Serves 4-5; Preparation: 50 minutes; Cooking: 5 minutes; Level of difficulty: Simple

Mix the parmesan with the breadcrumbs and eggs in a mixing bowl. § Soften the beef marrow by heating it gently in a small saucepan and then combine with the breadcrumbs. § Add the nutmeg, lemon zest, and salt and set aside for 30 minutes. § Press the mixture through a food mill, fitted with the disk with the largest holes, to produce short, cylindrical dumplings, about 1½ in (4 cm) long. Cut them off with the tip of a sharp knife as they are squeezed out of the mill. If the mixture is too stiff, add a little broth; if too soft, add some more breadcrumbs. § Let the little worm-shaped dumplings fall directly into a saucepan of boiling stock and simmer until they bob up to the surface. § Turn off the heat; leave to stand for a few minutes and then serve.

■ INGREDIENTS

• 12 oz/375 g dried red kidney, cranberry, or white beans, soaked
• 4 sage leaves
• ½ cup/3 oz/90 g diced pancetta
• 1 small leek, 1 stalk celery, 1 carrot, sliced
• 7 oz/200 g Swiss chard/silverbeet, coarsely chopped
• ¼ teaspoon crushed chilies
• 1 clove garlic, crushed
• ¾ cup/5 oz/150 g spelt
• 6½ cups/2½ pints/1.5 liters boiling *Beef broth* (see recipe p. 14)
• 6 tablespoons extra-virgin olive oil
• salt and freshly ground white or black pepper
• dash of nutmeg

Wine: a dry, aromatic red (Elba Rosso)

■ INGREDIENTS

• 8 oz/250 g ground beef
• 3 eggs
• 3 tablespoons freshly grated pecorino cheese
• ½ clove garlic, minced
• 1 tablespoon finely chopped parsley
• freshly grated nutmeg
• salt
• 4 cups/1¾ pints/1 liter *Beef broth* (see recipe p. 14)
• 1 cup/8 oz/250 g soft fresh ricotta cheese
• 3 tablespoons breadcrumbs

Right: Zuppa di farro e verdure

STRACCIATELLA
Rag soup

The name comes from the fact that when the eggs are rapidly mixed into the broth they form strands or tatters, in other words, rags. Versions differ slightly from one region to the next. This Roman recipe is perhaps the most classic.

Serves 4; Preparation: 2 minutes; Cooking: 1-2 minutes; Level of difficulty: Simple

Put the eggs, parmesan, a dash of freshly grated nutmeg, salt and pepper in a bowl. § Whisk for a minute, until the mixture is well combined but not foamy. § Pour it into a pot containing the broth, over medium heat, and mix rapidly with the whisk. As soon as the broth begins to boil again, the soup is ready and should be served immediately.

■ INGREDIENTS

- 4 eggs
- 4 tablespoons freshly grated parmesan cheese
- dash of nutmeg
- salt and freshly ground white pepper
- 5 cups/2 pints/1.2 liters boiling *Beef* or *Chicken broth* (see recipes pp. 14, 16)

Wine: a light medium or sweet white (Bianco Capena)

ACQUACOTTA
Cooked water

This soup was originally prepared with water, a few herbs, oil, eggs, and stale bread. It was a staple in the diet of the butteri *or cowboys of the Tuscan Maremma. It has become much richer over the years and there are many different versions.*

Serves 4; Preparation: 15 minutes; Cooking: 45 minutes; Level of difficulty: Medium

Plunge the tomatoes into boiling water for 10 seconds, then into cold water. Slip off the skins and cut in half horizontally. Squeeze out some of the seeds and cut the flesh in pieces. § Heat the oil in a large pot, add the onions and sauté over medium heat, stirring frequently, until they are soft and translucent. § Add the tomatoes, celery, and basil, and cook for 20 minutes; the sauce should be fairly thick. § Season with salt and pepper, add the broth and continue cooking for 20 minutes. § Lower the heat to the minimum. Break the eggs carefully into the soup, not too close together and taking care not to break the yolks. After 2–3 minutes the eggs will have set but still be soft. § Arrange the slices of bread in individual soup bowls and ladle out the soup with one or two eggs per serving. Sprinkle with pecorino and serve.

■ INGREDIENTS

- 14 oz/450 g ripe tomatoes
- 2 onions, sliced
- 4–5 tablespoons extra-virgin olive oil
- 2 celery stalks, cleaned and finely chopped
- 10 basil leaves
- 5 cups/2 pints/1.2 liters *Beef broth* (see recipe p. 14)
- salt and freshly ground black pepper
- 4–8 eggs
- 4–8 slices dense grain, home-style bread, toasted
- 4 tablespoons freshly grated pecorino cheese

Wine: a dry white (Galestro)

Right:
Stracciatella

■ INGREDIENTS

- 8 oz/250 g ground beef
- 3 eggs
- 3 tablespoons freshly
  grated pecorino cheese
- ½ clove garlic, minced
- 1 tablespoon finely
  chopped parsley
- freshly grated nutmeg
- salt
- 4 cups/1¾ pints/1 liter
  Beef broth (see recipe p. 14)
- *Beef broth* (see recipe p. 14)
- 1 cup/8 oz/250 g soft
  fresh ricotta cheese
- 3 tablespoons breadcrumbs

Minestra pasquali
Sicilian Easter soup

Serves 4; Preparation: 10 minutes; Cooking: 5 minutes; Level of difficulty: Simple

Combine the meat in a bowl with one egg, the cheese, garlic, parsley, nutmeg, and salt. § Mix well and shape heaped teaspoonfuls into little meatballs. § Bring the broth to a boil in a large saucepan. Drop in the meatballs and cook for 4–5 minutes. § Beat the remaining eggs and combine with the ricotta, breadcrumbs, and salt to make a smooth, creamy mixture. § Pour the egg mixture into the broth and stir with a fork for about 1 minute, until the egg sets into tiny shreds. § Serve hot.

RISI E BISI
Rice and pea soup

Serves 4; Preparation: 10 minutes; Cooking: 30 minutes; Level of difficulty: Simple

Melt half the butter in a pot with the oil. Add the onion and sauté until soft and translucent. § Add the parsley and garlic and sauté for 2–3 minutes. § Add the peas and a few tablespoons of the boiling broth, cover and cook over low heat for 8–10 minutes. § Stir in the remaining broth and the rice and cook for 13–14 minutes. § Taste to see if the rice is cooked. Season with salt. § Add the remaining butter and finish cooking. This will take another 2–3 minutes, depending on the rice. § Add the parmesan, mix well, and serve.

■ INGREDIENTS

- ¼ cup/2 oz/60 g butter
- 3 tablespoons extra-virgin olive oil
- 1 onion, finely chopped
- ½ clove garlic, minced
- 1 tablespoon finely chopped parsley
- 2½ cups/12 oz/375 g shelled baby peas
- 5 cups/2 pints/1.2 liters *Beef broth* (see recipe p. 14)
- 1¼ cups/8 oz/250 g short-grain rice
- salt
- 4 tablespoons freshly grated parmesan cheese

Wine: a dry white (Soave)

PANCOTTO
Bread and garlic soup

This is a very old peasant recipe from Tuscany.

Serves 4; Preparation: 8-10 hours to soak the fava beans; Cooking: 3 hours; Level of difficulty: Simple

Sauté the garlic in the oil for 2–3 minutes. § Pour in the broth and add the bread. Cook over medium-low heat for 15 mintues, stirring all the time. § Add the cheese, cover and set aside for 10 minutes before serving.

■ INGREDIENTS

- 4 cloves garlic, minced
- 6 tablespoons extra-virgin olive oil
- 8 oz/250 g day-old bread
- 5 cups/2 pints/1.2 liters boiling *Beef broth* (see recipe p. 14)
- salt and freshly ground black pepper
- 6 tablespoons freshly grated parmesan cheese

MINESTRA DI FAVE
Fava bean soup

Serves 4; Preparation: 8-10 hours to soak the fava beans; Cooking: 3 hours; Level of difficulty: Simple

Soak the fava beans in enough cold water to cover them amply for 8–10 hours. § Drain and transfer to a heavy-bottomed pan or earthenware pot. Add enough salted water to cover them by about 2 in (5 cm). § Cook over low heat for 3 hours, stirring frequently and mashing the fava beans with a fork. They should be completely disintegrated when cooked. § Add the oil, salt, and pepper and serve immediately.

■ INGREDIENTS

- 14 oz/450 g dry fava/broad beans
- 5–6 tablespoons extra-virgin olive oil
- salt and freshly ground black pepper

Wine: a dry red (Cacc'e Mmitte di Lucera)

Right: *Risi e bisi*

Macco di fave
Crushed fava beans

The origins of this dish go back to Ancient Roman times when mushes based on legumes or grains were an important part of the diet. The name comes from maccare *or "to crush". It is common, with variations, throughout southern Italy. This recipe comes from Calabria.*

Serves 4; Preparation: 15 minutes + 8-10 hours to soak the fava beans; Cooking: 3 hours; Level of difficulty: Simple

Soak the fava beans in enough cold water to cover them amply for 8–10 hours. § Combine the drained fava beans with 2 tablespoons of the oil, the tomatoes, onion, and celery in a heavy-bottomed pan or earthenware pot. Add 9 cups/3½ pints/2 liters of water. § Partially cover and cook over low heat for 3 hours, stirring frequently and mashing the fava beans with a fork. They should be a soft purée. § When cooked, add salt, pepper, and the remaining oil. § Serve the grated pecorino passed separately at table.

INGREDIENTS

- 1½ cups/8 oz/250 g dry fava/broad beans
- 5 tablespoons extra-virgin olive oil
- 7 oz/200 g peeled and chopped fresh or canned tomatoes
- 1 large red onion, thinly sliced
- 3 celery stalks, chopped
- salt and freshly ground black pepper
- 4 tablespoons freshly grated aged pecorino cheese (optional)

Wine: a dry red
(San Severo Rosso)

Canederli
Bread dumpling soup

Serves 4; Preparation: 45 minutes; Cooking: 15 minutes; Level of difficulty: Medium

Combine three-quarters of the milk with the bread in a large bowl and let stand for at least 30 minutes, mixing once or twice. The bread should become soft but not too wet. If necessary, add the remaining milk. § Squeeze out the excess milk by hand and put the bread back in the bowl, discarding the milk first. § Gradually add the eggs, sausage, pancetta, prosciutto, onion, half the parsley, and 3 scant tablespoons of flour, stirring continuously until the mixture is firm but elastic. If needed, add a little more flour. § In the meantime, bring 3 cups/24 fl oz/750 ml of water to a boil with 2 tablespoons of salt in a fairly deep pot. § Make small balls about 2 in (5 cm) in diameter with the bread mixture and dust with flour. § When they are all ready, drop the *canederli* into the boiling water. Turn the heat up to high until the water begins to boil, then lower the heat slightly and cook for 15 minutes. § Remove from the water with a skimmer. Drain, transfer to a tureen, and ladle in the boiling broth. Garnish with the parsley and serve piping hot.

INGREDIENTS

- 1¼ cups/10 fl oz/300 ml whole/full cream milk
- 8 oz/250 g dense grain, home-style, stale bread, cut in pieces
- 2 eggs
- 3 oz/90 g fresh Italian pork sausage meat
- ⅓ cup/3 oz/90 g finely chopped smoked pancetta
- ⅓ cup/3 oz/90 g finely chopped prosciutto
- 1 tablespoon finely chopped onion
- 2 tablespoons finely chopped parsley
- ¾ cup/2½ oz/75 g all-purpose/plain flour
- salt
- 5 cups/2 pints/1.2 liters boiling *Beef broth* (see recipe p. 14)

White: a dry white (Terlano)

INGREDIENTS

- 4 eggs
- 7 oz/200 g all-purpose/plain flour
- 2 cups/16 fl oz/500 ml whole/full cream milk
- 2 tablespoons finely chopped parsley
- salt and black pepper
- ¼ cup/2 oz/60 g butter
- 5 cups/2 pints/1.2 liters *Beef broth* (see recipe p. 14)
- 2 tablespoons chives

Above: *Canederli*

MINESTRA DI FRITTATA
Omelet soup

Serves 4; Preparation: 45 minutes; Cooking: 15 minutes; Level of difficulty: Medium

Combine the eggs, flour, milk, parsley, salt, and pepper in a bowl. § Heat the butter in a skillet (frying pan) and add tablespoons of the egg and flour mixture to make little "omelets." When cooked on both sides set aside to cool. § Roll the omelets up and slice thinly (they should look like tagliolini when unrolled). § Transfer to a heated soup tureen and pour the boiling beef broth over the top. § Sprinkle with the finely chopped chives and serve hot.

FRITTATINE IN BRODO
Crêpes in broth

■ INGREDIENTS

- 3 eggs
- 5 oz/150 g freshly grated pecorino cheese
- ½ tablespoon finely chopped parsley
- salt
- dash of nutmeg
- ⅔ cup/5 fl oz/150 ml whole/full cream milk
- 6–7 tablespoons all-purpose/plain flour
- 2 tablespoons/1 oz/30 g butter
- 5 cups/2 pints/1.2 liters boiling *Chicken broth* (see recipe p. 16)

Wine: a dry white (Trebbiano d'Abruzzo)

Serves 4; Preparation: 10 minutes; Cooking: 30 minutes; Level of difficulty: Medium

Beat the eggs in a bowl with 1 heaping tablespoon of pecorino, the parsley, salt, nutmeg, and one-third of the milk. § Gradually add the flour, alternating with the remaining milk. The batter should be fairly liquid. § Melt a quarter of the butter in a small, nonstick skillet (frying pan), about 6–7 in (15–18 cm) in diameter. When it is sizzling hot, pour in two spoonfuls of batter. § Tip the skillet and rotate, so that the batter spreads out to form a very thin crêpe. After less than a minute, turn it over with a spatula and cook for another minute or less on the other side. § Slide it onto a plate and repeat, adding a dab of butter to the skillet each time, until all the batter has been used. Stack the crêpes up in a pile. These quantities should make about 12 crêpes. § Dust each one with ½ tablespoon of pecorino. Roll them up loosely and arrange in individual soup bowls, three per person. § Pour the boiling broth over the top and serve with the remaining cheese.

PAPPA CON IL POMODORO
Bread soup with tomato

■ INGREDIENTS

- 8 oz/250 g dense grain, home-style bread, cut in slices 1½ in/3.5 cm thick and cubed
- 8 tablespoons extra-virgin olive oil
- 3 cloves garlic, crushed
- 2 bay leaves
- salt and freshly ground black pepper
- 14 oz/450 g firm ripe tomatoes

Wine: a dry white (Bianco Vergine Val di Chiana)

This Tuscan soup is a delicious way of using up leftover bread.

Serves 4; Preparation: 15 minutes; Cooking: 20-25 minutes: Level of difficulty: Simple

Put the diced bread in a preheated oven at 325°F/160°C/gas 3 for 10 minutes to dry it out, but without toasting. § In the meantime, plunge the tomatoes into boiling water for 10 seconds and then into cold. Peel and cut them in half horizontally. Squeeze gently to remove most of the seeds and chop the flesh into small pieces. § Pour 6 tablespoons of the oil into a heavy-bottomed pan or earthenware pot and add the garlic and bay leaves. § As soon as the oil is hot, add the diced bread and cook over medium-low heat for 3–4 minutes, stirring frequently. § Season with salt and pepper. § Stir in the tomatoes and, using a ladle, add about 2 cups /16 fl oz/500 ml of water. § Cook for 15 minutes, stirring occasionally. If the soup becomes too thick, add a little more water (remember, however, that traditionally this soup is very thick). § Drizzle the remaining oil over the top and serve hot.

Right:

Pappa con il pomodoro

■ INGREDIENTS

- 3½ lb/1.3 kg clams in shell
- 3 cloves garlic, crushed
- ½ cup/4 fl oz/125 ml extra-virgin olive oil
- 12 oz/375 g coarsely chopped tomatoes
- salt and freshly ground black pepper to taste
- ½ cup/4 fl oz/125 ml dry white wine
- 3 tablespoons finely chopped parsley
- 5 thick slices dense grain, home-style bread, toasted

ZUPPA DI VONGOLE
Clam soup

Serves 4; Preparation: 30 minutes + 1 hour to soak the clams; Cooking: 25 minutes; Level of difficulty: Medium

Soak the clams in cold water to eliminate sand, then rinse in plenty of cold water, discarding any that are open. § Sauté the garlic in the oil in a large heavy-bottomed pan for 1–2 minutes. Add the tomatoes, season with salt and pepper, and simmer for 10 minutes. § Add the clams, cover and cook until they have all opened (discard any that do not open). § Add the wine and simmer for 10 minutes. § Arrange the toasted bread in individual soup bowls and ladle the clam soup over the top. Sprinkle with the parsley and serve.

DADOLINI IN BRODO
Dice in beef or chicken broth

■ INGREDIENTS
- 3 large eggs
- 2 tablespoons/1 oz/30 g melted butter
- ¾ cup/3 oz/90 g freshly grated parmesan cheese
- ¾ cup/3 oz/90 g all-purpose/plain flour
- salt
- dash of nutmeg
- 6½ cups/2½ pints/ 1.5 liters *Beef* or *Chicken broth* (see recipes pp. 14, 16)

Wine: a dry white (Verduzzo)

Serves 4; Preparation: 10 minutes; Cooking: 1 hour; Level of difficulty: Simple

Combine the eggs, lukewarm melted butter, parmesan, salt, and nutmeg to taste in a bowl. Mix well with a fork, then slowly add the flour to the mixture, making sure that no lumps form. § Pour into a lightly buttered square or rectangular nonstick pan, large enough for the mixture to spread out to about ¾-in (2-cm) deep. § Bake in a preheated oven at 300°F/150°C/gas 2 for 1 hour. § Cut into squares when cool. Add to the tureen and pour the boiling broth in over the top. § Serve immediately.

ZUPPA MARICONDA
Dumplings in meat or chicken broth

■ INGREDIENTS
- 7 oz/200 g day-old bread, without the crust, broken into pieces
- 1¼ cups/10 fl oz/300 ml whole/full cream milk
- ¼ cup/2 oz/60 g butter
- 3 eggs
- 5 tablespoons freshly grated parmesan cheese
- dash of nutmeg
- salt and freshly ground white pepper (optional)
- 6½ cups/2½ pints/ 1.5 liters *Beef* or *Chicken broth* (see recipes pp. 14, 16)

Wine: a light, dry white (Collio Goriziano)

Serves 4; Preparation: 40 minutes + 1 hour in the refrigerator; Cooking: 5-7 minutes; Level of difficulty: Simple

Put the bread in a bowl with the milk to soften. After 15–20 minutes, drain and squeeze out some, but not all, of the milk. § Melt the butter in a nonstick skillet (frying pan). Add the bread and let it dry out over low heat, mixing well. This will take 2–3 minutes. The bread should stay soft because it will have absorbed the butter. § Transfer to a bowl and add the eggs, parmesan, nutmeg, and salt and pepper to taste. Mix well to obtain a smooth mixture. § Cover with plastic wrap or a plate and place in the refrigerator for 1 hour. § Take teaspoonfuls of the mixture to make small dumplings, about the size of a large marble, and line them up on a clean work surface. § Bring the broth to a boil in a fairly deep pot and add the dumplings. § Lower the heat as soon as the broth begins to boil again. When the dumplings are cooked they will rise to the surface. § Serve hot, with extra grated parmesan, if desired.

MINESTRINA IN BRODO
Pasta and meat, chicken, fish, or vegetable broth

■ INGREDIENTS
- 4 cups/1¾ pints/1 liter *Broth* (see recipes pp. 14, 16)
- 8 oz/250 g tiny pasta shapes
- freshly grated parmesan cheese

Serves 4; Preparation: 5 minutes + time to make the broth; Cooking: 5-10 minutes; Level of difficulty: Simple

Prepare the broth. § Put the broth in a saucepan, add the pasta, and simmer until the pasta is cooked *al dente*. § Sprinkle with parmesan and serve.

Right: Dadolini in brodo

■ INGREDIENTS

- 1 lb/500 g white or red
  kidney beans, canned, or
  soaked and precooked
- 1 onion, finely chopped
- 1 tablespoon finely
  chopped fresh rosemary
- 4 tablespoons extra-virgin
  olive oil
- 1 ripe tomato, chopped
- salt and freshly ground
  black pepper
- 7 oz/200 g of small,
  tubular pasta

Wine: a dry white (Tocai di Lison)

Minestra di pasta e fagioli
Pasta and bean soup

Serves 4; Preparation: 5 minutes; Cooking 25 minutes + overnight soaking and cooking if using dried beans; Level of difficulty: Simple

Purée three-quarters of the beans in a food mill or blender. § Combine the onion and rosemary in a heavy-bottomed pan with the oil and sauté briefly over high heat. Before the onion begins to change color, add the puréed beans, tomato, and, if necessary, one or two cups of water. Season with salt and pepper and simmer over medium-low heat for about 15 minutes. § Add the pasta and remaining whole beans, and cook for 6–7 minutes, or until the pasta is cooked. Serve hot.

■ INGREDIENTS

- 1¾ cups/10 oz/300 g dry
  garbanzo beans/chick peas
- 7 oz/200 g young Swiss
  chard/silverbeet
- 4 tablespoons extra-virgin
  olive oil
- 1 onion, finely chopped
- 1–2 whole cloves garlic,
  lightly crushed
- 3–4 anchovy fillets in oil
- 3 plum tomatoes, peeled
  and chopped
- salt and freshly ground
  black pepper
- 4–8 slices dense grain,
  home-style bread, toasted
- 4 tablespoons freshly
  grated pecorino cheese

Wine: a dry white (Montecarlo)

Left: *Cacciucco di ceci*

Cacciucco di ceci
Garbanzo bean soup

Serves 4; Preparation: 30 minutes + 12 hours to soak the garbanzo beans; Cooking: 3½ hours; Level of difficulty: Medium

Place the garbanzo beans in a bowl and add enough cold water to cover them by at least 2 in (5 cm). Soak for 12 hours. § About 3½ hours before you intend to serve the soup, put the Swiss chard, well rinsed but not drained dry, in a pot and cook, covered, for 5 minutes over medium heat. Set aside. § Heat the oil in a large, heavy-bottomed pan or earthenware pot. Add the onion and garlic and sauté until the onion is soft and translucent. § Add the anchovy fillets, mashing them with a fork as you stir. § Drain the garbanzo beans and add to the pot, together with the chard and the liquid it was cooked in, and the tomatoes. Season with salt and pepper, stir, and add about 9 cups/3½ pints/2 liters of hot water. § Cover the pot and simmer over medium heat for at least 3 hours. The garbanzo beans should be very tender. § Arrange the toast in individual soup bowls and ladle the soup over the top. § Sprinkle with the pecorino and serve.

Minestra di riso e patate
Rice and potato soup

Serves 4; Preparation: 20 minutes; Cooking: 20-25 minutes; Level of difficulty: Simple

Put the pancetta, onion, and rosemary in a pot and sauté over low heat for 2–3 minutes, stirring frequently. § Add the potatoes and the broth. As soon as it begins to boil, add the rice, stir once or twice and cook for 15 minutes. § Taste for salt and to see if the rice is cooked. Add the parsley just before serving, and pass the cheese separately.

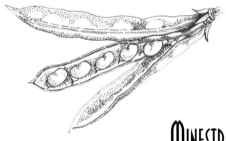

Minestra di riso e fagioli
Rice and bean soup

Cannellini or white beans are not available fresh throughout the year, and soaking and cooking dried beans requires time and forethought. This recipe for a typically Tuscan soup is based on canned beans.

Serves 4; Preparation: 25 minutes; Cooking: 40-45 minutes; Level of difficulty: Medium

Put the oil, pancetta, onion, celery, garlic, parsley, basil, chilies, and sage in a pot, preferably earthenware. Cook over low heat for 7–8 minutes, stirring occasionally. § In the meantime plunge the tomatoes into boiling water for 10 seconds, then into cold. Peel them and cut in half horizontally. Squeeze lightly to remove most of the seeds. Chop the flesh coarsely and stir them into the pot. § Simmer for 15 minutes, covered, stirring occasionally. § Add the beans and boiling broth and cook for another 5 minutes. § Add the rice which will take about 15 minutes to cook. If necessary, add a little more boiling broth or water (although bear in mind that the soup should be quite thick). Season with salt and serve hot.

VARIATIONS
– Use one 14-oz/450-g can of tomatoes, well drained and chopped, in place of the fresh tomatoes.
– This soup can be served lukewarm or cold (at room temperature) particularly in summer. In that case cook the rice for just 10 minutes.

■ INGREDIENTS

- ⅓ cup/2 oz/60 g finely chopped lean pancetta
- ½ onion, finely chopped
- 1 tablespoon finely chopped rosemary leaves
- 2 medium potatoes, peeled and sliced
- 1 cup/7 oz/200 g short-grain rice
- 6½ cups/2½ pints/1.5 liters boiling *Beef broth* (see recipe p. 14)
- salt
- 1 tablespoon coarsely chopped parsley
- 4 tablespoons freshly grated parmesan cheese

Wine: a dry white (Valdadige)

■ INGREDIENTS

- 3 tablespoons extra-virgin olive oil
- ⅓ cup/2 oz/60 g finely chopped lean pancetta
- 1 medium onion, 1 celery stalk, finely chopped
- 1 clove garlic, finely chopped
- ½ tablespoon finely chopped parsley
- 6 basil leaves, torn
- ¼ teaspoon crushed dried chilies
- 1 sage leaf, finely chopped
- 3 medium tomatoes
- two 14-oz/450-g cans white beans, drained
- 5 cups/2 pints/1.2 liters *Beef broth* (see recipe p. 14)
- 1 cup/7 oz/200 g short-grain rice
- salt

Wine: a dry red (Rosso delle Coline Lucchesi)

Right: *Minestra di riso e patate*

ZUPPA DI CIPOLLE
Onion soup

Serves 4; Preparation: 15 minutes; Cooking: 40 minutes; Level of difficulty: Simple

Combine the onions, oil, celery, and carrot in a deep, heavy-bottomed saucepan or earthenware pot. Cover and sauté over low heat, stirring frequently. § After 20 minutes season with salt and pepper. § Continue cooking, stirring and adding a spoonful or so of the boiling broth, for another 20 minutes. § Dilute with the remaining broth. § Place the toast in a tureen or individual soup bowls and pour the soup over the top. Sprinkle with the pecorino and serve.

ZUPPA DI VALPELLINE
Valpelline soup

This delicious soup comes from a village called Valpelline in the Valle d'Aosta in the northwest.

Serves 4; Preparation: 20 minutes; Cooking: 1 hour; Level of difficulty: Medium

Clean the cabbage and cut in quarters, discarding the core so that the leaves are no longer attached. § Melt the lard in a saucepan over low heat, add the cabbage leaves, cover and cook for 10–15 minutes, stirring occasionally. § Dry the bread out in a preheated oven at 300°F/150°C/gas 2 for 15 minutes. Make sure it doesn't get too dark. § Arrange a layer of toasted slices on the bottom of a large ovenproof baking dish and drizzle with 2 tablespoons of pan juices. Cover with one-third of the prosciutto and one-third of the cabbage. Season with a sprinkling of the spices and distribute one-third of the fontina on top. Repeat the procedure twice. § Before adding the last layer of fontina, pour on as much broth as needed to just cover the layers. § Arrange the remaining fontina on the top and dot with dabs of butter. § Place the dish in a preheated oven at 300°F/150°C/gas 2 and gradually increase the temperature (in 15 minutes it should reach 400°F/200°C/gas 6). Cook for 30–40 minutes. § Serve hot straight from the oven.

■ INGREDIENTS

- 2 lb/1 kg red onions, cut in thin slices
- 7 tablespoons extra-virgin olive oil
- 1 small celery stalk, finely chopped
- 1 small carrot, finely chopped (optional)
- salt and pepper
- 5 cups/2 pints/1.2 liters *Beef broth* (see recipe p. 14)
- 4 slices dense grain, home-style bread, toasted
- 4 tablespoons freshly grated pecorino cheese

Wine: a dry white (Bianco dei Colli Maceratesi)

■ INGREDIENTS

- 1 medium savoy cabbage
- ¼ cup/1 oz/30 g lard
- 8–10 slices dense grain, home-style bread, toasted
- ½ cup/4 fl oz/125 ml pan juices from a roast
- 5 oz/150 g prosciutto, finely chopped
- dash of nutmeg
- dash of ground cloves
- dash of ground cinnamon
- 7 oz/200 g fontina cheese, cut in thin slivers
- 5 cups/2 pints/1.2 liters warm *Beef broth* (see recipe p. 14)
- 2 tablespoons/1 oz/30 g butter

Wine: a dry, fruity white (Blanc de Morgex)

Right: *Zuppa di cipolle*

■ INGREDIENTS

- 2 lb/1 kg turnips, cleaned and cut in half vertically, then sliced
- 5 oz /150 g diced lean pancetta
- 2 oz/60 g finely chopped lard
- 1 clove garlic, finely chopped
- 9 cups/3½ pints/2 liters boiling *Beef broth* (see recipe p. 14)
- 4–8 slices toasted bread
- salt and freshly ground black pepper
- 5 tablespoons freshly grated parmesan cheese

Wine: a dry white
(Bianco di Custoza)

■ INGREDIENTS

- 1 oz/30 g dried porcini mushrooms
- ½ tablespoon finely chopped calamint or parsley
- 1 clove garlic, finely chopped
- 5 tablespoons extra-virgin olive oil
- 1¼ lb/650 g porcini (or white) mushrooms, thinly sliced
- ½ cup/4 fl oz/125 ml dry white wine
- 5 cups/2 pints/1.2 liters boiling *Vegetable broth* (see recipe p. 14)
- 1 tablespoon all-purpose/ plain flour
- salt and freshly ground pepper
- 4 slices toasted bread

Wine: a light, dry rosé
(Colli Altotiberini Rosato)

Left: *Zuppa di funghi*

ZUPPA DI RAPE
Turnip soup

A rustic, winter soup from Piedmont in the north.

Serves 4; Preparation: 20 minutes; Cooking: 30 minutes: Level of difficulty: Simple

Put the turnips, pancetta, lard, and garlic in a heavy-bottomed saucepan. Add the broth, cover, and simmer over low heat for 30 minutes. § Season with salt and pepper. § Arrange the toast in individual soup bowls, sprinkle with half the cheese, and pour the soup over the top. § Serve the rest of the cheese passed separately.

VARIATIONS
– Sauté the pancetta, lard, and garlic for 4–5 minutes. Add the turnips, stir and sauté 2 more minutes before adding the broth.
– Serve the soup in a tureen, alternating a layer of toast sprinkled with cheese with 2 ladles of soup.

ZUPPA DI FUNGHI
Mushroom soup

If you can't get fresh porcini, use the same quantity of white mushrooms.
In this case, double the quantity of dried porcini.

Serves 4; Preparation: 40 minutes; Cooking: 35-40 minutes; Level of difficulty: Medium

Soak the dried porcini mushrooms in 1 cup/8 fl oz/250 ml of tepid water for 30 minutes, then drain and chop finely. § Strain the water in which they were soaked and set aside. § Sauté the calamint (or parsley) and garlic with 4 tablespoons of oil in a heavy-bottomed saucepan over medium heat for 30 seconds. § Add the dried mushrooms, and after a couple of minutes, the fresh mushrooms. Sauté for about 5 minutes, stirring occasionally. § Pour in the wine, and after a couple of minutes, begin gradually adding the broth and mushroom water. § Simmer for about 25 minutes. § Heat the remaining oil in a skillet (frying pan) over low heat. Add the flour and brown slightly, stirring carefully. § Remove the skillet from the heat and add 3–4 tablespoons of the mushroom liquid, mixing well so that no lumps form. § Pour this mixture into the soup. Cook another 2–3 minutes, stirring continuously. § Arrange the bread in individual soup bowls, or in a tureen, and pour the soup over the top.

Zuppa di acciughe
Fresh anchovy soup

Serves 4; Preparation: 30 minutes; Cooking: 25 minutes; Level of difficulty: Medium

Combine the oil, onion, celery, carrot, parsley, garlic, and chilies in a heavy-bottomed saucepan or earthenware pot and sauté over low heat for 6–7 minutes or until the mixture turns soft. § Plunge the tomatoes into a pot of boiling water for 10 seconds and then into cold. Drain and peel. § Cut them in half horizontally, and squeeze to remove some of the seeds. Chop coarsely. § Add to the pan and continue cooking for about 10 minutes. § Add the anchovies, pour in the wine, and stir carefully. § Simmer for 5–8 minutes over low heat, adding the boiling water a little at a time. Don't stir during this stage, just shake the pan occasionally. § Pour the soup into individual soup bowls over the slices of toasted bread and serve.

■ INGREDIENTS

- 4 tablespoons extra-virgin olive oil
- ½ small onion, ½ celery stalk, ½ small carrot, all finely chopped
- ½ tablespoon finely chopped parsley
- 1 clove garlic, finely chopped
- ¼ teaspoon crushed chilies
- 2 medium-large tomatoes
- 2 lb/1 kg fresh anchovies, without their heads, split, cleaned, and boned
- 1 cup/8 fl oz/250 ml dry white wine
- 2 cups/16 fl oz/500 ml salted, boiling water
- salt
- 4-8 slices toasted bread

Wine: a dry white (Pigato di Albenga)

Zuppa di moscardini
Octopus soup

Moscardini are a kind of tiny octopus. If you can't get them fresh or frozen, use very small squid in their place. To clean them, turn the head inside out like a glove, remove the inner organs, and discard the eyes and the beak (the white ball in the middle of the base of the tentacles).

Serves 4; Preparation: 20 minutes; Cooking: 40 minutes; Level of difficulty: Simple

Plunge the tomatoes into boiling water for 10 seconds, then into cold, slip off the skins, and cut into pieces. § Heat the oil with the parsley and garlic in a heavy-bottomed saucepan or an earthenware pot. § Add the moscardini and braise for 3 minutes over medium heat, stirring continuously. § Add the wine and when this has evaporated, add the tomatoes, chilies, and a little salt. § Stir one last time and cover the pot— the *moscardini* produce a good deal of liquid which, together with that of the tomatoes, has to be kept from evaporating. Cook for 30 minutes, shaking the pot frequently. § Finally, taste for salt and pour the soup over slices of toasted bread in a tureen or individual plates.

■ INGREDIENTS

- 4 medium tomatoes, ripe and firm
- 4 tablespoons extra-virgin olive oil
- 1 tablespoon finely chopped parsley
- 1 clove garlic, finely chopped
- 1½ lb/750 g moscardini, cleaned, rinsed, and cut in pieces
- ½ cup/4 fl oz/125 ml dry white wine
- ¼ teaspoon crushed chilies
- salt
- 4–8 slices toasted bread

Wine: a dry white (Vernaccia di San Gimignano)

VARIATIONS
- Add 1 teaspoon of fresh finely chopped rosemary with the tomatoes.
- For extra fragrance, add 2 tablespoons of olive oil just before serving.

Right: *Zuppa di moscardini*

Rice and Risotti

Rice is such a versatile food and the possibilities for serving it Italian-style are almost endless. Remember that only short-grain rice is grown in Italy; long-grain varieties are not suitable for these recipes.

Insalata di riso Arcobaleno
Rainbow rice salad

Serves 4; Preparation: 30 minutes; Cooking: 15 minutes; Level of difficulty: Simple

Bring 2½ quarts/5 pints/3 liters of salted water to a boil. Add the rice, stir once or twice, and allow 13–15 minutes cooking time from when the water comes to a boil again. The rice should be *al dente* but not too firm. § Drain, pass under cold running water for 30 seconds to stop cooking. Drain again very thoroughly and transfer to a large salad bowl. § Season with oil, lemon juice, and pepper to taste. § Just before serving, add the remaining ingredients and toss well.

■ INGREDIENTS

- 1¼ cups/8 oz/250 g short-grain rice
- 4 tablespoons extra-virgin olive oil
- 2 tablespoons lemon juice
- salt and freshly ground white pepper
- 2 medium tomatoes, cubed
- 6–8 red radishes, sliced
- 2 celery stalks, sliced
- 6 pickled gherkins, sliced
- 8 small white pickled onions, quartered
- 1 tablespoon salted capers
- 10 green olives in brine, pitted and quartered
- 2 tablespoons golden raisins/sultanas, rinsed and drained
- ½ cup/4 oz/125 g parmesan cheese, flaked

Wine: a dry white (Pinot Bianco)

Insalata di riso semplicissima
Simple rice salad

This is a basic Italian rice salad. The possible variations are almost infinite — from dressing the salad with mayonnaise or French mustard, to adding tuna fish, leftover roast chicken, hard-cooked (hard-boiled) eggs, artichoke hearts, or different kinds of cheese. Use your imagination and experiment to create your own favorite variations.

Serves 4; Preparation: 30 minutes; Cooking: 15 minutes; Level of difficulty: Simple

Bring 2½ quarts/5 pints/3 liters of salted water to a boil. Add the rice, stir once or twice, and allow 13–15 minutes cooking time from when the water comes to a boil again. The rice should be *al dente* but not too firm. § Drain, pass under cold running water for 30 seconds to stop cooking. Drain again very thoroughly and transfer to a large salad bowl. § Toss with the oil immediately. § Just before serving add the remaining ingredients and mix well.

■ INGREDIENTS

- 1¼ cups/8 oz/250 g short-grain rice
- 4 tablespoons extra-virgin olive oil
- 2 medium firm tomatoes
- 1 medium cucumber, peeled and cubed
- 1 tablespoon capers
- 10 green or black olives, pitted and chopped
- 4 oz/125 g emmental cheese, cubed
- 6 leaves basil, torn

Wine: a dry white (Sauvignon)

Right: Insalata di riso semplicissima

■ INGREDIENTS

- 1 onion, finely chopped
- 3 tablespoons extra-virgin olive oil
- 2 tablespoons/1 oz/30 g butter
- 2 cups/14 oz/450 g arborio rice
- 5 cups/2 pints/1.2 liters *Beef broth* (see recipe p. 14)
- 3 heads of red radicchio, cut in short strips
- sprigs of rosemary and parsley, finely chopped

Risotto con radicchio
Radicchio risotto

Serves 4; Preparation: 10 minutes; Cooking: 25 minutes; Level of difficulty: Simple
Sauté the onion in the oil and butter in a heavy-bottomed pan. § Add the rice and stir for 2 minutes. § Stir in a little broth followed by the radicchio. Gradually add the rest of the broth, stirring almost continuously. § Season to taste with salt and freshly ground black pepper. § Stir in the rosemary and parsley just before serving. § Serve hot.

■ INGREDIENTS

• 1¾ lb/800 g raw shrimp
  in shell

• juice of 1 lemon, plus 3
  tablespoons

• 6 tablespoons extra-virgin
  olive oil

• 2 cups/14 oz/450 g
  short-grain rice

• 4 tablespoons coarsely
  chopped arugula/rocket

• salt and freshly ground
  white pepper

Wine: a dry white (Pinot Bianco)

■ INGREDIENTS

• 2 eggplants/aubergines

• 2 cloves garlic, mincd

• 1 tablespoon parsley,
  finely chopped

• ⅓ cup/3 fl oz/90 ml
  extra-virgin olive oil

• 2 cups/14 oz/450 g
  arborio rice

• 5 cups/2 pints/1.2 liters
  Beef broth (see recipe p. 14)

■ INGREDIENTS

• 2 cups/14 oz/450 g
  short-grain rice

• ¼ cup/2 oz/60 g butter

• 1 onion, finely chopped

• 1 oz/30 g pine nuts

• 8 chicken livers, chopped

• salt and freshly ground
  white pepper

• 5 tablespoons dry marsala

• 5 tablespoons dry white wine

Wine: a dry white (Müller Thurgau)

Left: Insalata di riso con gamberetti

Insalata di riso con gamberetti
Rice salad with shrimp

Serves 4; Preparation: 30 minutes; Cooking: 15-20 minutes; Level of difficulty: Medium

Cook the shrimp in 9 cups/3½ pints/2 liters of salted, boiling water and the juice of 1 lemon for 5 minutes. § Drain, let the shrimp cool, then shell (detach the head, press the tail with two fingers at its base, and the body will slip out.) Place in a bowl with almost all the oil. § Cook the rice in 2½ quarts/5 pints/3 liters of salted, boiling water, allowing 13–15 minutes cooking. § Drain the rice and pass under cold running water. Drain thoroughly and transfer to the bowl with the shrimp. § Mix carefully, adding salt and pepper to taste. Add the remaining lemon juice and oil. § Just before serving, add the arugula and mix again.

Risotto con melanzane
Eggplant risotto

Serves 4; Preparation: 10 minutes + 1 hour for the eggplants; Cooking: 15 minutes; Level of difficulty: Simple

Cut the aubergines into cubes, sprinkle with salt and place on a slanted cutting board so that the bitter liquid they produce can run off. § Sauté the the garlic and parsley in the oil in a heavy-bottomed pan. § Add the eggplant and cook over medium heat until the eggplants are soft. § Stir in the rice and cook for 2 minutes. § Gradually stir in the broth. The rice will be cooked in about 15–18 minutes. § Season with salt and pepper and serve hot.

Riso con fegatini
Rice with chicken livers

Serves 4; Preparation: 10 minutes; Cooking: 15 minutes; Level of difficulty: Simple

Pour the rice into 9 cups/3½ pints/2 liters of salted, boiling water and stir well. Allow 13–15 minutes cooking time. § Sauté the onion in the butter in a heavy-bottomed pan for 3 minutes. § Turn the heat up to medium-high, add the chicken livers, pine nuts, salt, and pepper. Stir for 1–2 minutes to brown, then add half the marsala and wine. Stir again before adding the rest. § Cook for 6–7 minutes, stirring occasionally. § When the rice is cooked, drain thoroughly and transfer to a serving dish. § Pour the chicken liver sauce over the top and serve hot.

RISO ALL'UOVO
Rice with egg and cream

Serves 4; Preparation: 2 minutes; Cooking: 13-15 minutes; Level of difficulty: Simple

Cook the rice in 9 cups/3½ pints/2 liters of boiling, salted water for 13–15 minutes. § When the rice is almost ready, beat the egg yolks, cream, parmesan, and a dash of pepper to a cream in a bowl. § Drain the rice thoroughly and transfer to a heated serving dish. § Season with the sauce and dabs of butter. Stir quickly and serve immediately.

■ INGREDIENTS

• 2 cups/14 oz/450 g short-grain rice
• 3 fresh egg yolks
• scant ½ cup/3½ fl oz/100 ml light/single cream
• 4 tablespoons freshly grated parmesan cheese
• freshly ground white pepper
• 2 tablespoons/1 oz/30 g butter

Wine: a dry white (Traminer)

RISOTTO CON LE PERE
Pear risotto

Serves 4; Preparation: 2 minutes; Cooking: 13-15 minutes; Level of difficulty: Simple

Peel, core, and cube the pears. § Sauté the onion until translucent in the butter in a heavy-bottomed pan. § Stir in the rice and cook for 2 minutes, then add the wine. § When the wine has all been absorbed, add a ladle full of boiling broth and the pears. § Complete cooking, gradually adding the remaining broth. Season to taste. § Add the taleggio and liquer shortly before serving. § Stir well and serve hot.

■ INGREDIENTS

• 14 oz/450 g pears
• 1 onion, finely chopped
• 2 tablespoons/1 oz/30 g butter
• 2 cups/14 oz/450 g arborio rice
• 1 cup/8 fl oz/250 ml dry white wine
• 6½ cups/2½ pints/1.5 liters *Vegetable broth* (see recipe p. 14)
• 3 oz/90 g creamy taleggio cheese
• 2 tablespoons Williams pear liqueur

RISO INTEGRALE CON SALSA DI POMODORO
Brown rice with tomato sauce

For winter meals, serve the brown rice hot with Simple tomato sauce. *In summer, when fresh tomatoes are readily available and soaring temperatures make life in the kitchen unpleasant, serve with* Fresh tomato sauce *on hot or cold brown rice.*

Serves 4; Preparation: 25 minutes; Cooking: 45 minutes; Level of difficulty: Simple

Cook the rice in 9 cups/3½ pints/2 liters of salted, boiling water, stirring once or twice. It will be cooked in about 45 minutes. § Prepare the tomato sauce. § When the rice is done, drain thoroughly, and transfer to a large bowl. § Pour the remaining oil over the rice and toss vigorously. § Add the tomato and herb mixture, toss carefully and serve.

■ INGREDIENTS

• 2 cups/14 oz/450 g brown rice
• 1 quantity *Fresh* or *Simple* tomato sauce (see recipes p. 2)

Wine: a light, dry rosé (Chiaretto del Garda)

Right: *Riso integrale con salsa di pomodoro crudo*

Risotto con asparagi
Asparagus risotto

The delicate flavors in this risotto call for high-quality, fresh asparagus.

Serves 4; Preparation: 15 minutes; Cooking: 25 minutes; Level of difficulty: Medium

Rinse the asparagus and trim the stalks to ½ in (1 cm) before the white part begins. Cut the green tips in two or three pieces. § Melt three-quarters of the butter in a deep, heavy-bottomed saucepan. Add the onion and sauté for 1 minute; then add the asparagus and sauté for 5 minutes. § Add the rice and pour in the wine. Stir well. § When the wine has been absorbed, begin adding the boiling broth, a little at a time, stirring frequently. § The risotto will be cooked in 15–18 minutes. § Add the remaining butter and the parmesan. Mix well. § Check the seasoning and add salt and pepper if required.

■ INGREDIENTS

- 1¾ lb/800 g asparagus
- ¼ cup/2 oz/60 g butter
- ½ onion, finely chopped
- 1¾ cups/12 oz/375 g arborio rice
- ½ cup/4 fl oz/125 ml dry white wine
- 5 cups/2 pints/1.2 liters hot *Chicken* or *Beef broth* (see recipes pp. 14, 16)
- 4 tablespoons freshly grated parmesan cheese
- salt and freshly ground white pepper

Risotto alla sbirraglia
Chicken risotto

*Served with a green salad, this nourishing risotto is a meal in itself. It takes its name from the Austrian soldiers (*sbirri*) who occupied northern Italy in the 19th century. They were apparently very fond of it.*

Serves 4; Preparation; 10 minutes: Cooking: 1 hour; Level of difficulty: Medium

Melt three-quarters of the butter with the oil in a deep, heavy-bottomed saucepan. Add the celery, onion, and carrot and sauté for 2 minutes over low heat. § Season the chicken with salt and pepper and place the pieces in the saucepan in a single layer. Increase the heat and brown, turning as required. § After 8–10 minutes begin sprinkling with wine. Cover and continue cooking, gradually adding the wine, for 25–30 minutes. § To test if the chicken is cooked, pierce with a fork or toothpick. The liquid that forms around the hole should be transparent rather than pink. § Remove the chicken and set aside in a warm oven or on a dish set over a pot of very hot water and covered with another dish. § Place the rice and chicken livers in the pan with the cooking juices and cook for 1 minute. § Gradually stir in the boiling broth. Continue cooking until the rice is tender, stirring frequently (it will take about 15–18 minutes). § Just before serving add the remaining butter and parmesan and mix well. § Transfer the risotto to a serving dish and arrange the pieces of chicken on top.

■ INGREDIENTS

- ¼ cup/2 oz/60 g butter
- 3 tablespoons extra-virgin olive oil
- 1 celery stalk, 1 onion, 1 carrot, finely chopped
- 1 chicken, ready to cook, weighing about 2 lb/1 kg, cut in 8 pieces
- salt and freshly ground white pepper
- 1 cup/8 fl oz/250 ml dry white wine
- 1¾ cups/12 oz/375 g arborio rice
- 6½ cups/2½ pints/1.5 liters boiling *Beef broth* (see recipe p. 14)
- 1 chicken liver, cleaned and finely chopped
- 2 tablespoons freshly grated parmesan cheese

Wine: a dry white (Galestro)

Right: *Risotto con asparagi*

INGREDIENTS

- 5 tablespoons extra-virgin olive oil
- ½ onion, finely chopped
- 1¾ cups/12 oz/375 g arborio rice
- 5 bay leaves
- 2 cups/16 fl oz/500 ml dry white wine
- 3 cups/24 fl oz/750 ml *Beef broth* (see recipe p. 14)
- dash of nutmeg
- salt

Wine: a dry white (Orvieto)

RISOTTO CON ALLORO
Risotto with bay leaves

To savor the full flavor of this fragrant risotto, serve without adding parmesan cheese.

Serves 4; Preparation: 5 minutes; Cooking: 20 minutes; Level of difficulty: Simple

Heat the oil in a large, heavy-bottomed saucepan and sauté the onion until it is soft and translucent. § Add the rice and bay leaves. Stir for 2 minutes and then begin adding the wine, a little at a time. § When the wine has been absorbed, add the nutmeg and continue cooking. Keep adding broth until the rice is cooked. It will take about 15–18 minutes. § Serve hot.

RISOTTO AL PREZZEMOLO E BASILICO
Basil and parsley risotto

This traditional recipe contains all the fragrance of the Italian Riviera.

Serves 4; Preparation: 10 minutes; Cooking: 25 minutes; Level of difficulty: Simple

Dissolve the marrow in a heavy-bottomed saucepan over low heat. § Add the butter, oil, and garlic, and sauté for 1 minute. § Add the rice and cook for 2 minutes, stirring continuously. § Begin adding the broth, a little at a time, stirring frequently. § The rice will take about 15–18 minutes to cook. § A few minutes before the rice is ready, add the basil and parsley. § Taste for salt and pepper. § Add the pecorino as the final touch and serve hot.

RISO ARROSTO
Roasted rice

The original recipe for this Ligurian specialty calls for the juices produced by a roast. Nowadays butter or oil are generally used instead.

Serves 4; Preparation: 35 minutes; Cooking: 45-50 minutes; Level of difficulty: Medium

Sauté the onion, sausage, mushrooms, artichokes, and peas in a large, heavy-bottomed pan in three-quarters of the oil. Season with salt and pepper. § Add the broth, cover, and continue cooking for about 10 minutes. § In the meantime, bring 5 cups/2 pints/1.2 liters of salted water to a boil, pour in the rice and cook for 7–8 minutes. § Drain partially (leave some moisture). Transfer to the saucepan with the sauce and stir. Add the cheese and mix well. Transfer to an ovenproof dish greased with the remaining oil. § Bake in a preheated oven at 400°F/200°C/gas 6 for about 20 minutes. The rice will have a light golden crust when ready.

VARIATION
– If fresh porcini mushrooms are unavailable, use 1 oz/30 g dried porcini. Soak for at least 30 minutes in a cup of tepid water, then drain, chop coarsely, and combine with 1½ cups/4 oz/125 g sliced white mushrooms.

■ INGREDIENTS

- 2 tablespoons finely chopped ox-bone marrow
- 2 tablespoons/1 oz/30 g butter
- 3 tablespoons extra-virgin olive oil
- 2 cloves garlic, minced
- 1¾ cups/12 oz/375 g arborio rice
- 6½ cups/2½ pints/1.5 liters *Vegetable broth* (see recipe p. 14)
- 1 tablespoon each basil and parsley, finely chopped
- salt and white pepper
- 3 tablespoons freshly grated pecorino cheese

Wine: a dry white (Trebbiano)

■ INGREDIENTS

- 4 tablespoons extra-virgin olive oil
- 1 onion, finely chopped
- 5 oz/150 g Italian pork sausages, skinned and crumbled
- 2½ cups/7 oz/200 g porcini mushrooms, sliced
- 2 artichokes, trimmed and thinly sliced
- 2 tablespoons peas
- salt and pepper
- 1 cup/8 fl oz/250 ml *Beef broth* (see recipe p. 14)
- 1¾ cups/12 oz/375 g short-grain rice
- 3 tablespoons freshly grated pecorino cheese

Wine: a dry white (Vermentino)

Right: *Risotto al prezzemolo e basilico*

Risotto ai carciofi
Artichoke risotto

It is extremely important to clean the artichokes properly, discarding the tough tips, outer leaves and fuzzy choke. The inner hearts should be cut into slices less than ⅛ in (3 mm) thick.

Serves 4; Preparation: 20 minutes; Cooking: 30 minutes; Level of difficulty: Medium

Clean the artichokes as described above and place in a bowl of cold water with the lemon juice. Soak for 10–15 minutes so they will not discolor. § Melt the butter in a large, heavy-bottomed saucepan. Add the onion and sauté for a few minutes. § Drain the artichoke slices and add to the onion; sauté for another 5 minutes. § Add the rice and stir for 2 minutes. Increase the heat slightly, and begin adding the boiling broth, a little at a time, until the rice is cooked. It will take about 15–18 minutes. Season with salt and pepper. § Add the parsley and pecorino at the last minute. Mix well to create a creamy risotto.

VARIATION
– For a slightly different flavor, replace half the butter with 3 tablespoons of extra-virgin olive oil.

Riso alla biellese
Rice with butter and cheese

This dish comes from Piedmont and Valle d'Aosta, in northwestern Italy, where it was traditionally served at wedding banquets.

Serves 4; Preparation: 5 minutes; Cooking: 13-15 minutes; Level of difficulty: Simple

Pour the rice into 9 cups/3½ pints/2 liters of salted, boiling water and stir once or twice. Allow 13–15 minutes cooking time from when the water comes to a boil again. § A couple of minutes before the rice is cooked, melt the butter in a saucepan until it turns golden brown. § Drain the rice over the serving bowl so it fills with the hot cooking water. Don't drain the rice too thoroughly. § Throw out the water in the bowl which is now nicely warmed and put in the rice, alternating it with spoonfuls of the cheese. Drizzle with piping hot butter, stir quickly, and serve immediately, passing the pepper separately.

■ INGREDIENTS

- 6–7 artichokes, trimmed and sliced
- juice of 1 lemon
- 3 tablespoons/1½ oz/45 g butter
- ½ onion, finely chopped
- 1¾ cups/12 oz/375 g arborio rice
- 6½ cups/2½ pints/1.5 liters boiling water or *Vegetable broth* (see recipe p. 14)
- salt and freshly ground black pepper
- 1 tablespoon finely chopped parsley
- 4 tablespoons freshly grated parmesan or pecorino cheese

Wine: a dry white (Vernaccia di San Gimignano)

■ INGREDIENTS

- 2 cups/14 oz/450 g short-grain rice
- ⅓ cup/3 oz/90 g butter
- 5 oz/150 g fontina cheese, cubed
- freshly ground white pepper (optional)

Wine: a dry red (Freisa)

Right: *Risotto ai carciofi*

Risotto con finocchi
Risotto with fennel

To make this simple and delicate risotto, it is essential to have truly tender fennel bulbs. Be sure to discard all the tough and stringy outer leaves.

Serves 4; Preparation: 15 minutes; Cooking: 25 minutes; Level of difficulty: Simple

Cut the cleaned fennel bulbs vertically into slices about ⅛-in (3-mm) thick. § Melt half the butter in a large, heavy-bottomed saucepan together with the oil. Add the onion, celery, and fennel and sauté for 5–7 minutes. § Add the rice and cook for 1 minute over medium heat; then begin adding the boiling broth, a little at a time, stirring frequently until the rice is cooked. It will take about 15–18 minutes. The risotto should be creamy but not too liquid. § Finally, add the remaining butter and the parmesan and mix well. § Season with salt and pepper and serve hot.

■ INGREDIENTS

- 4–5 fennel bulbs, cleaned
- ¼ cup/2 oz/60 g butter
- 2–3 tablespoons extra-virgin olive oil
- 1 small onion, finely chopped
- 1 small stalk celery, finely chopped
- 1¾ cups/12 oz/375 g arborio rice
- 6½ cups/2½ pints/1.5 liters boiling *Beef broth* (see recipe p. 14)
- salt and freshly ground white pepper
- 4 tablespoons freshly grated parmesan cheese

Wine: a dry white (Soave)

Risotto con le quaglie
Risotto with quail

In Lombardy quail are often served with Risotto alla milanese; *a combination that works well. This one is more delicate and, I think, more harmonious.*

Serves 4; Preparation: 15 minutes; Cooking: 40 minutes; Level of difficulty: Medium

Season the quail inside and out with salt and pepper. Put the sage leaves inside. § Wrap the breasts with slices of pancetta or salt pork secured with two or three twists of white thread. § In a large, heavy-bottomed saucepan melt half the butter together with the oil. Add the quail and brown well on all sides over medium heat. This will take about 6–7 minutes. § Sprinkle the birds with the brandy and when this has evaporated, lower the heat, partially cover and cook, adding a spoonful of broth occasionally. The birds will be cooked in about 15 minutes. § Remove the quail and set aside in a warm oven or on a plate set over a pot of very hot water. § Add the rice to the juices left in the saucepan and stir well for 2 minutes. § Gradually stir in the broth. The rice will be cooked in 15–18 minutes. § At the last moment, stir in the remaining butter and the cheese. § Serve the rice with the quail arranged on top. Remove the thread but leave the salt pork or pancetta in place.

■ INGREDIENTS

- 4 quail ready to be cooked
- salt and freshly ground white pepper
- 4 leaves sage
- 4 slices salt pork or pancetta
- 3 tablespoons/1½ oz/45 g butter
- 2 tablespoons extra-virgin olive oil
- 3 tablespoons brandy
- 1¾ cups/12 oz/375 g arborio rice
- 6½ cups/2½ pints/1.5 liters boiling *Beef broth* (see recipe p. 14)
- 4 tablespoons freshly grated parmesan cheese

Wine: a dry white (Cortese di Gavi)

Right:
Risotto con finocchi

INGREDIENTS

- 1 oz/30 g dried porcini mushrooms
- 5 tablespoons extra-virgin olive oil
- 1 small onion, finely chopped
- ½ cup/4 fl oz/125 ml dry white wine
- 1¾ cups/12 oz/375 g arborio rice
- 5 cups/2 pints/1.2 liters *Vegetable broth* (see recipe p. 14)
- 2 tablespoons finely chopped parsley
- salt

Wine: a dry white (Pinot Grigio)

RISOTTO AI FUNGHI
Mushroom risotto Venetian-style

There are many different recipes for mushroom risotto. This one comes from the city of Venice.

Serves 4; Preparation: 30 minutes; Cooking: 25-30 minutes; Level of difficulty: Medium

Soak the mushrooms for 30 minutes in 1 cup/8 fl oz/250 ml of tepid water. Drain, reserving the water, and chop coarsely. § Strain the water in which the mushrooms were soaked and set it aside. § Heat the oil in a large, heavy-bottomed saucepan. Add the onion and sauté over low heat until it is soft and translucent. § Add the mushrooms and sauté for 2–3 minutes. § Add the rice and stir for 2 minutes over medium heat. Add the wine gradually, and when it has been absorbed, stir in the mushroom water. § Begin adding the broth a little at a time until the rice is cooked. It will take about 15–18 minutes. § Add the parsley just before the rice is cooked and mix. § Season with salt to taste and serve hot.

VARIATION
– Add 4 tablespoons of freshly grated parmesan at the end, or pass separately at the table.

INGREDIENTS

- ¼ cup/2 oz/60 g butter
- 1 onion, finely chopped
- 1¾ cups/12 oz/375 g arborio rice
- ½ cup/4 fl oz/125 ml dry white wine
- 6½ cups/2½ pints/1.5 liters *Chicken* or *Beef broth* (see recipes pp. 14, 16)
- dash of nutmeg (optional)
- 4 tablespoons freshly grated parmesan cheese
- sale and freshly ground white pepper

Wine: a light, dry red (Gutturnio)

Left:
Risotto ai funghi

RISOTTO BIANCO AL PARMIGIANO
Simple risotto with parmesan cheese

Serves 4; Preparation: 5 minutes; Cooking: 25 minutes; Level of difficulty: Medium

Melt half the butter in a large, heavy-bottomed saucepan. Add the onion and sauté over low heat until soft and translucent. § Add the rice, increase the heat, and stir for 2 minutes. § Pour in the wine, and when it has been completely absorbed, gradually stir in the boiling broth. Stir frequently, adding the nutmeg, if liked. § When the rice is almost cooked (it will take about 15–18 minutes), add a little over half the parmesan. § Taste for salt and, finally, add the remaining butter in dabs, mixing well. § Serve with the remaining parmesan passed separately.

VARIATION
– After the wine has evaporated, add 2 tablespoons of tomato paste. This will give you *Risotto rosso alla piemontese* or "Red risotto Piedmont-style". In this case, use a little less parmesan.

RISOTTO AI FORMAGGI
Cheese risotto

Many different combinations of cheeses can be used in this recipe. These four go particularly well together, but feel free to experiment with others.

Serves 4; Preparation: 15 minutes; Cooking: 35 minutes; Level of difficulty: Simple

Put the rice into 9 cups/3½ pints/2 liters of salted, boiling water and stir once or twice. Cook for 13–15 minutes. § Butter an ovenproof baking dish with a little butter. § Mix the breadcrumbs with 1 tablespoon of the parmesan. § Melt two-thirds of the remaining butter in a saucepan, and add the sage or rosemary, the nutmeg, and garlic, if liked. Sauté until golden brown. § When the rice is cooked, drain well and transfer to a bowl. § Stir in the cheeses and sausage. § Remove the herbs from the butter and add to the rice. Stir rapidly. § Transfer the mixture to a baking dish. Smooth the surface, sprinkle with the mixed breadcrumbs and parmesan, and dot with dabs of the remaining butter. § Bake in a preheated oven at 400°F/200°C/gas 6 for 15 minutes, or until a golden crust has formed.

■ INGREDIENTS

- 1¾ cups/12 oz/375 g arborio rice
- ¼ cup/2 oz/60 g butter
- 1 tablespoon breadcrumbs
- 5 leaves fresh or dried sage, or 1 sprig rosemary
- 1 clove garlic (optional)
- 2 oz/60 g emmental cheese, 2 oz/60 g smoked scamorza cheese, 2 oz/60 g fontina cheese, chopped
- ¾ cup/2 oz/60 g freshly grated parmesan cheese
- 5 oz/150 g Italian pork sausages, skinned and crumbled
- dash of nutmeg (optional)

Wine: a dry red (Cabernet)

RISOTTO AL GORGONZOLA
Gorgonzola risotto

Rice and gorgonzola cheese make a tasty partnership. Choose the best soft and creamy cheese.

Serves 4; Preparation: 10 minutes; Cooking: 25 minutes; Level of difficulty: Simple

Melt the butter in a large, heavy-bottomed saucepan. § Add the onion and sauté over low heat until soft and translucent. § Add the rice and cook, stirring constantly, for 2 minutes. § Increase the heat slightly and pour in the wine. § When the wine has been absorbed, begin adding the boiling broth, a little at a time and stirring frequently. § The rice will take about 15–18 minutes to cook. § About 3–4 minutes before it is ready, add the gorgonzola and mix well. Season with salt and pepper. § Add the parmesan and serve.

VARIATIONS
– Replace the gorgonzola with the same quantity of well-ripened taleggio; in this case add half a finely chopped garlic clove and a dash of nutmeg to the onion before adding the rice.
– Stir in 2–3 tablespoons of fresh cream just before serving.

■ INGREDIENTS

- 3 tablespoons/1½ oz/45 g butter
- ½ small onion, finely chopped
- 1¾ cups/12 oz/375 g arborio rice
- ⅔ cup/5 fl oz/150 ml dry white wine
- 6½ cups/2½ pints/1.5 liters *Beef broth* (see recipe p. 14)
- 8 oz/250 g gorgonzola cheese, chopped
- salt and freshly ground white pepper
- 4 tablespoons freshly grated parmesan cheese

Wine: a dry red (Merlot)

Right:
Risotto al gorgonzola

RISOTTO CON LENTICCHIE
Creamy lentil risotto

Serves 4; Preparation: 10 minutes; Cooking: 20-25 minutes; Level of difficulty: Simple

Heat the butter and oil in a large, heavy-bottomed saucepan. Add the onion and garlic and sauté for 5 minutes over low heat. § Increase the heat slightly and pour in the rice. Cook for 2 minutes, stirring continuously. § Add the boiling broth little by little, stirring frequently. After about 10 minutes, add the drained lentils and continue cooking. The rice will be ready in about 15–18 minutes. § Add half the cheese and season with salt and pepper. § Mix well until creamy and serve. The remaining cheese can be served separately at table.

VARIATION
– Add 1 tablespoon of tomato paste with the lentils.

■ INGREDIENTS

- 3 tablespoons/1½ oz/45 g butter
- 3 tablespoons extra-virgin olive oil
- 1 onion, finely chopped
- 1 clove garlic, minced
- 1¾ cups/12 oz/375 g arborio rice
- 6½ cups/2½ pints/1.5 liters Beef broth (see recipe p. 14)
- one 14-oz/450-g can lentils
- 5 tablespoons freshly grated pecorino or parmesan cheese
- salt and freshly ground white or black pepper

Wine: a dry red (Rosso Conero)

RISOTTO CON I PEOCI
Risotto with mussels

This recipe comes from Veneto, the region around the city of Venice.
In local dialect mussels are called peoci.

Serves 4; Preparation: 20 minutes + 1 hour soaking for mussels; Cooking: 20 minutes; Level of difficulty: Medium

Soak the mussels in a large bowl of water for at least an hour to purge them of sand. Pull off their beards, scrub and rinse well in abundant cold water. § Combine the mussels and the whole clove of garlic in a large, shallow skillet (frying pan). Place over high heat and shake the skillet and stir with a wooden spoon until all the mussels are open. This will take about 2–3 minutes. Discard any that have not opened. § Drain the mussels. Set aside a dozen of the largest, in their shells, to use as a garnish. § Take the remaining mussels out of their shells and put them in a bowl. § Strain the liquid left in the pan through a fine cloth or sieve and

■ INGREDIENTS

- 3½ lb/1.7 kg mussels in shell
- 2 cloves garlic, 1 of which finely chopped
- scant ½ cup/3½ fl oz/100 ml extra-virgin olive oil
- ½ small onion, finely chopped
- 1¾ cups/12 oz/375 g arborio rice
- scant ½ cup/3½ fl oz/100 ml dry white wine
- 3½ cups/26 fl oz/800 ml boiling water
- salt and freshly ground pepper
- 2 tablespoons finely chopped parsley

Wine: a dry white
(Tocai Isonzo)

set it aside, discarding the garlic. § Sauté the onion and chopped garlic in the same skillet for a few minutes. § Add the rice and cook, stirring continuously, for 2 minutes. § Increase the heat slightly and pour in the wine. When all the wine has been absorbed, begin slowly adding the mussel liquid and then boiling water as required, stirring frequently, until the rice is cooked. This will take about 15–18 minutes. § Add the mussels and stir well. Sprinkle with the parsley and season with salt and pepper. § Transfer to a serving dish and garnish with the whole mussels. § Serve hot.

VARIATION
– At the last minute add 2 tablespoons/1 oz/30 g of butter and 4 tablespoons of freshly grated parmesan cheese. Many consider this quite unorthodox, but the Venetians think otherwise.

Above:
Risotto con lenticchie

Risotto al limone
Lemon risotto

The distinctive flavor of this risotto does not combine well with any wine.
Serve with cool, sparkling mineral water with slices of lemon.

Serves 4; Preparation: 10 minutes; Cooking: 25 minutes; Level of difficulty: Simple

Sauté the onion in the oil for a few minutes over medium-low heat in a large, heavy-bottomed saucepan until it is soft and translucent. § Increase the heat slightly and add the rice; stir for 2 minutes. § Add the wine and, when it has been absorbed, gradually add the boiling broth as required. § After about 10 minutes, add the lemon rind, stirring well. § The rice will take about 15–18 minutes to cook. § Season with salt and pepper to taste. Add the lemon juice and parsley, stir well and serve.

■ INGREDIENTS

- ½ small onion, finely chopped
- 4 tablespoons extra-virgin olive oil
- 1¾ cups/12 oz/350 g arborio rice
- scant ½ cup/3½ oz/100 ml dry, light white wine
- 6½ cups/2½ pints/1.5 liters *Beef broth* (see recipe p. 14)
- grated rind and juice of 1 large lemon
- salt and freshly ground white pepper
- 1 tablespoon finely chopped parsley

Risotto alla milanese
Milanese-style risotto

This is a traditional Milanese dish. Debate has always raged about whether wine should be added or not (and if so, whether it should it be red or white). Try it with both, and without, and decide for yourselves.

Serves 4; Preparation: 10 minutes; Cooking: 25 minutes; Level of difficulty: Medium

Melt half the butter with the marrow in a large, heavy-bottomed saucepan. § Add the onion and sauté over low heat until it is soft and translucent. § Add the rice and cook over medium heat for 2–3 minutes, stirring continuously. § Pour in the wine, if used, and when it has been absorbed, add the broth, a little at a time, stirring continuously. If wine is not used, begin directly with the broth. Increase the heat slightly. § The rice will take about 15–18 minutes to cook. After 15 minutes, add half the parmesan. § Add the saffron 1 minute before the rice is ready. Taste for salt. § Add the remaining butter in dabs just before serving and mix well. The risotto should be very creamy, because of the slow and gradual release during cooking of the starch that binds the rice together. § Serve with the remaining parmesan passed separately.

■ INGREDIENTS

- ¼ cup/2 oz/60 g butter
- 2½ tablespoons finely chopped ox-bone marrow
- 1 small onion, finely chopped
- 2 cups/14 oz/450 g arborio rice
- ½ cup/4 fl oz/125 ml white or red wine (optional)
- 9 cups/3½ pints/2 liters boiling *Beef broth* (see recipe p. 14)
- 6 tablespoons freshly grated parmesan cheese
- ½ teaspoon powdered saffron
- salt

Wine: a dry white (Riesling dell'Oltrepò Pavese)

VARIATION
– Add shavings of white truffle to the risotto just before serving.

Right:
Risotto al limone

Left

Risotto con pancetta e prosciutto

Risotto con pancetta e prosciutto
Risotto with pancetta and prosciutto

Serves 4; Preparation: 15 minutes; Cooking: 25–30 minutes; Level of difficulty: Medium

Melt the butter in a large, heavy-bottomed saucepan, add the onion and after 1 minute the pancetta. Sauté over low heat, stirring occasionally, until the onion is soft and translucent. § Add the rice and cook for 2 minutes, stirring continuously. § Increase the heat slightly and pour in the wine. When it has been absorbed, gradually add the hot broth as required until the rice is cooked. This will take about 15–18 minutes. § Three minutes before the rice is cooked, add a dash of freshly grated nutmeg, pepper to taste, the ham, cream, and cheese, mixing carefully to combine the ingredients well. Finally, taste for salt. § Serve hot.

VARIATIONS
– Add 2 tablespoons/1 oz/30 g of butter instead of the cream.
– Emmental cheese, or scamorza or some other similar type of cheese, in flakes or shavings, can be used instead of the parmesan.

Risotto alla milanese 'al salto'
Milanese-style risotto the day after

In Milan this was once the classic dish to order after an evening at the theater. It is prepared with leftover Risotto alla milanese, *so make a double quantity and serve this one the day after. In the original recipe the portions are prepared individually, but since not everyone is able to deal with four skillets (frying pans) at once, I have simplified things a little.*

Serves 4; Preparation: 5 minutes; Cooking: 15 minutes; Level of difficulty: Simple

§ Melt a quarter of the butter in each of two nonstick skillets (frying pans) 12–13 in (30 cm) in diameter. § Divide the rice into two portions and flatten each out so as to have two round cakes about 1 in (2.5 cm) thick. § Cook them in the skillets over high heat for about 5 minutes, so that a crisp crust forms. § Turn them with the help of a plate and slip them back into the skillets in which you have melted the remaining butter. § When both sides are crisp and deep gold in color, sprinkle with the parmesan and cut each one in half. § Serve immediately.

Risotto con mozzarella e panna
Risotto with mozzarella cheese and cream

Because of its delicate flavor, this recipe requires very fresh mozzarella if it is to be a success.

Serves 4; Preparation: 5 minutes; Cooking: 20-25 minutes; Level of difficulty: Simple

Melt the butter in a large, heavy-bottomed saucepan. Add the onion and sauté over low heat for a couple of minutes until the onion is soft and translucent. § Add the rice and cook for 2 minutes, stirring continuously. § Pour in the wine and when this has been absorbed, gradually add the broth, a little at a time, until two-thirds have been used. § After about 10 minutes add half the cream, stir well and then add the other half. § After 2–3 minutes add the mozzarella. § Continue cooking for about 15–18 minutes by which time the rice should be cooked. Stir in the remaining broth as required. § Season with salt and pepper. Serve the risotto with the grated parmesan passed separately.

■ INGREDIENTS

- 2 tablespoons/1 oz/30 g butter
- ½ onion, finely chopped
- 1¾ cups/12 oz/375 g arborio rice
- ½ cup/4 fl oz/125 ml dry white wine
- 4 cups/1¾ pints/1 liter *Beef* or *Chicken broth* (see recipes pp. 14, 16)
- ⅔ cup/5 fl oz/150 ml light/single cream
- 8 oz/250 g mozzarella cheese, cubed
- salt and freshly ground white pepper
- 4 tablespoons freshly grated parmesan cheese

Wine: a dry white (Ischia Bianco)

Risotto alla piemontese
Piedmont-style risotto

Thin shavings of white truffles, sprinkled on the risotto just before serving are the perfect complement to this dish. Cooking time for the sauce is about 10 minutes, so it can be prepared when the risotto is well-advanced in its cooking and needs less attention.

Serves 4; Preparation: 15 minutes + 3 hours soaking time; Cooking: 25 minutes; Level of difficulty: Complicated

Put the fontina in a bowl and cover it with the milk. Set aside for 3 hours. § When the fontina has been soaking for 2½ hours, prepare the risotto. § When the fontina is ready, melt the butter (which must not bubble) in a double boiler or saucepan and add the fontina and about half of the milk in which it was soaked. Stir carefully with a wooden spoon or a whisk over very low heat until the cheese melts and the mixture is creamy. § Add the first egg yolk and mix thoroughly before adding the second. Repeat this procedure before adding the third, mixing rather quickly to achieve a smooth, creamy sauce. § Season with salt and pepper (if serving with truffles, add less salt and pepper than you normally would). § Transfer the risotto to a serving dish and pour the sauce over the top. § Serve immediately.

■ INGREDIENTS

- 10 oz/300 g fontina cheese, cut in thin slices
- scant 1 cup/7 fl oz/200 ml milk
- 1 quantity *Risotto bianco al parmigiano* (see recipe p. 155)
- 3 tablespoons/1½ oz/45 g butter
- 3 egg yolks, at room temperature
- salt and freshly ground white pepper

Wine: a dry red (Nebbiolo)

Right:
Risotto con mozzarella e panna

Risotto all'Onegliese

Risotto with tomato and mushrooms

This dish, originally from the village of Oneglia, in Liguria, has spread all along the Italian Riviera.

Serves 4; Preparation: 30 minutes; Cooking: 35 minutes; Level of difficulty: Medium

Soak the mushrooms in a bowl of warm water for about 30 minutes until they have softened; then drain and chop coarsely. § If using fresh tomatoes, plunge them for 10 seconds into a pot of boiling water and then into cold. Peel and cut them in half horizontally. Squeeze to remove at least some of the seeds and then chop finely. § If using canned tomatoes, partially drain them and chop finely. § In a heavy-bottomed saucepan, sauté the onion in the oil until translucent. Add the mushrooms and, after another minute or so, the tomatoes. § Cook the sauce for 10 minutes, covered, then add the rice and stir well. § When part of the liquid has been absorbed, begin to add the boiling water, pouring it in a little at a time and stirring frequently. The rice will be cooked in about 15–18 minutes. § Just before it is ready, season with salt and pepper. § Serve the rice, passing the grated cheese separately.

■ INGREDIENTS

- ⅔ oz/20 g dried mushrooms
- 14 oz/450 g peeled and chopped fresh or canned tomatoes
- 1 small onion, finely chopped
- scant ½ cup/3 fl oz/90 ml extra-virgin olive oil
- 1¾ cups/12 oz/375 g arborio rice
- 5 cups/2 pints/1.2 liters boiling water
- salt and freshly ground black pepper
- 4 tablespoons freshly grated pecorino or parmesan cheese

Wine: a dry white (Pigato di Albenga)

Ris in Cagnon

Rice with butter

A simple and pleasant dish from Lombardy, the region around Milan.

Serves 4; Preparation: 5 minutes; Cooking: 15 minutes; Level of difficulty: Simple

Cook the rice in about 9 cups/3½ pints/2 liters of salted, boiling water, stirring a couple of times until it is cooked. It will take about 13–15 minutes. § Just before the rice is ready, slowly melt the butter in a saucepan with the garlic (remove after 1 minute) and sage leaves. The butter should turn dark golden brown. § Drain the rice thoroughly and transfer to a serving dish or individual plates. § Sprinkle with the parmesan and drizzle with the hot butter, with or without the sage leaves.

■ INGREDIENTS

- 2 cups/14 oz/450 g arborio rice
- ¼ cup/2 oz/60 g butter
- 1 clove garlic, cut in half
- 6 sage leaves (fresh or dried), whole or crumbled
- 5 tablespoons freshly grated parmesan cheese

Wine: a dry white (Lugana)

Right:
Risotto all'onegliese

RISOTTO AL VINO
Risotto with wine

Try to find a Barolo or a Chianti wine for this dish. The wine can be added a third or a quarter of a cup at a time, or alternately with the broth.

Serves 4; Preparation: 10 minutes; Cooking: 25 minutes; Level of difficulty: Simple

Melt three-quarters of the butter in a large, heavy-bottomed saucepan. Add the onion, celery, and carrot, and sauté over low heat for 5 minutes. § Increase the heat slightly, add the rice, and cook for 2 minutes, stirring continuously. § Gradually stir in the wine. § When this has been absorbed, begin adding the broth. § It will take about 15–18 minutes for the rice to cook. Season with salt and pepper. § Add the remaining butter just before serving. § The parmesan can either be added at this point or passed separately at table.

VARIATION
— For *Risotto allo champagne* use the same quantity of high quality, dry sparkling wine or champagne in place of the red wine.

■ INGREDIENTS

- ¼ cup/2 oz/60 g butter
- ½ onion, finely chopped
- 1 celery stalk, finely chopped
- 1 small carrot, scraped and finely chopped
- 1¾ cups/12 oz/375 g arborio rice
- 1¼ cups/10 fl oz/300 ml dry, full-bodied wine
- 5 cups/2 pints/1.2 liters boiling *Beef* or *Chicken broth* (see recipes pp. 14, 16)
- 4 tablespoons freshly grated parmesan cheese
- salt and freshly ground black pepper

Wine: a light, dry red (Gutturnio)

PANISSA
Risotto with beans

This is a hearty winter dish from the area around Vercelli, in the north. Traditionally, it is served with a generous sprinkling of pepper rather than with the usual grated cheese. If you can't get cotenna, just leave it out. The flavor will be a little different, but still very good.

Serves 4; Preparation: 30 minutes; Cooking: 1¼ hours; Level of difficulty: Medium

Put the beans in a pot with the broth and the cotenna. Cover and simmer over low heat for 50 minutes. § Take out the cotenna, dice, and return to the pot. § Place the salt pork and pancetta in a heavy-bottomed saucepan over low heat. When the fat has melted a little, add the onion and sauté for 5 minutes, stirring frequently. § Pour in the rice and stir for 2 minutes. § Add the wine, half at a time. § When it has been absorbed, begin adding, one ladle at a time, the hot beans and their broth. § Stir continuously until the rice is cooked. It will take about 15–18 minutes. § Season with salt and pepper. The risotto should be creamy but not too liquid. § Serve hot.

VARIATION
— If using dry beans, soak in cold water for 10–12 hours, then cook slowly with the cotenna for a couple of hours. Continue as above.

■ INGREDIENTS

- 8 oz/250 g fresh cranberry or red kidney beans, shelled
- 2 oz/60 g fresh cotenna, scraped
- 5 cups/2 pints/1.2 liters *Vegetable broth* (see recipe p. 16)
- ½ onion, finely chopped
- ⅓ cup/3 oz/90 g finely chopped salt pork/lard
- ⅓ cup/3 oz/90 g finely chopped lean pancetta
- 1¾ cups/12 oz/375 g arborio rice
- scant 1 cup/7 fl oz/200 ml robust red wine
- salt and freshly ground white or black pepper

Wine: a dry red (Grignolino)

Right: *Panissa*

RISOTTO NERO CON LE SEPPIE
Black risotto with ink squid

For first-timers, the color of this extraordinary risotto may be a little surprising. If possible, get your fish vendor to clean the ink squid, making sure the internal ink sacs are set aside without being broken.

Serves 4; Preparation: 25 minutes; Cooking: about 1¼ hours; Level of difficulty: Medium

To clean the ink squid, detach the head (the part with the tentacles) from the body by grasping the two parts with your hands and tugging sharply. The insides and two sacs will come out attached to the head. One of the sacs has the ink and the other is dark yellow. Some people also use the latter but the flavor is rather strong and it is better to discard it with the insides. Carefully separate the ink sacs from the squid and set them aside in a cup with 2–3 spoonfuls of cold water. Discard the eyes and the beaks at the base of the tentacles. Open the body at the side with kitchen scissors and extract the bone. Rinse the body and head well and cut into 1¼-in (3-cm) strips. § In a large, heavy-bottomed saucepan heat the oil and add the onion, parsley, and ink squid. § Cover and cook for 15 minutes over low heat, stirring once or twice. § Add the tomato paste, wine, and ½ cup/4 fl oz/125 ml hot water, and continue cooking, covered and over low heat, for 20–40 minutes, stirring occasionally. It is hard to give an exact time because this depends on the ink squid. Test them with a fork after 20 minutes; if they seem fairly tender, go on to the next stage (if cooked too long, ink squid become hard and rubbery). § In the meantime cut the ink sacs with scissors and collect the ink in a bowl, diluting with 2 cups/16 fl oz/500 ml of cold water. Throw the empty sacs away. § When the ink squid are tender, pour the black liquid into the saucepan, raise the heat slightly, and bring to a boil. § Cook for 5 minutes then add the rice. § Continue cooking, stirring frequently, and adding more boiling water if the mixture becomes too dry. § The rice will take about 15–18 minutes to cook. The risotto should be very creamy. § Taste for salt and pepper and serve hot.

■ INGREDIENTS

- 2 fresh ink squid (weighing about 1½ lb/750 g)
- scant ½ cup/3½ fl oz/100 ml extra-virgin olive oil
- 1 small onion, finely chopped
- 1 clove garlic, finely chopped
- 1 tablespoon finely chopped parsley
- 1 tablespoon tomato paste
- ½ cup/4 fl oz/125 ml dry white wine
- 1¾ cups/12 oz/375 g arborio rice
- salt and freshly ground white pepper

Wine: a dry white (Locorotondo)

Right:
Risotto nero con le seppie

- 1 quantity *Milanese-style risotto* (see recipe p. 160)
- 6 chicken livers
- 2 tablespoons/1 oz/30 g butter
- ½ cup/4 fl oz/125 ml dry white wine
- 1 grated lemon rind
- salt and freshly ground black pepper
- 1 tablespoon finely chopped parsley

Wine: a dry red (Nebiolo)

RISOTTO ALLA MILANESE CON SALSA DI FEGATINI
Milanese-style risotto with chicken liver sauce

Serves 4; Preparation: 35 minutes; Cooking: 30 minutes; Level of difficulty: Medium

Prepare the *Milanese-style risotto*. § Wash the chicken livers under cold running water for about 30 minutes to remove all the blood. § Chop the livers coarsely and sauté in the butter for about 5 minutes over medium heat. § Add the wine and, when it evaporates, the lemon rind. Season with salt and pepper. § Place the risotto in a heated serving dish and distribute the liver sauce on top. § Sprinkle with the parsley and serve hot.

■ INGREDIENTS

- 3 tablespoons/1½ oz/45 g butter
- ½ onion, finely chopped
- 1 celery stalk, chopped
- 1 leek, (white part only), sliced
- 8 oz/250 g fresh spinach, cooked, squeezed dry and finely chopped
- 1¾ cups/12 oz/375 g arborio rice
- 6½ cups/2½ pints/1.5 liters boiling *Beef* or *Vegetable broth* (see recipes pp. 14)
- salt and freshly ground white pepper
- nutmeg (optional)
- 4 tablespoons freshly grated parmesan cheese

Wine: a dry white
(Valcalepio Bianco)

RISOTTO CON SPINACI
Spinach risotto

Serves 4; Preparation: 20 minutes; Cooking: 25 minutes; Level of difficulty: Medium

Melt two-thirds of the butter in a large, heavy-bottomed saucepan, add the onion, celery, and leek and sauté for 3–4 minutes over low heat. § Add the spinach, stir well and sauté for 2 minutes. § Add the rice and after 1 minute begin adding the boiling broth, a little at a time, until the rice is cooked. It will take about 15–18 minutes. § Season with salt and pepper and a dash of nutmeg (if liked). § Add the remaining butter and the parmesan, mix carefully, and serve.

VARIATIONS
– If fresh spinach is not available, use 6 oz/175 g of frozen spinach instead.
– Replace one-third of the parmesan with 1 tablespoon of soft, fresh ricotta cheese.
– Just before serving, add 2–3 tablespoons of cream to the risotto, in addition to, or instead of, the remaining butter.

■ INGREDIENTS

- 10 oz/300 g fresh cranberry or red kidney beans, shelled
- 1 small onion
- 4 sage leaves (or ½ bay leaf)
- 4 oz/125 g green beans
- 1¾ cups/12 oz/375 g short-grain rice
- 5 tablespoons extra-virgin olive oil
- salt and freshly ground black pepper

Wine: a dry white
(Cortese di Gavi)

Left:
Risotto con spinaci

INSALATA DI RISO E FAGIOLI
Rice and bean salad

Serves 4; Preparation: 10 minutes; Cooking: 40-50 minutes; Level of difficulty: Simple

Place the beans in a pot with the onion and sage (or bay leaf), and add enough cold water to cover them by about 2 in (5 cm). § Cover and cook over medium-low heat for about 40 minutes. Taste one to see if they are tender. § Season with salt just before removing from heat (if the salt is added earlier the skin of the beans will become tough). § Clean and rinse the green beans and cut them into 2–3 pieces. § About 20–25 minutes before the cranberry or kidney beans are ready, bring a saucepan containing 9 cups/3½ pints/2 liters of salted water to a boil and add the rice and green beans. Cook over medium heat, stirring occasionally. § Drain the rice and green beans and transfer to a salad bowl. § Drain the cranberry or kidney beans. Discard the onion and sage (or bay leaf), and add to the rice, stirring rapidly. § Season with the oil and pepper. § This salad can be served hot or warm.

Risotto con zucca
Risotto with squash

*This exquisite dish of Venetian origin has almost been forgotten.
It is so delicious that it really deserves a revival.*

Serves 4; Preparation: 15 minutes; Cooking: 30 minutes; Level of difficulty: Medium

Put the squash in a large, heavy-bottomed saucepan with the garlic, oil, and half the butter. Sauté, stirring, over medium heat for 8–10 minutes. § Add the rice and cook for 2 minutes, stirring continuously. § Add the boiling broth gradually, stirring frequently. § The squash will start to disintegrate, as it should. § The rice will cook in about 15–18 minutes. It should be quite creamy when ready. § Stir in the remaining butter, the parsley, parmesan, salt and pepper, and serve immediately. § Pass extra grated parmesan separately at table.

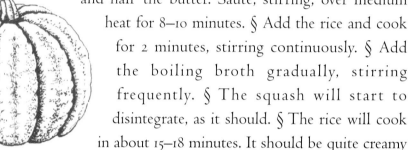

■ INGREDIENTS

- 10 oz/300 g yellow squash (hubbard or pumpkin) cleaned and diced
- 1 large clove garlic, finely chopped
- 3 tablespoons extra-virgin olive oil
- 3 tablespoons/1½ oz/45 g butter
- 1¾ cups/12 oz/375 g arborio rice
- 5 cups/2 pints/1.2 liters *Beef broth* (see recipe p. 14)
- salt and freshly ground white pepper
- 1 tablespoon finely chopped parsley
- 4 tablespoons freshly grated parmesan cheese

Wine: a light, dry red (Bardolino)

Riso in salsa di acciughe
Rice in anchovy sauce

This dish combines the simple, summer flavors of the Italian Riviera with the salty taste of the open sea. Replace the salt-preserved anchovies with those kept under oil for a milder dish.

Serves 4; Preparation: 5-7 minutes; Cooking: 15 minutes; Level of difficulty: Simple

Bring 9 cups/3½ pints/2 liters of salted water to a boil. Add the rice, stir once or twice, and allow 13–15 minutes cooking time from when the water comes to a boil again. § While the rice is cooking, rinse the anchovies under cold running water and divide into fillets, removing the bones. § Rinse the capers and chop finely with the anchovies. § Heat the oil in a small skillet (frying pan), add the capers and anchovies and cook over low heat for 2–3 minutes. § Add the lemon juice just before removing from heat. § Drain the rice well and transfer to a serving dish or individual plates. Pour the sauce over the top. § Garnish with the lemon and serve hot.

■ INGREDIENTS

- 2 cups/14 oz/450 g short-grain rice
- 5 tablespoons extra-virgin olive oil
- 4 anchovies, preserved in salt
- 1 tablespoon capers
- ½ tablespoon lemon juice
- thin slices of lemon to garnish

Wine: a dry white (Cinqueterre)

Right:
Risotto con zucca

POLENTA

From its humble origins among the poorer peasants of northern Italy, polenta has gained an international reputation and a host of gourmet interpretations.

POLENTA CONDITA ALL'ANTICA
Polenta with traditional toppings

These simple recipes give us a taste of how polenta was served in peasant homes in times of yore. A rather soft polenta is needed, so use slightly less yellow cornmeal than in the basic recipe. The recipe for Basic polenta *is on p. 18.*

■ INGREDIENTS

- 1 quantity *Basic polenta* (see recipe p. 18)
- 4 cups/1½ pints/1 liter cold milk
- ¼ cup/2 fl oz/60 ml light/single cream

Wine: a light, dry red (Lambrusco)

■ INGREDIENTS

- 1 quantity *Basic polenta* (see recipe p. 18)
- ⅓ cup/3 oz/90 g butter
- 4 tablespoons freshly grated parmesan cheese

Wine: a dry red (Chianti Classico - Geografico)

■ INGREDIENTS

- 1 quantity *Basic polenta* (see recipe p. 18)
- 4 oz/125 g lard, 2 cloves garlic, 2 tablespoons parsley, finely chopped together

Wine: a dry, red (Grignolino)

Left: *Polenta e lardo*

POLENTA E LATTE
Polenta and milk

Serves 4-6; Preparation: 5 minutes; Cooking: 50-60 minutes; Level of difficulty: Simple

Prepare the polenta. § Pour the milk into a pitcher and then add the cream. § Pour the piping hot polenta into soup plates or, in the classic version, small bowls. § Serve the polenta and creamy milk separately, so that everyone can help themselves to as much as they like.

POLENTA CON BURRO E FORMAGGIO
Polenta with butter and cheese

Serves 4-6; Preparation: 5 minutes; Cooking: 50-60 minutes; Level of difficulty: Simple

Prepare the polenta. § Chop the butter in small pieces, dust with the parmesan and place half in individual soup plates. § Pour the polenta into the plates, and sprinkle with the remaining butter and parmesan. § This recipe is also good with the same quantity of gorgonzola cheese instead of parmesan.

POLENTA E LARDO
Polenta and lard

Serves 4-6; Preparation: 5 minutes; Cooking: 50-60 minutes; Level of difficulty: Simple

Prepare the polenta. § Mash the chopped lard, garlic, and parsley with the blade of a knife held flat to achieve a smooth, almost creamy, mixture. § Place half the mixture in the bottom of individual soup plates. § Pour the hot polenta into the plates and cover with the remaining mixture. § Serve.

Polenta d'Oropa
Oropa-style polenta

Oropa is a tiny locality in Piedmont, in northern Italy. Apart from this dish,
it is also famous for its beautiful religious sanctuary.

Serves 4; Preparation: 10 minutes; Cooking: 50 minutes; Level of difficulty: Medium

Use the first four ingredients to prepare the polenta as explained on p. 18. These quantities will make a rather soft polenta. § After the polenta has been cooking for about 30 minutes, add the toma and continue cooking for another 15 minutes, stirring energetically. § A few minutes before the polenta is cooked, slowly melt the butter in a small saucepan until it starts to bubble. § Pour the polenta into a large serving dish, dust with pepper and sprinkle with the parmesan. Drizzle the hot butter over the top and serve immediately.

VARIATION
– Toma cheese can be hard to find outside of northern Piedmont. Use the same quantity of fontina or fontal in its place.

■ INGREDIENTS

- 5 cups/2 pints/1.2 liters boiling water
- 2 pints/1.2 liters hot milk
- 1 tablespoon coarse sea salt
- 2½ cups/10 oz/300 g coarse-grain cornmeal
- 14 oz/450 g toma grassa cheese, cut in slivers
- 5 tablespoons freshly grated parmesan cheese
- ⅓ cup/3 oz/90 g butter
- freshly ground black pepper

Wine: a dry red
(Gamay della Valle d'Aosta)

Polenta di patate
Potato polenta

This delicious polenta comes from Trento in the northeast. It should be served with pickles,
particularly sweet-sour gherkins. For a complete meal, serve with barbecued pork ribs.

Serves 4; Preparation: 30 minutes; Cooking: 30-35 minutes; Level of difficulty: Medium

Mash the potatoes and transfer to the pot where the polenta is to be cooked. § Add the cornmeal and buckwheat flour, mix well, and continue to mix while adding the water. § Cook over medium-high heat, stirring frequently and energetically. § Melt the butter and oil over medium heat in a small saucepan. Add the onion and sauté until golden. § Add the butter and oil to the polenta which will have been cooking for about 10 minutes by this time. Stir continuously. § After 20 more minutes, add a little salt, a generous dash or two of pepper, and the cheese and continue stirring for 10 more minutes. § Serve immediately. If there is any left over, cut in slices when cold and serve broiled (grilled) or fried.

VARIATIONS
– Fine-grain yellow cornmeal can also be used.
– If you don't have buckwheat flour use a double quantity of cornmeal

■ INGREDIENTS

- 2¼ lb/1.2 kg potatoes, boiled and peeled, still hot
- ½ cup/2 oz/60 g coarse-grain cornmeal
- ½ cup/2 oz/60 g buckwheat flour
- 1 cup/8 fl oz/250 ml boiling water
- 3 tablespoons/1½ oz/45 g butter
- 3 tablespoons extra-virgin olive oil
- 2 onions, thinly sliced
- salt and freshly ground black pepper
- 4–5 oz/125-150 g fresh Asiago cheese, in slivers

Wine: a hearty, dry red
(Breganze Rosso)

Right:
Polenta d'Oropa

Polenta al taleggio
Polenta with taleggio cheese

Taleggio cheese comes from Lombardy. It should be creamy, fragrant, and well ripened.
If you can't get taleggio, use the same quantity of fontina cheese in its place.

Serves 4; Preparation: 10 minutes; Cooking: 1 hour; Level of difficulty: Simple

Use the first four ingredients to prepare the polenta as explained on p. 18. These quantities will make a rather soft polenta which will cook in about 45 minutes. § Lightly butter an ovenproof baking dish about 10 in (25 cm) in diameter and about 3 in (8 cm) deep. § When the polenta is ready, pour one-third into the dish, sprinkle with one-third of the parmesan, one-third of the taleggio, and one-third of the remaining butter, in dabs. Repeat this procedure twice. § Bake in a preheated oven at 400°F/200°C/gas 6 for about 15 minutes, or until the surface turns golden brown. § Serve hot.

■ INGREDIENTS

- 6½ cups/2½ pints/1.5 liters boiling water
- 3 cups/24 fl oz/750 ml milk
- 1 tablespoon coarse sea salt
- 2¾ cups/12 oz/375 g coarse-grain cornmeal
- 2 tablespoons/1 oz/30 g butter
- ½ cup/2 oz/60 g parmesan cheese, flaked
- 10 oz/300 g ripe taleggio cheese, without its crust and cut in slices

Wine: a dry red (Valcalepio Rosso)

Polenta con la luganega
Polenta with luganega sausage

Luganega is a type of fresh pork sausage found throughout northern Italy. If you can't find it,
replace it with another type of fresh Italian pork sausage and modify cooking method.

Serves 4; Preparation: 5 minutes; Cooking: 50 minutes; Level of difficulty: Medium

Prepare the polenta. § About 20 minutes before the polenta is cooked, pierce holes about 1 in (2.5 cm) apart in the casing of the luganega with a toothpick, so that the fat will drain out during cooking and the heat will penetrate to the inside. Don't use a fork as the holes will be too close together and the casing will probably break. § Roll the luganega up in a flat spiral, piercing it horizontally with two long thin wooden or metal skewers, placed crosswise, so it will keep its shape. § Melt the butter in a skillet (frying pan). Add the oil and rosemary, and then carefully add the sausage. Brown for 3–4 minutes over medium heat, then turn so it will brown on the other side. § Increase the heat and pour the wine into the pan; as soon as it is hot, lower the heat and cover the pan. § Sauté for about 10 minutes, turning the luganega again after the first 5 minutes. § When it is cooked, remove the skewers and cut the sausage into pieces about 2 in (5 cm) long. § Transfer the polenta to a wide serving dish and arrange the sausage pieces on top. § Discard the rosemary from the pan and drizzle the juices over the polenta. § Serve hot.

■ INGREDIENTS

- 1 quantity *Basic polenta* (see recipe p. 18)
- 1 lb/500 g luganega (or very fresh Italian pork sausage)
- 2 tablespoons/1 oz/30 g butter
- 1 tablespoon extra-virgin olive oil
- 1 small twig rosemary
- ⅔ cup/5 fl oz/150 ml dry white or red wine

Wine: a dry red
(Raboso del Piave)

Right:
Polenta con la luganega

- 9 cups/3½ pints/2 liters boiling water
- 1 tablespoon coarse sea salt
- 2¼ cups/10 oz/300 g coarse-grain cornmeal
- ⅔ cup/5 oz/150 g diced lean pancetta
- ¾ cup/3 oz/90 g freshly grated pecorino cheese
- 3 tablespoons/1½ oz/45 g butter
- 1 lb/500 g ripe tomatoes (or one 14-oz/450-g can)
- ½ onion, finely chopped
- 3 tablespoons extra-virgin olive oil
- ½ clove garlic, finely chopped
- 10 fresh basil leaves, torn

*Wine: a dry red
(Montescudaio Rosso)*

- 9 cups/3½ pints/2 liters boiling water
- 1 tablespoon coarse sea salt
- 2¼ cups/10 oz/300 g coarse-grain cornmeal
- 1 tablespoon extra-virgin olive oil
- 10 oz/300 g fresh Italian pork sausage, skinned and crumbled
- ½ cup/3 oz/90 g finely chopped salt pork
- ½ tablespoon finely chopped rosemary leaves
- 1 clove garlic, finely chopped
- 5 tablespoons freshly grated parmesan cheese

*Wine: a dry red
(Merlot Colli Bolognesi)*

Left: *Polenta alla Tosco-Emiliana*

POLENTA ALLA MAREMMANA
Maremma-style polenta

Serves 4; Preparation: 15 minutes; Cooking: 50 minutes; Level of difficulty: Simple

Use the first three ingredients to prepare the polenta as explained on p. 18. These quantities will make a very soft polenta. § Meanwhile prepare the sauce. Plunge the tomatoes into boiling water for 10 seconds, then into cold. Peel and chop coarsely. If using canned tomatoes, do not drain but chop them slightly. § In a saucepan, over low heat, sauté the onion in the oil until it is translucent. Add the garlic, tomatoes, and basil. § Turn up the heat a little and simmer the sauce for 15–20 minutes. § When the polenta is half cooked, add the pancetta, cheese, and pieces of butter; stir frequently. § When the polenta is ready, transfer to individual plates and spoon the tomato sauce over the top. § Serve hot.

POLENTA ALLA TOSCO-EMILIANA
Tuscan-Emilian-style polenta

A hearty, winter dish. Followed by a salad and fruit, it is a complete meal.

Serves 4; Preparation: 15 minutes; Cooking: 1 hour, 10 minutes; Level of difficulty: Medium

Use the first three ingredients to prepare the polenta as explained on p. 18. These quantities will make a very soft polenta which will cook in about 45 minutes. § Oil an ovenproof baking dish, large enough to contain the polenta in a 1-in (2.5-cm) layer. § Using a fork, carefully mix the sausage, salt pork, rosemary, and garlic together in a bowl. § When the polenta is cooked, pour it into the baking dish and smooth it out with a spatula. § Spread with the sausage mixture, gently pushing it into the polenta with your fingertips. § Bake in preheated oven at 400°F/200°C/gas 6, for 15 minutes. § Dust with the parmesan just before serving.

VARIATION
– If salt pork is not liked, omit and add extra sausage.

POLENTA PASTICCIATA ALLA MILANESE
Baked polenta, Milanese-style

Serves 4; Preparation: 1 hour; Cooking: 25-30 minutes; Level of difficulty: Medium

For the mushroom sauce: soak the mushrooms in 1 cup/8 fl oz/250 ml of tepid water for 30 minutes. Drain (reserving the liquid), squeeze out excess moisture, and chop coarsely. § Strain the water in which the mushrooms were soaked and set aside. § In a skillet (frying pan) melt two-thirds of the butter and sauté the onion for a few minutes over low heat; add the sausage, and the mushrooms with their water. § Cover and cook over medium heat for 30 minutes, stirring occasionally. Season with salt and pepper. (This sauce can be prepared ahead of time). § Prepare the béchamel sauce. § Butter an ovenproof baking dish about 8 in (20 cm) in diameter and 3 in (7.5 cm) deep. Cover the bottom with ¼-in (6-mm) thick slices of polenta. § Pour on one-third of the mushroom sauce, dust with one-third of the parmesan, arrange one-third of the gruyère on top and cover with one-third of the béchamel sauce. Repeat this procedure twice. § Bake in a preheated oven at 400°F/200°C/gas 6 for 25–30 minutes, or until the top is golden brown. § Serve hot.

■ INGREDIENTS

SAUCE:
- 1 oz/30 g dried porcini mushrooms
- 3 tablespoons/1½ oz/45 g butter
- 1 small onion, finely chopped
- 4–5 oz/125–150 g Italian pork sausage, skinned and crumbled
- salt and freshly ground black pepper
- 1 quantity *Béchamel sauce* (see recipe p. 22)
- 1 lb/500 g cold *Basic polenta* (see recipe p. 18)
- ¾ cup/3 oz/90 g freshly grated parmesan cheese
- 3½ oz/100 g gruyère cheese (or similar), cut in slivers

Wine: a dry red (Bonarda Oltrepò Pavese)

POLENTA PASTICCIATA AL FORMAGGIO
Baked polenta with cheese

*Always make a generous quantity of polenta,
there are so many delicious ways of using up any that is leftover.*

Serves 4; Preparation: 10 minutes; Cooking: 25-30 minutes; Level of difficulty: Simple

Cut the polenta into ¼-in (6-mm) thick slices, about 1¼ in (3 cm) long. § Butter an ovenproof baking dish deep enough for three layers of polenta. § Cover the bottom with slices of polenta, sprinkle with one-third of the parmesan, one-third of the gruyère, and dot with one-third of the butter. § Repeat this procedure twice. § Bake in a preheated oven at 400°F/200°C/gas 6 for 25–30 minutes, or until a golden crust has formed. § Serve hot.

■ INGREDIENTS

- 1 lb/500 g cold *Basic polenta* (see recipe p. 18)
- ⅓ cup/3 oz/90 g butter
- 6 tablespoons freshly grated parmesan cheese
- 4 oz/125 g gruyère cheese, cut in slivers

Wine: a dry red (Donnaz)

Right:
Polenta pasticciata alla milanese

POLENTA PASTICCIATA CON IL POMODORO
Baked polenta with tomato sauce

■ INGREDIENTS

- 1 quantity *Basic tomato sauce* (see recipe p. 2)
- 1 tablespoon extra-virgin olive oil
- 1 lb/500 g cold *Basic polenta* (see recipe p. 18)
- 10 oz/300 g mild provolone cheese, diced
- freshly ground black pepper (optional)

Wine: a light, dry red (San Colombano)

Serves 4; Preparation: 20 minutes; Cooking: 25-30 minutes; Level of difficulty: Simple

Prepare the tomato sauce. § Oil an ovenproof baking dish about 8 in (20 cm) in diameter and about 3 in (8 cm) deep. § Cover the bottom with ¼-in (6-mm) thick, short slices of the cold polenta, and scatter one-third of the diced provolone evenly on top. § Dust with pepper and drizzle with one-third of the tomato sauce. § Repeat this procedure twice, finishing up with a layer of sauce. § Bake in a preheated oven at 400°F/200°C/gas 6 for 25–30 minutes. § Serve piping hot straight from the oven.

> VARIATIONS
> – Replace the tomato sauce with 1 quantity of either of the meat sauces on p. 4.

POLENTA ALLA PIZZAIOLA
Polenta with pizza sauce

Children particularly love this delicious dish. It is also convenient because it can be prepared a few hours ahead, kept at room temperature, and then popped into the oven 20 minutes before serving.

Serves 4; Preparation: 10 minutes; Cooking: 1¼ hours; Level of difficulty: Medium

Use the first three ingredients to prepare the polenta as explained on p. 18. Cook for 50 minutes; it should be fairly solid but not too hard. § In the meantime prepare the sauce: cook the tomatoes in a small saucepan for 5 minutes over medium heat. § Add the garlic, oregano, and a little salt. Cover and cook over low heat for 15 minutes, stirring occasionally. § When

■ INGREDIENTS

- 9 cups/3½ pints/2 liters boiling water
- 1 tablespoon coarse sea salt
- 2¾ cups/12 oz/375 g coarse-grain cornmeal
- 4 tablespoons extra-virgin olive oil
- 2 cups/8 oz/250 g scamorza cheese, diced
- 8 anchovy fillets, preserved in oil, crumbled

Right:
Polenta pasticciata con il pomodoro

SAUCE:
- one 14-oz/450-g can tomatoes, partially drained and coarsely chopped
- 1 small clove garlic, finely chopped
- 1 teaspoon oregano
- salt
- 2 tablespoons extra-virgin olive oil

Wine: a dry white (Greco di Tufo)

the sauce is cooked, add the oil. The sauce can also be prepared ahead of time. § Oil an ovenproof baking dish large enough for a layer of polenta about 1¼ in (3 cm) thick with 2 tablespoons of the oil. § When the polenta is ready, transfer it to the dish and level with a spatula. § Cover the surface with the sauce. Distribute the diced scamorza evenly on top, add the anchovies, and drizzle with the remaining oil. § Cook in a preheated oven at 400°F/200°C/gas 6 for about 15 minutes. § If the dish was prepared ahead of time and the polenta is no longer hot, preheat the oven to 350°F/180°C/gas 4 and cook at that temperature for the first 10–15 minutes, then increase to 400°F/200°C/gas 6 for the last 5–10 minutes, otherwise a tough, unpleasant crust will form on the scamorza.

Polenta pasticciata in salsa di formaggio
Baked polenta in cheese sauce

Serves 4; Preparation: 20 minutes; Cooking: 30 minutes; Level of difficulty: Simple

Melt the butter in a saucepan. When it stops foaming, add the flour and cook over low heat for a couple of minutes, stirring well. § Begin to add the milk, a little at a time, stirring continuously. The sauce should be a smooth and fluid béchamel. Season with a little nutmeg. § Turn up the heat and add the cheeses, a handful at a time. Keep stirring so that they will melt and the sauce will stay smooth. § Butter an ovenproof baking dish large enough to contain the polenta and sauce in a layer about 2 in (5 cm) thick. § Cut the polenta into ¾-in (2-cm) cubes. § Cover the bottom with half the polenta cubes and pour half the sauce over the top. Arrange the remaining polenta on top and cover with the remaining sauce. § Bake in a preheated oven at 400°F/200°C/gas 6 for 25–30 minutes, or until the top has a golden crust.

■ INGREDIENTS

SAUCE:
- 2 tablespoons/1 oz/30 g butter
- 1 tablespoon all-purpose/plain flour
- 1 cup/8 fl oz/250 ml milk
- 5 oz/150 ml gorgonzola cheese, cut in pieces
- 5 oz/150 g emmenthal (or gruyère, or similar) cheese, thinly sliced
- 2–3 tablespoons freshly grated parmesan cheese
- dash of nutmeg

BASE:
- 1 tablespoon/½ oz/15 g butter
- 1 lb/500 g cold *Basic polenta* (see recipe p. 18)

Wine: a dry red (Barbacarlo Oltrepò Pavese)

Polenta con i funghi
Polenta with mushroom sauce

For a really tasty sauce, use highly prized wild mushrooms, such as porcini, shiitake, or chanterelle. If using cultivated varieties, combine with 1 oz/30 g of dried porcini mushrooms. Soak the dried porcini in a bowl of warm water for 30 minutes, chop coarsely and mix with the fresh mushrooms. The distinctive musky flavor of the dried porcini will add just the right amount of zest to the sauce.

Serves 4; Preparation: 20 minutes; Cooking: 50 minutes; Level of difficulty: Medium

Prepare the polenta. § To prepare the sauce: trim the stems of the mushrooms, rinse under cold running water and pat dry with kitchen towels. Slice thinly. § Heat the oil in a skillet (frying pan) over medium heat, add the garlic and sauté for 2–3 minutes, stirring often so that they don't burn. Discard. § Add the parsley (or calamint) and mushrooms and cook over high heat for 2–3 minutes. § Add the tomatoes and continue cooking over medium heat for 15–20 minutes, stirring frequently. § Transfer the polenta to a serving dish and pour the mushroom sauce over the top. § Serve hot.

■ INGREDIENTS

- 1 quantity *Basic polenta* (see recipe p. 18)

SAUCE:
- 14 oz/450 g mushrooms
- 4 tablespoons extra-virgin olive oil
- 2 cloves garlic
- 1 tablespoon finely chopped parsley or calamint
- 14 oz/450 g peeled and chopped canned or fresh tomatoes
- salt and freshly ground white pepper

Wine: a light, dry red (Bardolino)

Right: *Polenta con i funghi*

Polenta Taragna
Taragna polenta

This is a typical dish of the Valtellina, in Lombardy in the north. Truly hearty, it is made with buckwheat flour, once considered to be quite lowly, but now rising in popularity.

Serves 4; Preparation: 5 minutes; Cooking: 50 minutes; Level of difficulty: Medium

Bring the water and salt to a boil. § Sift in the flour, stirring with a wire whisk and add half the butter. § Cook, stirring frequently, as for a regular polenta (see p. 18), for 40 minutes. The buckwheat polenta will be rather soft. § Add the cheese and continue stirring over fairly low heat. § After a couple of minutes add the remaining butter. § After another 5–8 minutes the polenta will be ready. Not all the cheese will have melted and combined with the polenta. § Serve immediately.

VARIATION
– Replace one-third of the buckwheat flour with 1 cup/3½ oz/100 g of coarse-grain cornmeal.

■ INGREDIENTS

- 9 cups/3½ pints/2 liters water
- 1 scant tablespoon coarse sea salt
- 3 cups/10 oz/300 g buckwheat flour
- scant 1 cup/7 oz/200 g butter
- 7 oz/200 g fontina, asiago, or fontal cheese (or a mixture of the three), cut in slivers

Wine: a hearty red

Polenta fritta
Fried polenta

Leftover polenta, cut into slices about ½-in (1-cm) thick and fried, is delicious with many meat or game dishes. It also makes an ideal snack or appetizer by itself or with various toppings. Try it with any of the meat or tomato sauces on pp. 2–6, or with the mushroom sauce given on p. 12.

Serves 4; Preparation: 2 minutes; Cooking: 8 minutes; Level of difficulty: Simple

Heat enough lard or oil and butter in a skillet (frying pan) to cover the bottom by ¼ in (6 mm). § Add the rosemary, sage, and garlic. When the fat is hot, but not smoking, add the slices of polenta. § As soon as they are crisp and golden underneath, turn them over with a spatula and fry on the other side. It will take about 6–8 minutes. § Lift to let excess fat drip off and transfer to paper towels to absorb the rest. § Serve with a sprinkling of salt and pepper.

VARIATION
– Fry the slices as above in oil only and omit the rosemary, sage, garlic, salt and pepper. When cooked, sprinkle with sugar and a little cinnamon, and serve as a sweet or snack. This used to be a classic treat for children.

■ INGREDIENTS

- lard, or olive oil and butter, for frying
- 1 sprig rosemary
- 4 sage leaves
- 1 clove garlic
- 4–8, or more, slices of cold *Basic polenta* (see recipe p. 18)
- salt and freshly ground black pepper

Wine: depending on what is served with the polenta

Right:
Polenta fritta

CROSTONI DI POLENTA AL FORMAGGIO
Fried polenta with cheese topping

Use your imagination in making these slices of fried polenta, depending on what kinds of cheese are available and how much you want to use. Some good cheeses are: taleggio, gorgonzola, fontina, asiago, provola, scamorza (smoked or plain).

Serves 4; Preparation: 10 minutes; Cooking: 8 minutes; Level of difficulty: Simple

To prepare the cheese(s), remove the crust and chop into pieces if very soft, or in thin slices if harder. § Pour the oil into a skillet (frying pan) and when it is hot, but not smoking, add the slices of polenta together with the sage or rosemary. § Fry over high heat for 3 minutes or so. Turn the slices over with a spatula and cover with the cheese, leaving a small border around the edges. § Cover the skillet (frying pan) and cook for another 3 minutes so that the slices of polenta get crisp on the underside and the cheese melts. § Serve immediately, with a sprinkling of pepper if liked.

■ INGREDIENTS

- 8 or more slices of cold *Basic polenta* (see recipe p. 18), ¾ in/2 cm thick and about 4 in/10 cm long
- scant ½ cup/3½ fl oz/100 ml extra-virgin olive oil
- 4 sage leaves or 1 sprig rosemary
- choice of cheese (see introduction to recipe for some ideas)
- freshly ground white or black pepper (optional)

Wine: a dry red (Franciacorta Rosso)

POLENTA E FAGIOLI
Polenta and beans

This recipe comes from Veneto, the region around Venice, and ideally the marbled pink and white Lamon beans (a type of red kidney bean) should be used, but they are not easy to find. Use cranberry or red kidney beans in their place. If using dried beans, soak for 12 hours first and extend the cooking time to 1 hour.

Serves 4; Preparation: 5 minutes; Cooking: 1¼ hours; Level of difficulty: Medium

Put the beans in a pot that can hold about 4 quarts/8 pints/5 liters. Add the onion, pancetta, and bay leaf with enough cold water to cover the beans by at least 2 in (5 cm). § Cover and cook over low heat for about 30 minutes. § Sift the cornmeal into the pot very slowly, stirring with a whisk so that no lumps form. When all the cornmeal has been added, continue stirring with a long wooden spoon. § It will take about 40 minutes for the polenta to cook. It should be very soft; if it is too hard, add a little more boiling water. § Season with salt when almost cooked. § Shortly before the polenta is cooked, melt the butter in a small saucepan to a golden color. § Serve the polenta in individual plates, sprinkled with parmesan and drizzled with the hot butter.

■ INGREDIENTS

- 1 cup/7 oz/200 g fresh cranberry or red kidney beans, shelled
- ½ small onion, finely chopped
- ⅓ cup/1 oz/30 g finely chopped pancetta
- 1 bay leaf
- 2½ cups/10 oz/300 g fine-grain cornmeal
- salt
- ¼ cup/2 oz/60 g butter
- 8 tablespoons freshly grated parmesan cheese

Wine: a dry, fragrant red (Gutturnio)

Right:
Crostoni di polenta al formaggio

- 1 quantity *Basic polenta*
  (see recipe p. 18)
- 12 oz/375 g leeks, (white
  part only)
- 3 tablespoons/1½ oz/45 g
  butter
- 1½ cups/10 fl oz/300 ml
  light/single cream
- 5 tablespoons milk
- salt and freshly ground
  white pepper

Wine: a dry, lightly sparkling red
(Barbera del Monferrato Vivace)

Polenta con salsa di porri
Polenta with leek sauce

Serves 4; Preparation: 15 minutes; Cooking: 50 minutes; Level of difficulty: Simple

Prepare the polenta. § Cut the leeks into ⅛ in/2–3 mm thick slices. § Melt the butter in a heavy-bottomed saucepan over medium heat, add the leeks, cover and cook for 5 minutes, or until the leeks have wilted. § Season with salt and pepper. Add the cream and milk and cook for 20–25 minutes. § When the polenta is done (it should be very thick, almost stiff), turn it out onto a heated serving platter. § Serve hot with the leek sauce handed round separately in another heated serving dish.

VEGETABLE APPETIZERS

A salad or vegetable-based appetizer is a light and healthy way to begin a meal. A few of the recipes included in this chapter are fried or baked and thus heavier; in that case be sure to balance the meal by serving something light to follow.

OLIVE CONDITE
Hot and spicy green olives

■ INGREDIENTS

• 2¼ cups/10 oz/300 g
  pitted green olives

• 4 cloves garlic

• 1 twig fresh rosemary

• 1 tablespoon coarsely
  chopped fresh mint

• ½ teaspoon oregano

• ½ teaspoon crushed
  chilies

• 2 tablespoons extra-virgin
  olive oil

*Wine: a dry white
(Etna Bianco)*

This tasty dish comes from Sicily. In some parts of the island the olives will sometimes appear on your table served in tiny, hollowed-out bread rolls. The crusty bread helps offset some of the fire in the dressing. Use only the highest quality green olives packed in brine.

Serves: 4; Preparation: 10 minutes + 2 hours to marinate; Level of difficulty: Simple

Rinse the olives in cold water and pat dry with paper towels. § Lightly crush the olives with a meat-pounding mallet. § Use the same instrument to bruise the cloves of garlic. Place the olives and garlic in a serving dish. § Remove the rosemary leaves from the twig and add to the olives, together with the mint, oregano, chilies, and oil. Mix well and cover. Set aside in a cool place (not the refrigerator) for at least 2 hours before serving. § Serve with lots of crusty bread.

VARIATION
– Add 2 tablespoons finely chopped scallions/shallots.

BRUSCHETTA CON POMODORI FRESCHI
Bruschetta with fresh tomato topping

■ INGREDIENTS

• 4 slices *Bruschetta*
  (see recipe p. 20)

• 2 large ripe tomatoes

• 4 tablespoons extra-virgin
  olive oil

• 8 fresh basil leaves, torn

• 1 teaspoon oregano

• salt and freshly ground
  black pepper

*Wine: a dry white
(Orvieto Classico)*

If you want to prepare this dish ahead of time, keep the bruschette *and tomato mixture separate until just before serving, otherwise the dish will become soggy and unappetizing.*

Serves: 4; Preparation: 10 minutes; Cooking: 10 minutes; Level of difficulty: Simple

Prepare the *Bruschette*. § Dice the tomatoes into bite-size chunks. Place them in a bowl and mix with the oil, basil, oregano, salt and pepper. § Cover each bruschetta with a quarter of the tomato mixture. § Serve immediately.

VARIATIONS
– Add 1 cup/3½ oz/100 g diced mozzarella cheese to the tomato mixture.
– Add ⅓ teaspoon crushed chilies or 1 chopped fresh chili to the tomato mixture.
– Add 1 tablespoon small salted capers to the tomato mixture.

Right: *Olive condite*

■ INGREDIENTS

• 4 slices *Bruschetta*
  (see recipe p. 20)

• one 14-oz/450-g can
  white beans

• salt and freshly ground
  black pepper

• 1 tablespoon extra-virgin
  olive oil

Wine: a dry, young red
(Vino Novello)

BRUSCHETTA CON FAGIOLI
Bruschetta with white beans

Serves: 4; Preparation: 10 minutes; Cooking: 10 minutes; Level of difficulty: Simple

Prepare the *bruschette*. § Heat the beans in a small saucepan. Taste for salt; season if necessary. § When hot, pour over the *bruschette*. § Sprinkle with pepper and drizzle with oil. § Serve hot.

VARIATIONS
– Add 6 fresh sage leaves to the beans when heating.
– For homemade baked beans; cook 2 large diced tomatoes in the saucepan before adding the beans. Serve hot.

CAROTE ALL'OLIO, AGLIO E LIMONE
Carrot salad with garlic, oil, and lemon

This light, refreshing, and vitamin-packed salad is a perfect appetizer for hot summer evenings.

Serves: 4; Preparation: 10 minutes + 30 minutes to marinate; Level of difficulty: Simple

Place the carrots, garlic, parsley, and mint in a small salad bowl. Add the lemon juice, oil, salt and pepper to taste. Mix well. § Set aside for at least 30 minutes before serving.

■ INGREDIENTS

- 4 large carrots, coarsely grated
- 1 clove garlic, finely chopped
- 2 tablespoons finely chopped parsley
- 1 tablespoon finely chopped mint leaves
- juice of 1 lemon
- 3 tablespoons extra-virgin olive oil
- salt and freshly ground black pepper

Wine: a light, dry white (Soave)

PEPERONI ARROSTITI CON ACCIUGHE
Roasted bell peppers with anchovies

This dish is tastier if prepared the day before. Store in the refrigerator, but take out at least two hours before serving. If well covered with olive oil, roasted bell peppers with anchovies will keep for up to a week in the refrigerator.

Serves: 8; Preparation: 15 minutes + 2 hours to marinate; Cooking: 15–20 minutes; Level of difficulty: Simple

Cut the bell peppers in half lengthwise. Remove the seeds and pulpy core. Rinse under cold running water and pat dry with paper towels. Bake in a preheated oven at 400°F/200°C/gas 6 until the skins are wrinkled and slightly burned. Take the bell peppers out of the oven and leave to cool. Remove the charred skins with your fingers. § Cut the peeled bell peppers lengthwise into strips about 2 in (5 cm) wide. Choose a serving dish that will hold 4–5 layers of bell peppers and line the bottom with one layer. § Crumble 4 of the anchovy fillets in a small mixing bowl and add the garlic, parsley, capers, oregano, and oil. § Place a layer of this mixture over the bell peppers. Cover with another layer of bell peppers and anchovy mixture. Repeat the procedure until all the ingredients have been used. § Garnish the top layer with the remaining anchovy fillets and the basil. Set the dish aside to marinate for at least 2 hours before serving.

■ INGREDIENTS

- 2 yellow, 2 green, and 2 red bell peppers / capsicums, medium-size
- 8 anchovy fillets
- 4 cloves garlic, finely chopped
- 2 tablespoons finely chopped parsley
- 2 tablespoons capers
- ½ teaspoon oregano
- 4 tablespoons extra-virgin olive oil
- 8 fresh basil leaves, torn

Wine: a dry red (Chianti Classico)

Right:
Peperoni arrostiti con acciughe

Zucchine grigliate con menta fresca e aglio
Grilled zucchini with fresh mint and garlic

Serves 4; Preparation: 20 minutes + 2 hours to cool; Cooking: 10 minutes; Level of difficulty: Simple

Wash and dry the zucchini, trim the ends, and cut lengthwise into ¼-in (6-mm) thick slices. § Heat the grill pan to very hot and cook the slices for 2–3 minutes on each side. Remove and set aside to cool. § Put the oil in a bowl with the salt, parsley, and mint, and beat with a fork or whisk until well mixed. § Arrange the cold zucchini slices in a small, fairly deep-sided serving dish. Sprinkle with the garlic and grind the mixed pepper over the top. § Pour the oil mixture over the zucchini (make sure that the zucchini are well-covered with oil) and refrigerate for at least 2 hours before serving.

VARIATIONS
– Sprinkle 6 crumbled anchovy fillets over the zucchini together with the garlic.
– For a spicy dish, add ½ teaspoon crushed chilies to the oil and mix with the parsley, mint, and salt.

■ INGREDIENTS

• 8 zucchini/courgettes
• 12 tablespoons extra-virgin olive oil
• salt
• 2 tablespoons finely chopped parsley
• 1 tablespoon finely chopped fresh mint
• mixed red, black, green peppercorns
• 2 cloves garlic, finely chopped

Wine: a dry white (Trebbiano di Lugana)

Zucchine crude con maionese piccante
Marinated zucchini with spicy mayonnaise

Serves 4; Preparation: 20 minutes + 2 hours to marinate; Level of difficulty: Simple

Wash and dry the zucchini, trim the ends, and slice thinly (skin and all). § Place in a bowl, add the vinegar, and sprinkle with salt. Mix well and leave to marinate for at least 2 hours. § Prepare the mayonnaise and stir in the mustard. § Drain the zucchini, squeeze them gently in your hands to remove as much vinegar as possible. § Mix the zucchini with the spicy mayonnaise and transfer to a serving dish. § Garnish with sprigs of parsley and serve.

■ INGREDIENTS

• 4 large zucchini/courgettes
• 4 tablespoons white wine vinegar
• salt and freshly ground black pepper
• 1 quantity *Mayonnaise* (see recipe p. 16)
• 2 teaspoons hot mustard
• 8 sprigs parsley

Wine: a dry white (Traminer aromatico)

Right: *Zucchine grigliate con menta fresca e aglio*

INSALATA DI OVOLI
Caesar's mushroom salad

This eyecatching salad calls for very fresh Caesar's (also known as royal agaric) mushrooms. For a perfect salad, choose the ones with the caps still closed around the stems and serve them the same day they are purchased. They must be absolutely fresh.

Serves 4-6; Preparation: 10 minutes; Level of difficulty: Simple

Clean the mushrooms and rinse them carefully in cold water. Pat dry with paper towels. § Slice the mushrooms finely and arrange them on a serving dish. § Sprinkle with the walnuts and parmesan flakes. § Mix the oil, salt, pepper, and lemon juice in a bowl and pour over the mushrooms. § Serve immediately, or the flavor will begin to change.

VARIATIONS
– Add a finely chopped clove of garlic to the olive oil dressing.
– Replace the Caesar's mushrooms with the same quantity of closed white button mushrooms. In this case, serve on a bed of fresh, crisp arugula (rocket).

■ INGREDIENTS

- 14 oz/450 g Caesar's (royal agaric) mushrooms
- 1 cup/3½ oz/100 g shelled and chopped walnuts
- 1 cup/3½ oz/100 g parmesan cheese, flaked
- 6 tablespoons extra-virgin olive oil
- salt and freshly ground white pepper
- juice of 1 lemon

Wine: a dry, sparkling white (Asti Spumante brut)

CROSTONI CON UOVA E FUNGHII
Crostoni with eggs and mushrooms

Serves 4; Preparation: 10 minutes; Cooking: 15 minutes; Level of difficulty: Simple

Clean the mushrooms, wash them carefully, and pat dry with paper towels. § Slice the mushrooms and sauté in a skillet (frying pan) with half the butter and the thyme for about 10 minutes. § Add the ham and season with salt just before removing from heat. Mix well. § Toast the bread in the oven or under the broiler and set aside in a warm place. § Melt the remaining butter in a saucepan over medium-low heat, break in the eggs, and let them set slightly before breaking them up with a fork. Continue cooking and stirring until the eggs are cooked but still soft. Season with salt. § Arrange the toasted bread on a serving dish and cover each slice with a quarter of the egg mixture, followed by a quarter of the mushroom mixture. § Sprinkle with the parsley and pepper and serve.

■ INGREDIENTS

- 4 oz/125 g white mushrooms
- 3 tablespoons/1½ oz/45 g butter
- 1 teaspoon finely chopped fresh thyme
- 2 oz/60 g ham
- salt and freshly ground black pepper
- 4 large slices white or wholewheat bread
- 4 eggs
- 1 tablespoon finely chopped parsley

Wine: a dry red (Sangiovese di Romangna)

Right: Insalata di ovoli

■ INGREDIENTS

- 1¼ lb/625 g white mushrooms
- 4 cloves garlic, minced
- 8 tablespoons extra-virgin olive oil
- 1 bay leaf
- 2 cloves
- 10 black peppercorns
- ⅓ cup/3 fl oz/100 ml dry white wine
- salt
- juice of 1 lemon

Wine: a dry white (Orvieto)

FUNGHI INSAPORITI
Tasty braised mushrooms

Serves 4; Preparation: 10 minutes; Cooking: 20 minutes; Level of difficulty: Simple

Clean the mushrooms. Wash and dry them carefully, then peel and slice. § Sauté the garlic in a skillet (frying pan) with the oil for 2–3 minutes, then add the mushrooms, bay leaf, cloves, and peppercorns. § Cook over high heat for a few minutes, then add the wine, lemon juice, and salt. § Cover the skillet and finish cooking over medium-low heat. § Transfer the mushrooms to a serving dish and serve either hot or cold with fresh crunchy bread or toast.

Teglia di verdure ripiene al forno
Platter of stuffed vegetables

Serves 6-8; Preparation: 15 minutes; Cooking: 40-50 minutes; Level of difficulty: Simple

Blanch the zucchini in salted water for 5 minutes, drain, and cool. Cut in half horizontally, scoop out the pulp, and set aside. § Peel the onions and blanch in salted water for 5 minutes, drain, and cool. § Cut the onions in half horizontally and hollow them out, leaving ½-in (1-cm) thick sides. Chop the pulp and set aside. § Wash the tomatoes and cut them in half. Scoop out the pulp, and set aside. Be careful not to pierce the skin. § Cut the bell peppers in half and remove the seeds and core. § Beat the eggs in a bowl and add the bread crumbs, parsley, garlic, 6 tablespoons of parmesan, salt and bell pepper. § Stir in about half the tomato, zucchini, and onion pulp. Mix well until the mixture is smooth. § Fill the vegetables with the mixture and sprinkle with the remaining parmesan. § Pour the oil into a large ovenproof dish and arrange the vegetables in it. § Cook in a preheated oven at 400°F/200°C/ gas 6 for 30–40 minutes. § Serve piping hot.

■ INGREDIENTS

- 6 round zucchini/ courgettes
- 3 medium onions
- 3 medium tomatoes
- 1 red, 1 green, and 1 yellow bell pepper/ capsicum
- 3 eggs
- 2 cups/3½ oz/100 g bread crumbs
- 3 tablespoons finely chopped parsley
- 3 cloves garlic, finely chopped
- 8 tablespoons freshly grated parmesan cheese
- salt and freshly ground black pepper
- 6 tablespoons extra-virgin olive oil

Wine: a dry white (Soave Classico)

Insalata di pomodori e basilico
Tomato and basil salad

Tomato and basil salad is simple and typical of Italian summer cookery. It makes a tasty appetizer, a great side dish, or can be served between courses to revive the palate. Choose only the tastiest red tomatoes, and dress with the highest quality oil and the freshest of basil leaves.

Serves 4; Preparation: 15 minutes; Level of difficulty: Simple

Peel the garlic and rub the insides of a salad bowl with the clove stuck on a fork. § Wash, dry, and slice the tomatoes. Remove the seeds. § Sprinkle the slices with a little salt and place on a slightly inclined cutting board. Leave them for about 10 minutes so the water they produce can drain away. § Transfer to the salad bowl and sprinkle with the basil. § In a small bowl, beat the oregano, salt, pepper, and oil with a fork until well mixed. § Pour over the tomatoes and toss quickly. § Cover and set aside for about 15 minutes before serving.

■ INGREDIENTS

- 1 clove garlic
- 6 large tomatoes, firm and ripe
- salt and freshly ground black pepper
- 15 fresh basil leaves, torn
- dash of oregano
- 6 tablespoons extra-virgin olive oil

Wine: a dry, slightly sparkling white (Verdicchio)

Right:
Teglia di verdure ripiene al forno

■ INGREDIENTS

• 2 fennel bulbs
• 2 carrots
• 1 celery plant
• 1 Granny Smith apple
• 1 clove garlic, finely chopped
• salt and freshly ground black pepper
• 3 tablespoons of extra-virgin olive oil
• 5 oz/150g mild gorgonzola
• 1 tablespoon finely chopped parsley

*Wine: a dry white
(Tocai di San Martino della Battaglia)*

Insalata al Gorgonzola
Fennel, celery and carrots with apple and gorgonzola sauce

Serves 6; Preparation: 15 minutes; Level of difficulty: Simple

Discard the outer leaves of the fennel and halve the bulbs. Wash and cut into ⅛-in (3-mm) thick slices. § Trim the carrots, scrape, and cut in julienne strips. § Trim the celery, removing any damaged or tough outer leaves, and cut the stalks in slices like the fennel. § Wash the apple and cut in thin wedges. § Put the garlic, apple, and vegetables in a salad bowl and season with salt, pepper, and 2 tablespoons of olive oil. § Dice the gorgonzola and put it in a heavy-bottomed saucepan with 1 tablespoon of oil. Melt slowly over low heat, stirring continuously. § When it is barely lukewarm and has become creamy, pour it over the vegetables. § Sprinkle with the parsley and serve.

■ INGREDIENTS

• 5 oz/150 g gorgonzola cheese
• 7 oz /200 g ricotta cheese
• 4-5 tablespoons whole/full cream milk
• 1 small onion, very finely chopped
• dash of paprika
• 1 tablespoon extra-virgin olive oil
• 1 tablespoon celery, finely chopped
• salt and freshly ground black pepper
• 12 celery stalks
• 8 sprigs parsley

*Wine: a young, dry white
(Vermentino Ligure)*

Left: *Insalata al gorgonzola*

Coste di Sedano Farcite
Celery stalks filled with gorgonzola and ricotta

Serves 4-6; Preparation: 15 minutes + 1 hour in the refrigerator; Level of difficulty: Simple

Melt the gorgonzola in a heavy-bottomed saucepan over very low heat. § Remove from the heat when lukewarm and melted and add the ricotta and enough milk to obtain a creamy but dense mixture. § Add the onion, paprika, oil, finely chopped celery, salt and pepper. Mix well until smooth. § Cover and place in the refrigerator for about an hour. § Prepare the celery, removing the outer stalks and any stringy fibers. Rinse under cold running water, dry and slice into pieces about 2 in (5 cm) long. § Fill the celery stalks with the mixture and arrange on a serving dish. Garnish with the parsley and serve.

VARIATIONS
– Replace the onion with 1 tablespoon finely chopped mint, 1 tablespoon finely chopped parsley, and 1 finely chopped garlic clove.
– Slice a crisp, tangy eating apple into wedges and arrange on the serving dish with the celery.

INSALATA INVERNALE
Winter salad

This simple salad makes an excellent, light appetizer. For a richer dish, add a few sliced button mushrooms or diced mozzarella cheese. For best results, season with the mayonnaise just before serving.

Serves 4-6; Preparation: 30 minutes; Level of difficulty: Simple

Trim the artichokes and remove all leaves except the tender ones near the heart. Remove the tough outer leaves from the fennel bulb. § Wash and dry the artichoke and fennel hearts and cut in thin strips. § Peel the eggs and cut in thin slices. § Clean, wash, and slice the radishes. § Put all the vegetables in a bowl and season with the oil, salt, pepper, and vinegar. Toss well. § Prepare the mayonnaise. Using a hand whisk, mix the mayonnaise and cream. § Transfer the salad to a bowl, arrange the eggs on top, and dress with the mayonnaise. § Garnish with the parsley and serve immediately.

CROSTONI CON ASPARAGI
Crostoni with asparagus and orange sauce

Serves 6-8; Preparation: 30 minutes; Cooking: 30 minutes; Level of difficulty: Medium

Clean the asparagus, trim the stalks, and cook in a pot of salted, boiling water for 8–10 minutes. § Drain well and cut off all but the very tenderest part of the stalks and tips. § Squeeze the orange and set the juice aside. Cut half the rind into thin strips. § Blanch in a pot of boiling water for a few seconds. Drain and dry with paper towels. § Toast the bread and transfer to a serving dish. § Arrange the asparagus on the toast. § To prepare the sauce: place a large pan of water over medium heat. § Combine the egg yolks with a few pieces of butter, a dash of salt, and 1 tablespoon of water in a small pot. Beat well with a whisk. § Put the small pot in the larger one filled with water, keeping the heat low so the water doesn't boil. § As soon as the butter begins to melt, add the rest a little at a time, so that it is gradually absorbed, whisking all the time and taking care that the sauce never boils. § When the sauce is whipped and creamy, add another dash of salt and, very gradually, the orange juice, stirring carefully all the time. § Remove from the heat and stir in the sliced orange rind. § Pour the orange sauce over the *crostoni* and serve immediately.

■ INGREDIENTS

- 3 artichokes
- 1 fennel bulb
- 3 hard-cooked/hard boiled eggs
- 10 radishes
- 2 tablespoons extra-virgin olive oil
- salt and freshly ground black pepper
- 1 tablespoon white wine vinegar
- 1 quantity *Mayonnaise* (see recipe p. 16)
- 3 tablespoons fresh cream
- parsley, to garnish

Wine: a dry white (Orvieto Classico)

■ INGREDIENTS

- 3½ lb/1.5 kg asparagus
- 1 orange
- 12 slices plain or wholewheat bread
- 3 egg yolks
- ⅔ cup/5 oz/150 g butter, cut in small pieces
- salt

Wine: a dry white (Albano di Romagna)

Right:
Insalata di cetrioli e cipolle

■ INGREDIENTS

- 5 medium sweet red onions
- salt and freshly ground
  black pepper
- 4 tablespoons extra-virgin
  olive oil
- 1 tablespoon white wine
  vinegar
- 2 medium cucumbers
- 1 tablespoon capers
- 6 leaves fresh basil, torn

Wine: a dry white (Cirò)

INSALATA DI CETRIOLI E CIPOLLA
Cucumber and onion salad

This refreshing summer salad comes from Calabria, in the south of Italy.
It is really delicious when served with fresh ricotta or caprino cheese.

Serves 4-6; Preparation: 15 minutes + 30 minutes resting; Level of difficulty: Simple

Peel the onions and slice in thin wheels. § Put the onions in a salad bowl, sprinkle with the salt, pepper, vinegar, and oil. Toss well and set aside for 30 minutes. § Peel the cucumbers and slice very thinly. § Add the cucumbers and capers to the onions and toss well. § Garnish with the basil and serve.

Insalata di pere e peperoni
Pear and bell pepper salad

This salad can be made using bell peppers of one color, but it will be more attractive and appetizing if you use three different colors. Always choose fresh, fleshy bell peppers and firm, ripe pears. The salad must be served as soon as it is made, otherwise the pears will turn black.

Serves 4-6; Preparation: 15 minutes; Level of difficulty: Simple

Clean the bell peppers by removing the top, seeds, and core. § Wash and cut in short, thin strips. § Peel and core the pears and cut into match-size sticks. § Combine the pear and bell pepper strips in a salad bowl, and add the garlic, salt, pepper, parsley, and oil. § Serve immediately.

■ INGREDIENTS

- 3 medium bell peppers/ capsicums (1 red, 1 yellow, 1 green)
- 2 firm ripe pears
- 1 clove garlic, finely chopped (optional)
- salt and freshly ground black pepper
- 1 tablespoon finely chopped parsley
- 4 tablespoons extra-virgin olive oil

Wine: a dry, sparkling white (Asti Spumante)

Erbazzone emiliano
Vegetable omelet Emilia-Romagna style

Serves 4-6; Preparation: 15 minutes; Cooking: 30 minutes; Level of difficulty: Simple

Clean and wash the greens. Cook them in a pot of salted, boiling water for 8–10 minutes. § Drain well, squeeze out excess water, and chop finely. § Sauté the garlic, parsley, and onion in the lard (or butter) over medium heat until the onion is transparent. § Add the greens, season with salt and pepper, and cook for 5 minutes more. § In a bowl, beat the eggs until foamy, mix in the vegetables, and then add the parmesan, flour, and bread crumbs. § Heat the oil in a large skillet (frying pan) and add the mixture, taking care to spread it evenly in the pan. § Cook until it begins to turn brown underneath, then carefully detach it from the sides of the skillet using a wooden spoon and turn it over (with the help of a lid or plate). Brown on the other side. § Slide onto a serving dish and serve hot.

■ INGREDIENTS

- 1½ lb/750 g mixed fresh spinach and Swiss chard/silverbeet
- 4 cloves garlic, finely chopped
- 1 cups/1 oz/30 g finely chopped parsley
- 1 small onion, finely chopped
- ¼ cup/2 oz/60 g lard or butter
- salt and freshly ground black pepper
- 4 eggs
- 1 cup/4 oz/125 g freshly grated parmesan cheese
- 2 tablespoons all-purpose/plain flour
- 2 tablespoons bread crumbs
- 4 tablespoons extra-virgin olive oil

Wine: a young, dry red (Gutturnio dei Colli Piacentini)

Right:
Erbazzone Emiliano

■ INGREDIENTS

- 7 oz/200 g lollo rosso (or other leafy salad)
- 7 oz/200 g arugula/rocket
- salt and black pepper
- 6 tablespoons canned peas, well-drained
- 8 oz/250 g white mushrooms
- 1¼ cups/5 oz/150 g emmenthal cheese, diced
- 8 tablespoons extra-virgin olive oil
- 1 tablespoon white wine vinegar
- 4 hard-cooked/hard-boiled eggs, sliced
- 1 carrot, grated
- 8 radishes, finely sliced
- 1 tablespoon mustard
- 1 white truffle (optional)

Wine: a light, dry, sparkling white (Prosecco)

■ INGREDIENTS

- 1 lb/500 g dense grain, day-old bread
- 5 medium tomatoes
- 2 red onions
- 1 cucumber
- 12 leaves fresh basil, torn
- 6 tablespoons extra-virgin olive oil
- salt and freshly ground black pepper
- 1 tablespoon red wine vinegar

Wine: a dry red (Chianti dei Colli Senesi)

Left: *Panzanella*

INSALATA ARCOBALENO
Rainbow salad

If you like truffles, slice a white one very thinly and add it to the mushrooms. The salad will be even more fragrant and tasty.

Serves 4-6; Preparation: 20 minutes; Level of difficulty: Simple

Wash and dry the salad greens and cut in strips. § Arrange in the bottom of a salad bowl and season with salt and pepper. § Sprinkle the peas over the top. § Clean, wash, peel, and thinly slice the mushrooms. Place them in a bowl with the cheese. § Prepare a dressing by beating the oil, mustard, salt, and vinegar together in a bowl. Pour half of it over the mushrooms and toss well. § Sprinkle the mushroom mixture over the salad and cover with the eggs, carrots, and radishes. § Just before serving, drizzle with the remaining dressing and toss again. § Serve immediately.

PANZANELLA
Tuscan bread salad

Panzanella is a typical Tuscan dish. The ingredients used vary according to which part of Tuscany it is made in. The addition of cucumber, for example, is shunned in the area around Siena, while it is always included in Florence. The salad can be enriched by adding diced carrots, fennel, celery, hard-cooked (hard-boiled) eggs, capers, or pecorino cheese.

Serves 4-6; Preparation: 15 minutes + 15 minutes resting; Level of difficulty: Simple

Soak the bread in a bowl of cold water for at least 10 minutes. § Use your hands to squeeze out as much water as possible. Crumble the almost dry bread into a large salad bowl. § Slice the tomatoes and remove the seeds. Clean the onions and slice in thin wheels. Peel the cucumber and slice thinly. § Add the tomatoes, cucumber, basil, and onions to the bread. Season with salt, pepper, and 4 tablespoons of the oil and mix carefully. § Set aside in a cool place or the refrigerator for 15 minutes. § Add the vinegar and remaining oil just before serving.

Insalata di funghi porcini
Porcini mushroom salad

This mouthwatering salad is often served in Italy during the early summer months when porcini mushrooms are readily available. If you can't get porcini, you may want to experiment with other types of wild or cultivated mushrooms.

Serves 6; Preparation: 15 minutes; Level of difficulty: Simple

Clean the mushrooms, peel, rinse carefully under cold running water, and pat dry. § Without peeling, cut them in thin slices. § Wash the celery, remove any stringy fibers, and slice thinly. § Wash the lettuce hearts and slice thinly. § Place the lettuce in the bottom of a salad bowl and arrange the celery and mushrooms over the top. Cover with the parmesan. § In a small bowl, beat the oil, lemon juice, salt and pepper together with a fork. § Pour over the salad, toss carefully, and serve.

> VARIATION
> – Add ¾ cup/3½ oz/100 g of diced prosciutto and toss well.

■ INGREDIENTS

- 1 lb/500 g fresh porcini mushrooms
- 6 stalks celery
- 2 lettuce hearts
- 1 cup/3½ oz/100 g parmesan cheese, flaked
- 8 tablespoons extra-virgin olive oil
- juice of 1 lemon
- salt and freshly ground black pepper

Wine: a dry, young red (Vino Novello)

Funghi alle spezie
Mushrooms with bay leaf, cinnamon and garlic

Serves 4; Preparation: 25 minutes; Cooking: 20 minutes; Level of difficulty: Simple

Clean the mushrooms, peel, rinse under cold running water, and pat dry. § Put the bay leaf, cinnamon, and half the lemon juice in a pot full of water and bring to a boil. § Add the mushrooms and boil for 2–3 minutes. Drain well and cut the mushrooms in half. § Transfer to a skillet (frying pan) with the oil, the remaining lemon juice, salt, and peppercorns, and cook for 15 minutes. § Remove from the heat, drain, and set aside to cool. § Sprinkle with the parsley and garlic, and serve.

■ INGREDIENTS

- 1 lb/500 g button mushrooms
- 1 bay leaf
- 1 cinnamon stick
- juice of 1 lemon
- 6 tablespoons extra-virgin olive oil
- salt
- 10 black peppercorns, bruised
- 1 cup/1 oz/30 g finely chopped parsley
- 1 clove garlic, finely chopped

Wine: a dry, sparkling red (Lambrusco di Sorbara)

Right:
Insalata di funghi porcini

INGREDIENTS

- 12 slices mozzarella cheese
- 12 slices firm red tomato
- 1½ cups/7 oz/200 g mixed vegetables (onion, bell pepper/capsicum, celery, zucchini/courgette, carrots, finely chopped)
- 1 tablespoon capers
- 1 tablespoon extra-virgin olive oil
- salt and freshly ground black pepper
- 6 leaves fresh basil, torn

Mozzarella e pomodoro con verdure fresche
Mozzarella and tomato slices with fresh vegetables

These eyecatching mozzarella and vegetable slices make a light and tasty start to any meal. If you like garlic, add a clove (very finely chopped) to the vegetable mixture.

Serves 4-6; Preparation: 10 minutes; Level of difficulty: Simple

Arrange the slices of mozzarella on a serving dish and cover each one with a slice of tomato. § Combine the chopped vegetables in a bowl with the capers, salt, pepper, and oil. § Spread the vegetable mixture over the tomato. § Garnish with the basil and serve.

OLIVE ALL'ASCOLANA
Stuffed olives

This dish requires time and patience but these delicious little olives are so good that you will be tempted to make them again and again. The recipe comes from the Marches area in central Italy.

Serves 4-6; Preparation: 30 minutes; Cooking: 40 minutes; Level of difficulty: Medium

Sauté the beef and pork in a skillet (frying pan) with the olive oil for 5 minutes. Add the tomato paste and continue cooking for 15 minutes. § Add the chicken livers and cook for 5 minutes more. § Remove from heat, chop the meat very finely, and return to the skillet. § Soak the bread roll in cold water, squeeze out excess moisture, and crumble. § Add the bread, one of the eggs, the parmesan, salt, pepper, nutmeg, and cinnamon to the meat mixture. § Mix well with a fork and then stuff the pitted olives. § Arrange three bowls, the first with the flour, the second with 2 beaten eggs, and the third with the bread crumbs. § Dredge the olives in the flour, dip them in the egg and then in the bread crumbs. Remove excess crumbs by rolling them in your hands. § Deep-fry in a skillet with the frying oil. When a crisp, golden crust forms around each olive, remove from the pan with a slotted spoon. Place them on paper towels to drain excess oil. § Transfer to a serving dish, garnish with slices of lemon and parsley, and serve hot.

■ INGREDIENTS

- 1¼ cups/5 oz/150 g pork, coarsely chopped
- 1¼ cups/5 oz/150 g beef, coarsely chopped
- 4 tablespoons extra-virgin olive oil
- 2 tablespoons tomato paste
- ⅔ cup/3½ oz/100 g chicken livers, coarsely chopped
- 1 day-old bread roll
- 3 eggs
- 5 tablespoons freshly grated parmesan cheese
- salt and freshly ground black pepper
- nutmeg and cinnamon
- 60 giant green olives, pitted
- 1¼ cups/5 oz/150 g all-purpose/plain flour
- 2½ cups/5 oz/150 g bread crumbs
- 2 cups/16 fl oz/500 ml oil, for frying
- 1 lemon, sliced
- 8 sprigs parsley

Wine: a dry red (Rosso Conero)

POMODORINI CREMOSI
Cherry tomatoes filled with caprino cheese

Serves 4-6; Preparation: 20 minutes; Level of difficulty: Simple

Wash the tomatoes and dry well. § Turn them upside down and slice off a "lid." Set aside. § Using a small teaspoon, carefully remove the pulp. § Leave the tomatoes hole-side-down to drain for 10 minutes. § In a bowl, mix the oil, olives, garlic, basil, salt, pepper, cheese, and enough of the tomato pulp to make a smooth cream. Don't add all the tomato at once as it may make the cream too liquid. § Stuff the tomatoes with the cream filling. Place a "lid" on top of each and set aside in the refrigerator for 20 minutes before serving.

■ INGREDIENTS

- 12 cherry tomatoes
- ½ tablespoon extra-virgin olive oil
- 10 green olives, 1 clove garlic, finely chopped
- 6 fresh basil leaves, torn
- salt and freshly ground black pepper
- 8 oz/250 g caprino (or ricotta) cheese

Wine: a dry white (Verduzzo)

Right: *Olive alla marchigiana*

POLENTA FRITTA SPLENDIDA
Fried polenta with mushroom, peas, and cheese

Serves 4-6; Preparation: 15 minutes; Cooking: 30 minutes; Level of difficulty: Simple

Heat the oil in a skillet (frying pan) and add the mushrooms and peas. Mix well and cook over medium heat for 10 minutes. § Add the capers, salt and pepper. Cook for 5–10 minutes more, or until the vegetables are soft, stirring occasionally. § Lightly flour the polenta slices, dip them into the egg, and then into a bowl containing the bread crumbs. § Heat the frying oil in a deep-sided skillet (frying pan) until very hot and fry the slices of polenta until golden brown. § Drain on paper towels and arrange in a buttered baking dish. § Cover each slice with a spoonful of peas and mushrooms, and a slice of mozzarella. § Bake in a preheated oven at 400°F/200°C/gas 6 for about 10 minutes, or until the mozzarella is melted and golden. § Remove from the oven, sprinkle with the basil, and serve immediately.

■ INGREDIENTS

- 2 tablespoons extra-virgin olive oil
- 7 oz/ 200 g white mushrooms, sliced
- 8 oz/250 g fresh or frozen peas
- 1 tablespoon capers
- salt and freshly ground black pepper
- 4 tablespoons all-purpose/plain flour
- 6 large slices cold *Basic polenta* (see recipe p. 18)
- 1 egg, beaten
- 1 cup/3 oz/90 g bread crumbs
- 2 cups/16 fl oz/500 ml oil, for frying
- 3½ oz/100 g mozzarella
- 4 tablespoons finely chopped basil

Wine: a dry red (Chianti Classico)

POLENTA FRITTA CON SALSA DI FUNGHI PORCINI
Fried polenta pieces with porcini mushroom sauce

If you can't get fresh porcini for this mushroom sauce, combine 1 oz/30 g of soaked, dried porcini mushrooms with fresh white mushrooms.

Serves 6; Preparation: 30 minutes; Cooking: 40 minutes; Level of difficulty: Medium

Clean the mushrooms, rinse carefully under cold running water, and pat dry with paper towels. § Detach the stalks from the heads. § Sauté the garlic with the olive oil in a skillet (frying pan) over medium heat until golden brown. § Coarsely chop the mushrooms. § Add the stalks to the skillet first (they need longer to cook than the caps), and after about 5 minutes, add the caps. Add the calamint (or thyme) and season with salt and pepper. § Stir carefully for 4–5 minutes more. The time the porcini take to cook will depend on how fresh they are. Don't let them become mushy. § Heat the frying oil in a deep-sided skillet until very hot and fry the polenta slices until golden brown. § Spoon the mushroom sauce onto the polenta slices and serve hot.

■ INGREDIENTS

- 2 lb/1 kg porcini mushrooms
- 2 cloves garlic, minced
- 6 tablespoons extra-virgin olive oil
- 2 tablespoons finely chopped calamint or thyme
- salt and freshly ground black pepper
- 2 cups/16 fl oz/500 ml oil, for frying
- 6 large slices cold *Basic polenta* (see recipe p. 18)

Wine: a dry red (Nobile di Montepulciano)

Right: *Polenta fritta con salsa di funghi porcini*

CROSTINI SICILIANI
Sicilian-style crostini

■ INGREDIENTS

- 4–8 slices dense grain bread
- 1 cup/8 fl oz/250 ml oil, for frying
- 2 tablespoons vinegar
- 1 teaspoon sugar
- 1 teaspoon capers
- 1 teaspoon pine nuts
- 1 teaspoon raisins
- 1 teaspoon diced candied lemon peel
- 2 ripe tomatoes, diced

Wine: a dry red (Valpolicella)

Serves 4; Preparation: 10 minutes; Cooking: 10 minutes; Level of difficulty: Simple

Cut the slices of bread in half and remove the crusts. § Heat the oil in a skillet (frying pan) and fry the bread until golden brown on both sides. § Drain on paper towels. § Bring the vinegar, sugar, and 2 tablespoons of water to a boil, then add the capers, pine nuts, raisins, candied lemon peel, and tomatoes. § Cook for 5 minutes, stirring with care. § Spread the fried *crostini* with this mixture and serve hot.

ARANCINI DI RISO
Rice croquettes

Serves 4-6; Preparation: 20 minutes; Cooking: 55 minutes; Level of difficulty: Medium

Cook the rice in as you would a risotto (see, for example, *Risotto with bay leaves*, p. 147), using half the oil, then gradually stirring in the boiling broth as needed. When the rice is cooked, the liquid should all have been absorbed. § Sauté the onion in a skillet (frying pan) over medium heat with the oil until golden. § Wash the chicken livers, chop coarsely, and add to the skillet. Add the veal, peas, and wine. § When the liquid has evaporated, add the tomato pulp and season with salt and pepper. § Continue cooking, stirring often until the sauce is thick. § Combine the rice, parmesan, and butter in a bowl. § Mix well and mold into balls. Hollow out the center of each ball and fill with meat sauce and a piece of hard-cooked egg. § Close the rice around the filling. § Beat the raw eggs with a fork in a shallow dish. Dip the balls into the egg and then roll in bread crumbs. § Heat the oil in a deep-sided skillet and fry the balls until golden brown. § Drain on paper towels and serve piping hot.

■ INGREDIENTS

- 2 cups/14 oz/ 450 g short grain rice
- 4 tablespoons extra-virgin olive oil
- 2 cups/16 fl oz/500 ml *Beef broth* (see recipe p. 14)
- 1 small onion, chopped
- 4 oz/125 g chicken livers
- 2 oz/60 g ground veal
- 1½ cups/8 oz/250 g peas
- 2 tablespoons white wine
- 2 tablespoons tomato pulp
- salt and freshly ground black pepper
- 2 tablespoons freshly grated parmesan cheese
- 2 tablespoons/1 oz/30 g butter
- 2 hard-cooked/hard-boiled eggs
- 2 raw eggs
- 1½ cups/3 oz/90 g bread crumbs
- 2 cups/16 fl oz/500 ml oil, for frying

Wine: a dry red (Corvo Rosso)

CARCIOFI CON LA MOZZARELLA
Artichokes with mozzarella

Serves 4-6; Preparation: 20 minutes; Cooking: 40 minutes; Level of difficulty: Medium

Clean the artichokes by removing the stalks and tough outer leaves. Trim off the tops and place the hearts in a bowl of cold water with the lemon juice. § Mix the mozzarella with the parmesan, bread crumbs, and egg. Season with salt, pepper, and 1 tablespoon of oil. § Drain the artichokes, press out the water, dry, open and use a sharp knife to remove the centers. § Put some of the mozzarella mixture in each artichoke and set them upright, one next to the other, in an oiled braiser. § Pour the remaining oil over the top, add 2 glasses of water, cover and bring to a boil. § Transfer the braiser to a preheated oven at 350°F/180°C/gas 4 and cook the artichokes for about 40 minutes, basting them frequently with the liquid that settles in the bottom of the braiser. § Serve hot.

■ INGREDIENTS

- 8 artichokes
- juice of 1 lemon
- 4 oz/125 g mozzarella cheese, finely chopped
- 2 tablespoons freshly grated parmesan cheese
- 12 tablespoons bread crumbs
- 1 egg
- salt and freshly ground black pepper
- ½ cup/4 fl oz/125 ml extra-virgin olive oil

Wine: a dry white (Corvo)

Right: Arancini di riso

TESTE DI FUNGHI RIPIENE
Filled mushroom caps

■ INGREDIENTS
- 12 Caesar's/royal agaric mushrooms
- 1 clove garlic
- 2 slices bread, soaked in warm milk and crumbled
- salt and freshly ground black pepper
- 1 egg and 1 yolk
- 1 cup/4 oz/125 g freshly grated parmesan cheese
- dash of oregano
- 3 sprigs calamint or thyme
- 4 tablespoons extra-virgin olive oil

Wine: a dry white (Albenga)

Serves 4-6; Preparation: 30 minutes; Cooking: 30 minutes; Level of difficulty: Medium

Clean the mushrooms and carefully wash them under cold running water. Pat dry with paper towels and separate the stems from the caps. § Chop the stems, garlic, crumbled bread, salt and pepper together. § Transfer to a bowl and mix until the mixture has the consistency of a thick cream (add milk if it is too dry). § Stir in the eggs, parmesan, oregano, calamint (or thyme), and 1 tablespoon of oil. § Mix thoroughly and taste for salt. Fill the hollow of each mushroom cap with the mixture, and smooth the surface with a moistened knife blade. § Arrange the mushrooms in a lightly oiled ovenproof dish. § Drizzle with oil and bake in a preheated oven at 350°F/180°C/gas 4 for about 30 minutes. § Serve hot straight from the baking dish.

STRISCE COLORATE
Mixed baked vegetables

■ INGREDIENTS
- 1 yellow, 1 green, and 1 red bell pepper/capsicum
- 2 onions
- 1 large eggplant/aubergine
- 2 large zucchini/courgettes
- 6 plum tomatoes
- salt and freshly ground black pepper
- 3 tablespoons extra-virgin olive oil

Wine: a light, dry white (Soave Classico)

This dish can be really eyecatching. Be sure to arrange the vegetables in strips—a strip of onions, followed by one of green bell peppers, then zucchini, tomatoes, eggplant, red bell peppers, and lastly the yellow peppers. Not all the vegetable varieties are essential, but keep the idea of color in mind when choosing them and try to have at least two or three different colors.

Serves 4-6; Preparation: 30 minutes; Cooking: 1 hour; Level of difficulty: Simple

Wash the bell peppers, remove the seeds and cores, and cut into narrow strips, keeping the colors separate. § Clean the onions and cut into thin rings. § Cut the eggplant and the zucchini into julienne strips. § Cut the tomatoes in half, remove the seeds, and squeeze out excess water. Cut into small wedges. § Arrange the vegetables in strips (not layers), alternating the colors, in an ovenproof dish. § Season with salt and pepper, and drizzle with the oil. § Cover with aluminum foil and seal well around the edges of the dish. § Bake in a preheated oven at 325°F/160°C/gas 3 for about 1 hour. § Check the vegetables after 30 minutes and increase the heat if there is too much liquid or add a drop if they are too dry. When cooked, all the liquid should have been absorbed but the vegetables should not be dried out. § Serve hot or cold.

Right:
Strisce colorati

Sformato di fagiolini
Green bean mold

Serves 4-6; Preparation: 20 minutes; Cooking: 1¼ hours; Level of difficulty: Medium

Clean and wash the beans and cook for 10 minutes in lightly salted, boiling water. Drain and pass under cold running water. § Drain again and transfer to a dry kitchen towel. § Put the oil and half the butter in a skillet (frying pan). Add the onion, celery, and parsley, and when the onion begins to turn golden, add the beans. § Sauté so the beans can absorb the seasoning. § Dissolve the bouillon cube in the water and add. § Cover the pan and simmer for about 20 minutes. § Add the parmesan and pepper to the béchamel sauce. § Drain the beans and transfer to a bowl. Add half the béchamel sauce and the eggs. Mix well. § Butter a mold and sprinkle with the bread crumbs. Fill with the beans and cover with the remaining béchamel sauce. § Place a large container of cold water in a preheated oven at 350°F/180°C/gas 4. Place the mold pan in the water-filled container and cook *bain-marie* for 40 minutes. § Invert the mold onto a serving dish, slice and serve.

> VARIATIONS
> – Serve with 1 quantity of Basic tomato sauce (see recipe p. 2).
> – Add ¾ cup/3 oz/90 g diced ham to the skillet with the beans.

■ INGREDIENTS

- 14 oz/450 g fresh green beans
- 2 tablespoons extra-virgin olive oil
- ¼ cup/2 oz/60 g butter
- ½ onion, finely chopped
- 1 stalk celery, finely chopped
- 1 tablespoon finely chopped parsley
- ½ bouillon cube
- ½ cup/4 fl oz/125 ml boiling water
- 4 tablespoons freshly grated parmesan cheese
- salt and freshly ground black pepper
- ½ quantity *Béchamel sauce* (see recipe p. 22)
- 2 eggs, beaten
- 2 tablespoons bread crumbs

Wine: a dry white
(Bianco di Custoza)

Beignets di spinaci
Spinach fritters

Serves 4-6; Preparation: 15 minutes; Cooking: 30 minutes; Level of difficulty: Simple

Prepare the béchamel sauce. § Put the spinach in a pot to defrost over medium-low heat. § When the liquid has evaporated, squeeze dry and chop coarsely. § Return to the pot, add the butter and sauté for 5 minutes. § Remove from the heat and transfer to a bowl. § Add the béchamel sauce and mix well. Add the eggs, one at a time, and then the nutmeg, salt and pepper. Mix again until smooth. § Heat the frying oil in a deep-sided skillet (frying pan) until hot. § Add a few spoonfuls of the spinach mixture to the oil. Keep them well-spaced. § Turn the fritters as they cook so they turn golden on all sides. § Remove with a slotted spoon and place on paper towels to drain. § Repeat until all the fritters are cooked. § Sprinkle with salt and serve hot.

■ INGREDIENTS

- ½ quantity *Béchamel sauce* (see recipe p. 22)
- 1 lb/500 g frozen spinach
- 2 tablespoons/1 oz/30 g butter
- 2 egg yolks + 1 whole egg
- dash of nutmeg
- salt and freshly ground pepper
- 2 cups/16 fl oz/500 ml oil, for frying

Wine: a dry red
(Chianti Montalbano)

Right:
Sformato di fagiolini

■ INGREDIENTS

• 8 *Barchette* (see recipe p. 22)
• 1 quantity *Mayonnaise* (see recipe p. 16)
• 2 hard-cooked/hard-boiled eggs
• 1 tablespoon each finely chopped parsley and marjoram
• 1 small white truffle

Wine: a dry white (Tocai di Lison)

BARCHETTE CON MAIONESE AGLI AROMI
Barchette with herb mayonnaise and truffles

Serves 4; Preparation: 15 minutes + time to make mayonnaise and barchette; Level of difficulty: Simple
Prepare the *barchette* and set aside. § Prepare the mayonnaise. § Chop the eggs. § Transfer to a bowl and mix with the parsley, marjoram, and mayonnaise. § Fill the *barchette* with the sauce, arrange on a serving dish, and sprinkle with slivers of truffle. § Serve soon after filling so that the *barchette* are still crisp and fresh.

■ INGREDIENTS

- 4 large round tomatoes, ripe but firm
- salt and freshly ground black pepper
- 4 tablespoons finely chopped parsley
- 2 cloves garlic, finely chopped
- 1 cup/2 oz/60 g bread crumbs
- 1 tablespoon capers
- dash of oregano
- 4 tablespoons extra-virgin olive oil

Wine: a dry white (Greco di Tufo)

Pomodori alla Vesuviana
Baked Neapolitan-style tomatoes

Serves 4; Preparation: 20 minutes; Cooking: 30 minutes; Level of difficulty: Simple

Wash and dry the tomatoes and cut them in half horizontally. § Scoop out the seeds and part of the pulp and sprinkle the insides with a little salt and pepper. Turn them upside down and leave for 15 minutes to eliminate excess water. Pat dry with paper towels. § Combine the parsley, garlic, almost all the bread crumbs, capers, salt, pepper, and oregano in a bowl and mix well. § Fill the tomatoes with the mixture and arrange them in a well-oiled baking dish (use half the oil). § Drizzle with the remaining oil and bake in a preheated oven at 350°F/180°C/gas 4 for about 30 minutes. § Serve either hot or cold.

■ INGREDIENTS

- 1 Italian pork sausage
- 2 tablespoons/1 oz/30 g butter
- 5 oz/150 g ground veal
- 4 large onions
- 2 eggs
- salt and freshly ground black pepper
- dash of nutmeg
- 6 tablespoons freshly grated parmesan cheese
- 1 tablespoon finely chopped parsley
- 1 amaretti cookie/ macaroon, crumbled
- 1 tablespoon grappa
- 2 tablespoons bread crumbs

Wine: a dry red (Dolcetto d'Alba)

Left: *Cipolle ripiene dolce delicate*

Cipolle ripiene dolci delicate
Stuffed onions

Serves 4; Preparation: 15 minutes; Cooking: 1 hour; Level of difficulty: Simple

Peel and crumble the sausage and sauté in a skillet (frying pan) with half the butter. § Add the veal, stir well, and let brown slightly. Remove from the heat. § Peel the onions and cook for 10 minutes in a small pan of salted, boiling water. Drain well and pat dry with paper towels. § Cut the onions in half horizontally and carefully scoop out the center with a spoon. Chop the pulp finely and add to the meat and sausage mixture. § Stir in 1 egg, salt, pepper, nutmeg, 5 tablespoons of the parmesan, parsley, and the macaroon, and mix well. § Fill the onions with the mixture and arrange in a buttered baking dish. § Sprinkle with the grappa. § Beat the remaining egg to a foam and brush over the onions. Dust with the bread crumbs mixed with the remaining parmesan. Dab each onion with the remaining butter. § Bake in a preheated oven at 350°F/180°C/gas 4 for 45 minutes, or until a golden crust has formed on the surface. § Serve hot.

Egg and Cheese Appetizers

An almost endless variety of appetizers can be made using eggs and cheese. The following recipes are a selection of some personal favorites.

UOVA SODE CON SALSA DI PEPERONI
Hard-cooked eggs with bell pepper sauce

Serves 4-6; Preparation: 40 minutes; Cooking: 25-30 minutes; Level of difficulty: Simple

Combine the bell peppers, onion, garlic, parsley, and basil in a skillet (frying pan) with a dash of salt and the oil and sauté over medium heat. § To peel the tomatoes, bring a large pot of water to a boil. Plunge the tomatoes into the boiling water for 30 seconds and then transfer to cold water. The skins will slip off easily in your hands. § Cut the tomatoes in small dice and add to the saucepan. Cook over medium-low heat until the sauce is thick and smooth. § Add the vinegar and sugar, and mix well. Season with salt and pepper. § Remove from heat and set aside to cool. § Peel the hard-cooked eggs and cut in half lengthwise. § Remove the yolks, mash, and add to the tomato and bell pepper sauce. Mix well. § Fill the eggs with the mixture and arrange them on a serving dish. Pour any extra sauce over the top (or serve on slices of toasted bread or *bruschetta* with the eggs). § Place the eggs in the refrigerator for at least 30 minutes before serving.

■ INGREDIENTS

- 1 yellow and 1 red bell pepper/capsicum, finely chopped
- 2 white onions, finely chopped
- 2 cloves garlic, finely chopped
- 1 tablespoon finely chopped parsley
- 1 tablespoon finely chopped fresh basil
- salt and freshly ground black pepper
- 2 tablespoons extra-virgin olive oil
- 6 fresh tomatoes
- 1 tablespoon vinegar
- ½ tablespoon sugar
- 6 hard-cooked/hard-boiled eggs

Wine: a dry white (Vernaccia di San Gimignano)

CROSTINI AI QUATTRO FORMAGGI
Crostini with four cheeses

The four cheeses given here are suggestions since all cheeses are delicious when toasted on bread. Replace them with your particular favorites or with what you have in the refrigerator. Cheese crostini *also make a nourishing after-school or late night snack.*

Serves 4; Preparation: 10 minutes; Cooking: 15 minutes; Level of difficulty: Simple

Combine the cheeses in a bowl with the oil. Season with salt, oregano, and marjoram. § Mash the cheeses with a fork and mix well until you have a fairly smooth cream. If the mixture is too thick to spread, add more oil. § Spread on the bread and cut each slice in half to form a triangle. Grind a little black pepper over the top. Arrange the *crostini* on a baking sheet. § Bake in a preheated oven at 400°F/200°C/gas 6 for 10–15 minutes, or until the cheese is golden brown. § Serve hot.

■ INGREDIENTS

- 4 oz/125 g caprino cheese
- 1 cup/3½ oz/100 g grated parmesan cheese
- 3½ oz/100 g gorgonzola cheese, diced
- 3½ oz/100 g fontina cheese, grated
- 2 tablespoons extra-virgin olive oil
- salt and freshly ground black pepper
- dash of oregano
- 8 slices plain or wholewheat bread

Wine: a dry red (Lambrusco)

Right: *Uova sode con salsa di peperoni*

Formaggi misti al cumino
Mixed cheeses with cumin seeds

Serves 4; Preparation: 10 minutes + 4 hours in the refrigerator; Level of difficulty: Simple

Soften the butter over very low heat. § Combine the butter, ricotta, gorgonzola, mascarpone, garlic, cumin, parsley, and brandy in a bowl and mix well with a fork. Season with salt and pepper and continue mixing until smooth and creamy. § Place the mixture on a sheet of waxed paper and shape it into a log. § Wrap tightly in the paper and place in the refrigerator for at least 4 hours. § Unwrap and transfer to a serving dish. § Serve with fresh crunchy bread or toast.

PERE CON GORGONZOLA DOLCE
Pears with gorgonzola cheese

INGREDIENTS

- 4 large eating pears
- juice of 2 lemons
- 5 oz/150 g gorgonzola cheese
- 2 tablespoons light/single cream
- 4 tablespoons extra-virgin olive oil
- 1 tablespoon finely chopped mint, plus sprigs for garnishing
- salt and freshly ground white pepper

Wine: a dry white (Pinot Grigio)

Serves 4; Preparation: 25 minutes + 1 hour in the refrigerator; Level of difficulty: Simple

Wash the pears thoroughly, dry well, and remove the cores with a corer. § Brush the cavities with the juice of 1 lemon. § Combine the gorgonzola and cream in a bowl and mix until they form a smooth, thick cream. § Stuff the pears with the mixture, pressing it down so that the cavities are completely filled. § Place in the cold part of the refrigerator for at least an hour. § Combine the oil, remaining lemon juice, chopped mint, salt and pepper in a bowl and whisk until well mixed. § Use a sharp knife to cut the pears in thin round slices. § Arrange the rounds on individual serving dishes and spoon the sauce over the top. § Garnish with sprigs of mint and serve.

MOUSSE DI FORMAGGIO E NOCI
Cheese and walnut mousse

INGREDIENTS

- 3 large eating pears
- 7 oz/200 g ricotta cheese
- 8 oz/250 g each mascarpone and gorgonzola cheese
- 2 cups/10 oz/300 g walnuts, finely chopped
- freshly ground black pepper
- 2 tablespoons grappa
- 1 tablespoon/1 oz/30 g butter
- 2 tablespoons finely chopped chives

Wine: a dry white (Soave)

Serves 6; Preparation: 15 minutes + 1 hour in the refrigerator; Level of difficulty: Simple

Wash the pears, peel, core, and chop the pulp finely. § Combine the cheeses in a bowl, mix, then add the walnuts, pepper, and grappa. § Stir the pear pulp into the cheese mixture. § Butter six small molds and fill with the mixture. Place in the refrigerator for at least an hour. § Just before serving, invert the molds onto serving plates and garnish with the chives.

INSALATA DI ZUCCHINE TENERE
Baby zucchini with pecorino cheese

INGREDIENTS

- 14 oz/450 g baby zucchini/courgettes
- 5 oz/150 g pecorino romano cheese, flaked
- 4 tablespoons extra-virgin olive oil
- salt and freshly ground black pepper

Wine: a dry white (Lugana)

Serves 4; Preparation: 30 minutes; Level of difficulty: Simple

Wash the zucchini, trim the ends, and slice them very thinly. § Transfer to a serving dish and sprinkle with the pecorino. § Pour the oil over the top and sprinkle with salt and pepper. § Toss well and serve.

VARIATIONS
- Replace the pecorino cheese with the same quantity of parmesan.
- Add the juice of 1 lemon together with the oil.

Left: Pere con gorgonzola dolce

Peperoni ripieni di parmigiano e ricotta
Bell peppers filled with parmesan and ricotta

Be sure to choose rounded bell peppers that will sit upright in the baking dish during cooking.

Serves 4; Preparation: 15 minutes; Cooking: 35 minutes; Level of difficulty: Simple

Cut the tops off the bell peppers and discard the seeds and cores. § Wash them carefully under cold running water and pat dry with paper towels. § Combine the bread crumbs, parsley, mint, garlic, and parmesan in a food processor and blend until smooth. § Transfer the mixture to a large bowl and stir in the eggs and ricotta. Season with salt, pepper, and oil, and mix until smooth. § Fill the peppers with the mixture and arrange them in an ovenproof dish. § Cover with knobs of butter and cook in a preheated oven at 400°F/200°C/gas 6 for about 35 minutes, or until the bell peppers are cooked. § Serve hot or cold.

VARIATION
– For a more substantial dish, add 1 cup/5 oz/150 g finely chopped ham to the bread and parmesan mixture.

■ INGREDIENTS

- 4 yellow bell peppers/ capsicums
- 1 cup/3½oz/100 g bread crumbs
- 1 tablespoon finely chopped parsley
- 4 finely chopped mint leaves
- 1 clove garlic, finely chopped
- 1 cup/4 oz/125 g freshly grated parmesan cheese
- 2 eggs, beaten
- 7 oz/200 g ricotta cheese
- salt and freshly ground black pepper
- 2 tablespoons extra-virgin olive oil
- 3 tablespoons/1½ oz/45 g butter

Wine: a dry red (Carmignano)

Ricci di gorgonzola e sedano
Gorgonzola and celery served "porcupine-style"

Serves 4-6; Preparation: 20 minutes + 1 hour in the refrigerator; Level of difficulty: Simple

Melt the butter in a saucepan over low heat. § Combine the butter and gorgonzola in a bowl and mix well. § Gradually add the oil, lemon juice, and pepper, and stir carefully with a wooden spoon until the mixture becomes a thick cream. § Divide the cheese mixture in two equal parts and shape into balls. Wrap each ball in aluminum foil and place in the refrigerator for 1 hour. § Wash and dry the celery and chop into sticks about 3 in (8 cm) long and ¼ in (6 mm) wide. § Invert the bowl with the cheese onto a serving dish. Press pieces of celery into the cheese balls so that they stick out like a porcupine's quills. § Serve cold.

■ INGREDIENTS

- ¼ cup/2 oz/60 g butter
- 14 oz/450 g gorgonzola cheese
- 2 tablespoons extra-virgin olive oil
- 12 large stalks celery
- juice of 1 lemon
- freshly ground white pepper

Wine: a dry white (Fiano di Avellino)

Right:
Ricci di gorgonzola e sedano

■ INGREDIENTS

• 10 oz/300 g spring carrots

• 10 oz/300 g mascarpone
  cheese

• salt and freshly ground
  black pepper

• 4 slices *Bruschetta*
  (see recipe p. 20)

• sprigs of parsley, to
  garnish

Wine: a dry white
(Pinot Bianco)

BRUSCHETTE DI CAROTINE AL MASCARPONE
Bruschette with spring carrots and mascarpone cheese

Use the small, sweet carrots that appear in the markets in spring. The cheese and carrot mixture
is also good as a snack spread on crackers, toast, or crunchy fresh bread.

Serves 4; Preparation: 10 minutes; Level of difficulty: Simple
Wash the carrots thoroughly. § Grate them into a bowl and add the mascarpone, salt and pepper. Mix well. § Prepare the *bruschetta* and spread the mixture on the slices. § Garnish with the sprigs of parsley and serve.

INGREDIENTS

- 5 oz/150 g soft caprino cheese
- 4 tablespoons finely chopped fresh herbs (for example – parsley, chives, mint, thyme, marjoram, tarragon, dill, basil)
- 1 small canteloupe/rock melon, weighing about 12 oz/375 g
- 1 cucumber, peeled
- 4 tablespoons extra-virgin olive oil
- 5 oz/150 g purple grapes
- juice of 1 orange
- salt and freshly ground black pepper
- 12 cherry tomatoes
- 6 small radishes
- fresh spinach or grape leaves

Wine: a semisweet sparkling white (Moscato d'Asti Spumante)

INGREDIENTS

- 8 oz/250 g pecorino romano cheese
- 2 large eating pears
- 5 oz/150 g walnuts
- 1 bunch watercress
- 15 fresh spinach leaves
- 3 tablespoons extra-virgin olive oil
- juice of 1 small lemon
- salt and freshly ground black pepper
- 1 clove garlic, bruised

Wine: a dry or medium, slightly sparkling red (Freisa)

Left: *Palline di caprino e frutta*

PALLINE DI CAPRINO E FRUTTA
Caprino cheese and fruit salad

Serves 6; Preparation: 25 minutes; Level of difficulty: Simple

Use your hands to form the caprino into marble-size balls. Roll them in a dish filled with the chopped herbs until they are well coated. Set aside. § Use a small melon baller to make small balls from the canteloupe and cucumber. § Sprinkle the canteloupe balls with 1 tablespoon of orange juice and dust with the black pepper. § Drizzle the cucumber balls with salt and 1 tablespoon of oil. § Wash, dry, and remove the stem from the tomatoes. § Wash, dry, and trim the radishes, cutting off roots and leaves. § Wash and dry the grapes (you can peel them if you like). § Line a large serving bowl with grape leaves or fresh spinach leaves. § Arrange the cheese, vegetables and fruit on top. § Drizzle with the remaining oil and orange juice just before serving.

INSALATA DI PECORINO PERE E NOCI
Pecorino cheese, pear, and walnut salad

Serves 4-6; Preparation: 15 minutes; Level of difficulty: Simple

Chop the pecorino into ½-in (1-cm) dice. § Wash, peel and core the pears. Chop into ½-in (1-cm) dice. § Shell the walnuts and chop coarsely. § Wash and dry the watercress. § Arrange the dark green spinach leaves in the bottom of a salad bowl and add the pears, cheese, watercress, and walnuts. § Put the oil, lemon juice, salt, pepper, and garlic in a small jar. Screw the top down and shake vigorously for 2–3 minutes. When the dressing is well mixed, remove the garlic and drizzle over the salad. § Toss carefully, without disturbing the spinach leaves, and serve.

VARIATION
– Sprinkle 2 oz/60 g pitted and chopped black olives over the salad just before tossing.

Uova delle fate
Eggs fairy-style

These colorful eggs are perfect for a children's party. Served with a cool dry white wine, they also make an eyecatching appetizer for an adult or family meal.

Serves 4-6; Preparation: 20 minutes + 30 minutes in the refrigerator; Level of difficulty: Simple

Peel the hard-cooked eggs. Rinse under cold running water to remove any remaining pieces of shell and pat dry with paper towels. Cut a slice off the bottom of each egg so it will stand upright. § Prepare the mayonnaise and spread it over the bottom of a serving dish. Set the eggs, upright, in the mayonnaise, not too close to each other. § Cut the plum tomatoes in half, remove the pulp and seeds, and use the halves to put a "hat" on each upright egg. § Dot the tomato caps with lemon mayonnaise, squeezed from the tube, to look like the spots on mushrooms. § Sprinkle the parsley over the mayonnaise so that it looks like grass. § Garnish with the pieces of bell pepper and gherkin to look like flowers. § Place in the refrigerator for 30 minutes before serving.

■ INGREDIENTS

- 6 hard-cooked/hard-boiled eggs
- 1 quantity *Mayonnaise* (see recipe p. 16) + 1 tube lemon mayonnaise
- 3 red plum tomatoes
- 6 tablespoons finely chopped parsley
- ¼ red and ¼ yellow bell pepper/capsicum, cut in tiny diamond shapes
- 6 gherkins, sliced

Wine: a dry, slightly sparkling white (Galestro)

Ricotta alle erbe
Ricotta with herbs

This recipe comes from Trentino-Alto Adige in northeastern Italy. Its delicate flavor calls for the finest quality, freshest ricotta available. When the cheese and herbs are well mixed, store in the refrigerator for about an hour before serving so that the flavor of the herbs will have time to penetrate.

Serves 6; Preparation: 10 minutes + 1 hour in the refrigerator; Level of difficulty: Simple

Combine the ricotta, basil, and parsley in a bowl and mix well. § Add the bay leaves, fennel, salt and pepper, and mix again. § Place in the refrigerator. § Remove the bay leaves and garnish with sprigs of parsley. § Serve cold.

VARIATION
– Replace the basil with the same amount of finely chopped fresh mint.

■ INGREDIENTS

- 14 oz/450 g ricotta cheese
- 2 tablespoons finely chopped basil
- 2 tablespoons finely chopped parsley + sprigs to garnish
- 2 bay leaves
- 1 teaspoon fennel seeds
- salt and freshly ground black pepper

Wine: a dry white (Sauvignon)

Right:
Uova delle fate

Bigné al parmigiano
Parmesan puffs

Serves 4; Preparation: 10 minutes; Cooking: 30 minutes; Level of difficulty: Medium

Put the water in a small saucepan with 2 tablespoons of softened butter over medium heat. § When the water starts to boil, remove the pan from the heat and incorporate the sifted flour and a dash of salt, stirring constantly with a wooden spoon. § Return the saucepan to the heat and cook until the dough is thick, mixing all the time. § Remove from the heat and stir in the parmesan and a dash of paprika. Set aside to cool. § To blanch and peel the almonds, place them in a bowl and pour boiling water over the top so they are barely covered. Leave for 1 minute. Drain and rinse under cold water. Pat dry and slip off the skins. § Chop the almonds finely. § Add the eggs to the dough one at a time. Don't add the second until the first has been thoroughly incorporated. § Beat the dough vigorously. Transfer to a pastry bag with a smooth tube about ¼ in (6 mm) in diameter. § Butter a baking sheet and dust with flour. § Place marble-size balls of dough on the baking sheet and sprinkle with the almonds, making sure they stick to the puffs. § Bake in a preheated oven at 400°F/200°C/gas 6 for 15–20 minutes. The puffs will swell as they bake and dry. § Serve cool.

■ INGREDIENTS

- ⅔ cup/5 fl oz/150 ml cold water
- 3 tablespoons/1½ oz/45 g butter
- 1 cup/4 oz/125 g all-purpose/plain flour, plus 2 tablespoons for dusting the baking sheet
- salt
- ½ cup/2 oz/60 g freshly grated parmesan cheese
- dash of paprika
- ½ cup/2 oz/60 g sweet almonds
- 2 eggs

Wine: a dry sparkling white (Prosecco)

Pizzette semplici
Little pizzas with tomato, onion and mozzarella cheese

Serves 4; Preparation: 10 minutes + 2 hours resting; Cooking: 25-30 minutes; Level of difficulty: Simple

In a small bowl gently stir the yeast into half the warm water. Set aside to rest for 10 minutes. § Sift a quarter of the flour into a large bowl and make a well in the center. Add the olive oil. § Gradually stir in the water and yeast and the flour, adding as much of the remaining water as necessary to obtain a smooth, firm dough. § Add 2 pinches of salt. § Turn the dough out onto a clean, lightly floured counter. Form it into a ball and then knead and fold until a smooth, elastic dough has been obtained. §

■ INGREDIENTS

BASE
- 1 oz/30 g active dry yeast
- about 1 cup/8 fl oz/250 ml warm water
- 4 cups/1 lb/500 g all-purpose/plain flour
- 2 tablespoons extra-virgin olive oil
- salt

Right:
Pizzette semplici

TOPPING

- 1 14-oz/450 g can peeled and chopped tomatoes
- 1 tablespoon capers
- 1 clove garlic and 1 onion finely chopped
- generous dash oregano
- salt and freshly ground black pepper
- 5 oz/150 g mozarella cheese, diced

Wine: a light, dry red (Vino Novello)

Sprinkle with flour and wrap the dough in a clean tea towel. Place in a warm spot in the kitchen (or wrap in a woolen garment) and leave to rise until it has doubled in size. This will take about 1½–2 hours. § Mix the tomatoes, capers, garlic, onion, oregano, salt, and pepper together in a bowl. § Oil a baking sheet. § Break the dough into four pieces and, using kneading movements, press each one out to form a small round pizza. § Distribute the tomato mixture evenly over the top of each. § Bake in a preheated oven at 400°F/200°C/gas 6 for 20–25 minutes. § Remove from the oven and sprinkle with the mozzarella. Return to the oven for about 5 minutes, or until the mozzarella has melted and browned a little. § Take the pizzas out of the oven and serve hot or cold.

CREMA DI UOVA E PEPERONI
Egg and bell pepper cream

Egg and bell pepper cream makes a refreshing and unusual antipasto *for summer dinner parties. However, I strongly recommend that you try it out a few times before the invitations go out. A lot depends on the quantity of water the bell peppers produce during cooking and the size of the eggs. You really must make the dish a couple of times and learn for yourself how to adjust the ingredients to suit each time. Good luck!*

Serves 4-6; Preparation: 50 minutes + 2 hours in the refrigerator; Cooking: 30 minutes; Level of difficulty: Complicated

Wash the bell peppers, dry, and remove the seeds and cores. Cut into small pieces, keeping the colors separate. § Place 2 tablespoons of oil in three separate saucepans, divide the onion in three parts, and sauté a part in each. § When the onion is transparent, add salt, pepper, 2 tablespoons of water, and bell peppers, keeping the colors separate in each pan. § Cover each pan and cook over medium heat for about 30 minutes, or until the bell peppers are soft and well-cooked. § Remove the pans from the heat and let the mixtures cool. § Blend the contents of each pan separately in a food processor until a smooth purée. § Soften the gelatin in a little water. § Heat the milk in a pot, but don't let it boil. § Beat the egg yolks in a bowl and add the hot milk a bit at a time, stirring continuously. Season with salt and pepper. § Transfer to a saucepan and heat to just below boiling point, stirring frequently. Add the gelatin. § Remove from the heat and beat with a fork so that the gelatin dissolves. § Pour equal parts of the mixture into three different bowls and let cool. § Add one color of bell pepper purée to each and stir. § Whip the cream to stiff peaks and fold in equal parts to each of the three bowls. § Moisten a rectangular mold with water and pour in the yellow mixture. Place the mold in the refrigerator for 10 minutes. § Remove and pour in the red mixture. Return the mold to the refrigerator for 10 more minutes. § Remove again and add the green mixture. § Refrigerate for at least 2 hours. § Just before serving, dip the mold for a second in hot water and invert the cream on a serving dish.

■ INGREDIENTS

- 2 lb/1 kg bell peppers/ capsicums (equal quantities red, yellow, and green)
- 6 tablespoons extra-virgin olive oil
- 1¾ cups/14 fl oz/450 ml whipping cream
- salt and freshly ground white pepper
- 1 medium-large onion, finely chopped
- 1 oz/30 g gelatin
- 3 cups/24 fl oz/750 ml milk
- 6 egg yolks

Wine: a dry white (Cortese di Gavi)

Right:
Crema di uova e peperoni

BOMBOLINE DI PARMIGIANO
Fried parmesan puffs

Serves 6; Preparation: 20 minutes; Cooking: 20 minutes; Level of difficulty: Medium

Combine the water with the salt and butter in a saucepan and bring to a boil. § Add the sifted flour all at once, remove from the heat, and stir vigorously with a wooden spoon. § When the mixture is smooth, return to the heat and cook till the batter pulls away from the sides of the pan. Set aside to cool. § Add the eggs one at a time and mix each one in before adding the next. § Add the cheeses and nutmeg. § Mold the mixture into marble-size balls. § Heat the oil in a deep-sided skillet (frying pan) until very hot and fry the puffs a few at a time until golden brown. § Place on paper towels to drain, sprinkle with salt, and serve hot.

CRÊPES AI QUATTRO FORMAGGI
Crêpes with four-cheese filling

Serves 6; Preparation: 20 minutes + 1 hour for the crêpes; Cooking: 20 minutes; Level of difficulty: Medium

Beat the eggs in a bowl with a fork or whisk. § Sift the flour and salt into another bowl and stir the milk in gradually so that no lumps form. When it is smooth, pour it into the eggs. § Beat vigorously, then cover the bowl with plastic wrap and let stand in the coldest part of the refrigerator for about 40–50 minutes. § Before using, beat again for a few seconds. § Set a crêpe pan on the heat and grease well. Use a small ladle to pour 1–2 scoops of batter into the pan. Rotate the pan so that the batter covers the bottom evenly. § When the crêpe has set, turn it over using a spatula, your hands, or by flipping it. § When golden on both sides, slide it onto a plate. § Keep making crêpes until the batter is finished. Remember to grease the pan for each new crêpe. § Prepare the béchamel sauce. § Add half the parmesan, the gruyère, fontina, and gorgonzola to the béchamel. Cook over low heat until the cheeses have blended in with the sauce. § Spread 2–3 tablespoons of the cheese mixture on each crêpe. Roll the crêpes up and place them in a lightly buttered ovenproof dish. § Cover with the remaining cheese sauce and sprinkle with the remaining parmesan. Grind a little black pepper over the top and add several tiny knobs of butter. § Bake in a preheated oven at 350°F/180°C/gas 4 for 15 minutes, or until the topping is golden brown. § Serve piping hot straight from the oven.

■ INGREDIENTS

- scant 1 cup/7 fl oz/200 ml water
- 1 teaspoon salt
- 3 tablespoons/1½ oz/45 g butter
- 1 cup/4 oz/125 g all-purpose/plain flour
- 4 eggs
- 1 cup/4 oz/125 g freshly grated parmesan cheese
- 2 oz/60 g grated emmenthal cheese
- dash of nutmeg
- oil, for frying

Wine: a dry red (Grignolino)

■ INGREDIENTS

- 3 eggs
- ¾ cup/3 oz/90 g all-purpose/plain flour
- 1½ cups/12 fl oz/375 ml whole/full cream milk
- knob of butter to grease the crêpe pan
- 1 quantity *Béchamel* (see recipe p. 22)
- salt and freshly ground black pepper
- generous ½ cup/2½ oz/75 g freshly grated parmesan cheese
- 2½ oz/75 g freshly grated gruyère cheese
- 2½ oz/75 g diced fontina cheese
- 2½ oz/75 g diced gorgonzola cheese

Wine: a young, dry red (Roero)

Right: Crêpes ai quattro formaggi

CROSTINI PUGLIESI
Mozzarella crostini Puglia-style

■ INGREDIENTS

- 1 onion, finely chopped
- 4 tablespoons extra-virgin olive oil
- 14 oz/450 g peeled and chopped canned tomatoes
- 6 leaves fresh basil, torn
- 1 teaspoon dried oregano
- salt
- 4 slices plain or wholewheat bread
- 5 oz/150 g mozzarella cheese, thinly sliced

Wine: a dry rosé (Lizzano)

Serves 4; Preparation: 15 minutes; Cooking: 45 minutes; Level of difficulty: Simple

Sauté the onion in half the oil until transparent. § Add the tomatoes, basil, half the oregano, and salt, and simmer for 30 minutes. § Cut the slices of bread in half, cover with the mozzarella, and place in an oiled baking dish. Sprinkle with the remaining oregano, drizzle with the rest of the oil, and bake in a preheated oven at 400°F/200°C/gas 6 until the bread is crisp and the mozzarella melted. § Remove from the oven and spread with the tomato sauce. § Serve hot.

Malfatti di parmigiano e spinaci
Parmesan and spinach dumplings

Malfatti in Italian means "badly made" and refers to the fact that these little dumplings are similar to the stuffing used for ravioli. They are badly made because they lack their pasta wrappings. In Tuscany they are sometimes called Strozzaprete, *or "priest chokers," although the origin of this name remains obscure.*

Serves 6; Preparation: 20 minutes; Cooking: 20 minutes; Level of difficulty: Medium

Cook the spinach in a pot of salted, boiling water until tender (3–4 minutes if frozen, 8–10 minutes if fresh). Drain well and squeeze out excess moisture. Chop finely. § Mix the spinach with the ricotta, eggs, parmesan (reserving 2 tablespoons), and nutmeg. Season with salt and pepper. § Mold the mixture into walnut-sized balls. § Bring a large pot of salted water to a boil, add the dumplings, and cook until they rise to the surface. § Remove with a slotted spoon and place in a serving dish. § Melt the butter and sage together, season with salt and pepper, and pour over the dumplings. § Sprinkle with the remaining parmesan and serve hot.

> VARIATION
> – The dumplings make a delicious winter *antipasto* when baked. When the dumplings are cooked, drain well and place them in an ovenproof baking dish. Pour the melted butter and sage sauce over the top (or replace with 1 quantity *Basic tomato sauce*–see recipe p. 2). Sprinkle with ½ cup/2 oz/60 g freshly grated parmesan and bake in a preheated oven at 350°F/180°C/gas 4 for about 15 minutes, or until the topping is golden brown.

- INGREDIENTS
- 1½ lb/750 g fresh or 1 lb/500 g frozen spinach
- 5 oz/150 g ricotta cheese
- 1 egg and 1 yolk
- 1 cup/4 oz/125 g freshly grated parmesan cheese
- dash of nutmeg
- salt and freshly ground black pepper
- 2 tablespoons butter
- 5 fresh sage leaves, torn

Wine: a young, dry red (Vino Novello)

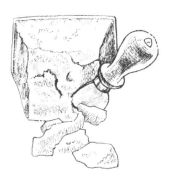

Fritta di mozzarella e polenta
Fried mozzarella and polenta cubes

This is a good way to use up leftover polenta.

Serves 6; Preparation: 10 minutes; Cooking: 15 minutes; Level of difficulty: Simple

Chop the polenta and the mozzarella into cubes about 1 in (2.5 cm) square. § Grind the pepper over the mozzarella. § Place a cube of mozzarella between two cubes of polenta and thread them together with a wooden toothpick. § Heat the oil in a deep-sided skillet (frying pan) until very hot. § Cook the polenta and cheese cubes until they turn golden. § Drain on paper towels, sprinkle with a little salt, and serve immediately.

- INGREDIENTS
- ½ quantity cold *Basic polenta* (see recipe p. 18)
- 6 oz/180 g mozzarella cheese
- freshly ground white pepper
- 2 cups/16 fl oz/500 ml oil, for frying

Wine: a dry red (Chianti)

Right:
Malfatti di parmigiano e spinaci

Rotolone d'uovo
Omelet roll

Serves 6; Preparation: 20 minutes + 4 hours in the refrigerator; Cooking: 20 minutes; Level of difficulty: Medium

In a bowl whisk the eggs with the flour, parmesan, milk, and salt. § Melt the butter in a skillet (frying pan) and pour in the egg mixture. Cook until golden on one side, then flip and cook on the other. § Drain on paper towels and set aside to cool. § Prepare the mayonnaise and mix with the mustard and gherkins. § Arrange the ham on the omelet and spread with a layer of mayonnaise. Cover with the mortadella and roll the omelet up, being careful not to break it. § Wrap in aluminum foil and keep in the refrigerator for at least 4 hours. § Just before serving, cut the roll in slices and arrange on a serving dish. Garnish with radishes and cucumber.

■ INGREDIENTS

• 6 eggs
• 1 tablespoon all-purpose/plain flour
• 1 tablespoon freshly grated parmesan
• 2 tablespoons milk
• salt
• 2 tablespoons/1 oz/30 g butter
• ½ quantity *Mayonnaise* (see recipe p. 16)
• 1 tablespoon mustard
• 6 gherkins, finely chopped
• 3½ oz/100 g ham, sliced
• 3 oz/90 g mortadella, in a single thick slice
• 8 radishes, chopped
• 1 cucumber, finely sliced

Wine: a dry red (Merlot dell'Isonzo)

Parmigiana di zucchine
Zucchini and parmesan pie

Serves 6; Preparation: 20 minutes; Cooking: 35 minutes; Level of difficulty: Simple

Wash the zucchini and trim the ends. Slice lengthwise in ¼-in (6-mm) strips. § Heat the frying oil in a skillet (frying pan) and cook the zucchini for about 10 minutes, or until they are golden brown. § Drain well on paper towels and set aside in the warming oven. § Sauté the garlic and onion over medium heat in a skillet with the olive oil. § Remove the garlic and add the tomatoes, basil, and salt. Cook for 10 minutes, stirring from time to time with a wooden spoon. § Grease an ovenproof dish with a little olive oil and cover the bottom with a layer of tomato sauce. Add a layer of zucchini slices, another of tomato sauce, sprinkle with parmesan, and cover with a layer of mozzarella slices. Repeat until all the ingredients are used up, leaving a little mozzarella and parmesan for the topping. § Arrange knobs of butter and grind a little black pepper over the top. § Bake in a preheated oven at 350°F/180°C/gas 4 for 15 minutes, or until the topping is golden brown.

■ INGREDIENTS

• 1½ lb/750 g zucchini/courgettes
• 2 cups/16 fl oz/500 ml oil, for frying
• 2 cloves garlic
• 1 onion, finely chopped
• 1¾ cups/14 oz/450 g peeled and chopped fresh or canned tomatoes
• 8 fresh basil leaves, torn
• salt and freshly ground black pepper
• 1 tablespoon extra-virgin olive oil
• 12 tablespoons freshly grated parmesan cheese
• 7 oz/200 g mozzarella cheese, in thin slices
• 1 tablespoon/½ oz/15 g butter

Wine: a dry red (Elba rosso)

Right: *Parmigiana di zucchine*

Sformatini di semolino
Semolina molds

Serves 4; Preparation: 15 minutes + time for the meat sauce; Cooking: 30 minutes; Level of difficulty: Simple

Prepare the meat sauce. § Add a dash of salt to the milk and bring to a boil. § As the milk begins to boil, sift in the semolina, stirring constantly. Cook for about 10 minutes over low heat, stirring all the time. § Remove from the heat and add the nutmeg, half the butter, the parmesan, and 2 egg yolks. § Butter four pudding molds 4 in (10 cm) in diameter and sprinkle with bread crumbs. Line the sides and the bottom with the semolina mixture. § Put a piece of fontina and 1 tablespoon of meat sauce in the center of each one, then fill completely with semolina. § Bake in a preheated oven at 400°F/200°C/gas 6 for 15–20 minutes. § When cooked, remove from the oven and invert into a casserole. § Return to the oven for a few minutes so they will brown. § Serve hot with the remaining sauce.

■ INGREDIENTS

- 1 quantity *Bolognese* or *Quick meat sauce* (see recipes p. 4)
- salt and freshly ground black pepper
- 3 cups/24 fl oz/750 ml whole/full cream milk
- 1 cup/5 oz/150 g semolina
- dash of nutmeg
- scant ½ cup/3½ oz/100 g butter
- ¼ cup/1 oz/30 g freshly grated parmesan cheese
- 2 egg yolks
- 3½ oz/100 g fontina cheese
- 2 tablespoons bread crumbs

Wine: a dry , full-bodied red (Barolo)

Frittata di menta
Mint omelet

Serves 6; Preparation: 10 minutes; Cooking: 10 minutes; Level of difficulty: Simple

Beat the eggs in a bowl until foamy, then add the bread crumbs, pecorino, mint, parsley, and a dash of pepper and salt. § Heat the oil in a deep-sided skillet (frying pan) until very hot. § Pour in the egg mixture. Spread it out over the bottom and cook over medium heat until the underside turns golden brown. § Flip the omelet with the help of a lid or plate. Don't let it cook too much; a good *frittata* is supposed to be fairly soft. § Serve hot.

VARIATION

– For a completely different but equally delicious dish, replace the mint with 10 oz/300 g of fresh cauliflower florets. The cauliflower should be sautéed for 8–10 minutes in the oil before adding the egg mixture. Zucchini are also good when prepared in this way.

■ INGREDIENTS

- 6 eggs
- ½ cup/1 oz/30 g bread crumbs
- 1¼ cups/5 oz/150 g freshly grated pecorino cheese
- 12 mint leaves, finely chopped
- 2 tablespoons finely chopped parsley
- salt and freshly ground black pepper
- 4 tablespoons extra-virgin olive oil

Wine: a dry white (Bianco di Pitigliano)

Right:
Sformatini di semolino

■ INGREDIENTS

- 14 oz/450 g tasty
  provolone cheese
- 4 tablespoons extra-virgin
  olive oil
- 1 clove garlic, cut in two
- 1 tablespoon white wine
  vinegar
- 1 teaspoon oregano
- 1 teaspoon sugar

Wine: a dry red (Cirò)

Caciu all'Argintera
Sweet and sour fried cheese

This simple and tasty dish comes from Sicily, in the south.
Provolone is a hard cheese and will not melt during cooking.

Serves 4; Preparation: 5 minutes; Cooking: 15 minutes; Level of difficulty: Simple

Cut the cheese in slices about ¼-in (6-mm) thick. § Heat the oil and the garlic in a skillet (frying pan). As soon as it is hot, put in the slices of cheese and brown on both sides. § When they are uniformly browned, sprinkle with the vinegar and dust with the oregano and sugar. § Serve immediately.

CROSTATA DI FORMAGGIO ALLO ZAFFERANO
Saffron cheese pie

Serves 6; Preparation: 20 minutes + 1 hour in the refrigerator; Cooking: 45 minutes; Level of difficulty: Simple

Prepare the dough: mix the flour with the butter (set aside a knob), oil, salt, 1 whole egg and 1 yolk. Do not overmix as the dough could become hard. § Wrap in a sheet of waxed paper and place in the refrigerator for an hour. § For the filling: put the ricotta in a bowl and mash with a fork. Add the gruyère, softened butter, saffron and, one at a time, the egg yolks, mixing well. § Beat the egg whites until stiff and fold into the mixture. § Roll out the dough and line a buttered pie pan. § Fill with the cheese mixture. § Bake the pie in a preheated oven at 350°F/180°C/gas 4 for 45 minutes. § Serve hot or cold.

■ INGREDIENTS

DOUGH
- 4 cups/12 oz/375 g all-purpose/plain flour
- ¼ cup/2 oz/60 g butter, softened and chopped
- 2 tablespoons extra-virgin olive oil
- salt
- 1 egg and 1 yolk

FILLING
- 14 oz/450 g ricotta cheese
- 5 oz/150 g grated gruyère cheese
- scant ½ cup/3½ oz/100 g butter
- generous dash of saffron
- 6 eggs, separated

Wine: a dry white (Frascati)

TORTELLI DI FORMAGGIO
Cheese tortelli

Serves 6; Preparation: 20 minutes; Cooking: 20 minutes; Level of difficulty: Simple

Put the two cheeses, flour, parsley, fennel seeds, and nutmeg in a bowl. Add 3 of the eggs and half the bread crumbs and mix well. § Beat the remaining egg with a fork in a shallow dish. Season with salt and pepper. § Shape walnut-sized balls with the cheese mixture, dusting your hands with flour to facilitate the process. § Dip the balls first in the beaten egg, and then in the remaining bread crumbs. § Melt the butter in a skillet (frying pan), add the tortelli, and fry until golden brown. Drain on paper towels. § Transfer to a serving dish, sprinkle with salt, and serve hot.

■ INGREDIENTS

- 10 oz/300 g grated gruyère cheese
- ¾ cup/3½oz/100 g freshly grated parmesan cheese
- 2 tablespoons all-purpose/plain flour
- 1 tablespoon finely chopped parsley
- dash of fennel seeds
- dash of nutmeg
- 4 eggs
- 1½ cups/3 oz/90 g bread crumbs
- salt and freshly ground mixed pepper
- 2 tablespoons/1 oz/30 g butter

Wine: a dry red (Dolcetto)

Right: *Crostata di formaggio allo zafferano*

Bocconcini di formaggio e prosciutto
Ham and cheese tidbits

Serves 4-6; Preparation: 10 minutes + 30 minutes resting; Cooking: 20 minutes; Level of difficulty: Simple

Mix the flour with the softened butter, 2 eggs, and a dash of salt. If necessary, add a little water and knead until the dough is smooth. § Wrap the dough in a cloth and set aside in a cool place for 30 minutes. § Roll out the dough in a thin sheet and cut into rectangles. § Cut the slices of ham and fontina to the same size as the pieces of dough. § Place pieces of ham, fontina, and anchovy on half the pieces of dough, cover with the remaining dough and press the edges together to seal. § Beat the remaining egg and brush the tops with it. § Place the tidbits on a buttered baking sheet and bake in a preheated oven at 350°F/180°C/gas 4 for 25 minutes, or until golden brown. § Serve hot.

■ INGREDIENTS
- 2½ cups/10 oz/300 g all-purpose/plain flour
- ⅔ cup/5 oz/150 g butter
- 3 eggs
- salt
- 10 oz/300 g ham, cut in thick slices
- 5 oz/150 g fontina cheese, sliced
- 8 anchovy fillets, crumbled

Wine: a dry, sparkling red (Lambrusco di Sorbara)

Insalata di uovo, provolone, mele e radicchio rosso
Egg, provolone, apple, and radicchio salad

Serves 4-6; Preparation: 15 minutes + 1 hour for the radicchio rosso; Level of difficulty: Simple

To clean the radicchio rosso, discard the outer leaves, wash several times, dry well and place in the bottom of a salad bowl. § Season with the lemon juice and half the oil, toss well and set aside for about an hour. § Slice the eggs with an egg cutter. § Peel the apples and dice. § Cut the provolone into cubes. § Add the eggs, apples, provolone, and olives to the salad bowl. § Mix the mustard, vinegar, remaining oil, salt and pepper together in a bowl. Beat vigorously with a fork and pour over the salad. § Toss well and serve.

■ INGREDIENTS
- 10 oz/300 g radicchio rosso
- juice of 1 small lemon
- 6 tablespoons extra-virgin olive oil
- 3 hard-cooked/hard-boiled eggs
- 3 crisp eating apples
- 7 oz/200 g provolone cheese
- 16 pitted and chopped large black olives
- 2 tablespoons hot mustard
- 1 tablespoon white wine vinegar
- salt and freshly ground black pepper

Wine: a dry white (Galestro)

Right: Insalata di uovo, provolone, mele e radicchio rosso

VARIATIONS
— Add a few chopped walnuts to give extra flavor to the salad.
— Replace the radicchio rosso with the same quantity of fresh spinach.

Barchette di formaggio

Cheese-filled barchette

A simple creamy cheese and béchamel filling highlights the delicate flavor of the pastry.
Experiment with mixes of your favorite cheeses.

Serves 4-6; Preparation: 20 minutes + time to make the barchette; Cooking: 20 minutes; Level of difficulty: Simple

Prepare the *barchette*. § Make a thick béchamel sauce. § Cut the cheeses in pieces, add to the béchamel sauce, and stir well over very low heat until melted. § Fill the *barchette* with the sauce and cook in a preheated oven at 350°F/180°C/gas 4 for a 5–10 minutes to brown. § Serve hot.

■ INGREDIENTS

• 12 *Barchette* (see recipe p. 22)

• 1 quantity *Béchamel sauce* (see recipe p. 22)

• 3 oz/90 g emmenthal cheese

• 7 oz/200 g mozzarella cheese

3 oz/90 g fontina cheese

Wine: a dry white (Corvo)

■ INGREDIENTS

- 3 cups/10 oz/300 g all-purpose/plain flour
- 3 cups/10 oz/300 g buckwheat flour
- ½ cup/4 fl oz/125 ml milk
- 8 oz/250 g diced fontina cheese
- ½ cup/4 oz/125 g butter
- dash of nutmeg
- salt and freshly grated black pepper
- 2 eggs (beaten) + 1 yolk
- 1¾ cups/3½ oz/100 g bread crumbs
- 2 cups/16 fl oz/500 ml oil, for frying

Wine: a dry red
(Chianti Classico)

■ INGREDIENTS

- 8 oz/250 g mozzarella cheese
- ½ cup/2 oz/60 g all-purpose/plain flour
- 2 eggs
- 1½ cups/3 oz/90 g bread crumbs
- 2 cups oil/16 fl oz/500 ml, for frying
- salt

Wine: a dry red
(San Severo Rosso)

■ INGREDIENTS

- 12 slices tomato
- 12 slices mozzarella
- 1 cup/8 oz/250 g mixed pickled vegetables

Wine: a light, sparkling red
(Lambrusco)

Left:
Barchette di formaggio

CROCCHETE DI FONTINA
Fontina croquettes

This dish is a rather filling antipasto *and should be followed by something light.*

Serves 6-8; Preparation: 15 minutes; Cooking: 15 minutes; Level of difficulty: Simple

Mix the two types of flour together in a saucepan. Stir in the milk, fontina, butter, nutmeg, salt and pepper. § Cook over low heat for about 20 minutes, stirring continuously until a fairly dense cream forms. § Remove from the heat and add the egg yolk, continuing to stir with a wooden spoon. Pour the mixture into a buttered dish and let cool. § Mold the mixture into small oblong croquettes, dip them in the beaten egg, and roll in the bread crumbs. § Heat the oil in a deep-sided skillet (frying pan) until very hot and fry the croquettes a few at a time until they are golden brown. § Sprinkle with a little salt and serve hot.

MOZZARELLA FRITTA
Fried mozzarella

Serves 4; Preparation: 5 minutes; Cooking: 10 minutes; Level of difficulty: Simple

Cut the mozzarella in rather thick slices and cover with flour. § Beat the eggs in a bowl and dip the slices in the egg and then in the bread crumbs. § Heat the oil in a deep-sided skillet (frying pan) until very hot and deep-fry the slices until golden brown on both sides. § Drain on paper towels, sprinkle with salt, and serve piping hot.

MOZZARELLA PICCANTE
Mozzarella and mixed pickled vegetables

Serves 4; Preparation: 10 minutes + 30 minutes in the refrigerator; Level of difficulty: Simple

Place a slice of mozzarella on each slice of tomato. § Purée the pickled vegetables together in a food processor. § Place a spoonful of vegetables on each slice of mozzarella. § Keep in the refrigerator for 30 minutes before serving.

Meat and Fish Appetizers

When serving a meat-based dish as an appetizer remember that meat is filling. If you are planning to follow it with pasta and a main dish in the traditional Italian manner, keep the quantities to tempting tidbit-size or your guests will spoil their appetites and all your hard work and planning will be wasted.

Italian seafood cookery is simpler than in most other cuisines. But it relies on the freshest, highest quality ingredients. With the exception of the smoked salmon, tuna fish, and salt cod, all the recipes in this section call for fresh fish. You may try them using frozen fish, but the results will not be as good. Be warned!

Cozze ripiene al forno
Stuffed baked mussels

■ INGREDIENTS

- 60 mussels in shell
- ½ cup/4 fl oz/125 ml dry white wine
- 3 day-old bread rolls
- 1 cup/8 fl oz/250 ml milk
- 4 tablespoons finely chopped parsley
- 4 cloves garlic, finely chopped
- 6 tablespoons freshly grated parmesan cheese
- 2 tablespoons extra-virgin olive oil
- salt and freshly ground black pepper

Serves 6; Preparation: 20 minutes + 1 hour to soak mussels; Cooking: 25 minutes; Level of difficulty: Simple

Soak the mussels in a large bowl of water for at least 1 hour to purge them of sand. Pull off their beards, scrub, and rinse well in abundant cold water. § Put the mussels in a large skillet (frying pan) over medium-high heat, sprinkle with the wine, and cover. § When all the shells are open (discard any that don't open), remove from the skillet. Discard all the empty half shells, keeping only those with the mussel inside. § Remove the crusts from the rolls and soak the insides in the milk for 10 minutes. Squeeze out excess moisture with your hands. § Combine most of the parsley and garlic in a bowl with the bread. Add 4 tablespoons of grated parmesan cheese, the oil, salt and pepper. Mix well. § Fill the shells with the mixture, then arrange them in a large, greased baking dish. Dust with the remaining parmesan and bake in a preheated oven at 400°F/200°C/gas 6 for about 15 minutes. § Just before serving, sprinkle the rest of the garlic and parsley on top, and serve hot.

Wine: a dry white (Cinqueterre)

Impepata di cozze
Mussels in pepper sauce

■ INGREDIENTS

- 60 mussels in shell
- 4 tablespoons finely chopped parsley
- 1 clove garlic, finely chopped
- 2 tablespoons extra-virgin olive oil
- salt
- 2 teaspoons freshly ground black pepper
- 6 slices *bruschetta* (see recipe p. 22)

This fiery dish makes a perfect appetizer when followed by oven-roasted fish. Vary the amount of pepper depending on your tastes.

Serves 6; Preparation: 10 minutes + 1 hour to soak mussels; Cooking: 10 minutes; Level of difficulty: Simple

Soak the mussels in a large bowl of water for at least an hour to purge them of sand. Pull off their beards, scrub, and rinse well in abundant cold water. § Sauté the parsley and garlic in a skillet (frying pan) with the oil for 4-5 minutes. Season with salt. § Add the mussels and cook over medium heat until they are all open. Discard any that haven't opened. § Add the pepper and cook for 2 minutes more, stirring all the time. § Prepare the *bruschetta* and place a slice in each serving dish. Cover with mussels and spoon some of the sauce from the skillet over each portion. § Serve hot.

Wine: a dry white (Corvo bianco)

Right: Impepata di cozze

VONGOLE IN SALSA DI PANNA FRESCA
Clams in fresh cream sauce

Serves 6; Preparation: 30 minutes + 1 hour to soak the clams; Cooking: 15 minutes; Level of difficulty: Simple

Soak the clams in a large bowl of water for at least an hour to remove any sand. Scrub and rinse well in abundant cold water. § Put them in a skillet (frying pan) with the wine, cover, and cook over medium-high heat. Take the clams out as they open. Arrange them on a serving dish and keep them in a warm place. § Strain the liquid left in the skillet and set aside to cool. § In the same sauté the onion and garlic in the butter until they turn golden. Add the flour and mix rapidly. § Gradually add the strained clam liquid and mix well until you have a thick, creamy sauce. Season with salt and pepper. § Beat the cream, egg, parsley, and lemon juice together and add to the clam sauce. Mix rapidly and then pour over the clams. § Serve at once.

COZZE GRATINATE AL FORNO
Baked mussels

Serves 4; Preparation: 30 minutes+1 hour to soak the mussels; Cooking: 15 minutes; Level of difficulty: Simple

Soak the mussels in a large bowl of water for at least an hour to purge them of sand. Pull off their beards, scrub, and rinse well in abundant cold water. § Transfer to a skillet (frying pan), cover, and cook over medium-high heat until they are all open. Discard any that haven't opened. § Set the liquid they produce aside. § Mix the parsley and garlic together in a bowl with the bread crumbs, 1 tablespoon of oil, salt and pepper. Strain the mussel liquid and add about 3 tablespoons to the bread mixture. Mix well. § Arrange the mussels in a buttered ovenproof dish. Fill each one with some of the mixture and drizzle with the remaining oil and lemon juice. § Bake in a preheated oven at 400°F/200°C/gas 6 for 15–20 minutes, or until the bread crumbs turn golden brown. § Serve hot.

■ INGREDIENTS

- 4 lb/2 kg clams in shell
- 1 cup/8 fl oz/250 ml dry white wine
- 1 medium onion, finely chopped
- 2 cloves garlic, finely chopped
- ¼ cup/2 oz/60 g butter
- 2 tablespoons all-purpose/plain flour
- salt and freshly ground black pepper
- 1¼ cups/10 fl oz/300 ml fresh light cream
- 1 egg, beaten
- 1 tablespoon finely chopped parsley
- juice of ½ lemon

Wine: a dry white (Roero Arneis)

■ INGREDIENTS

- 2 lb/1 kg fresh mussels
- 2 tablespoons finely chopped parsley
- 2 cloves garlic, finely chopped
- 1¾ cups/3 ½ oz/100 g bread crumbs
- 3 tablespoons extra-virgin olive oil
- salt and freshly ground black pepper
- 1 tablespoon butter
- juice of 1 small lemon

Wine: a dry white (Ischia bianco)

Right: *Vongole in salsa di panna fresca*

FRITTELLE DI BACCALÀ
Salt cod fritters

When buying salt cod, always choose meaty, cream-colored fillets. Avoid the brown ones.

Serves 4; Preparation: 15 minutes + 24 hours to soak cod; Cooking: 20 minutes; Level of difficulty: Simple

Put the salt cod in a bowl of cold water to soak a day ahead. § In a bowl combine the flour and enough of the water to obtain a thick batter. Add the olive oil, season with salt, and stir continuously for 5 minutes. § Wash the salt cod in running water, dry, and cut in pieces. § Heat the oil to very hot in a deep-sided skillet (frying pan), dip the pieces of salt cod in the batter, and deep-fry until golden brown. § Drain on paper towels, sprinkle with salt, and serve hot.

Calamari dolci delicati
Filled sweet squid

Serves 4; Preparation: 30 minutes; Cooking: 30 minutes; Level of difficulty: Simple

Choose small squid that are all about the same size. § To clean the squid, separate the tentacles and head from the body by grasping the head and pulling it apart from the body. Remove the ink sac from the head. Peel off the skin. Remove the bony part and clean out the insides. Rinse well in cold running water. § Cut off the tentacles and blanch the bodies in boiling water for 2–3 minutes. Set aside to cool. § Chop the tentacles in small pieces and put them in a bowl with the onion, raisins, pine nuts, bread crumbs, and egg. Mix well and season with salt and pepper. § Fill the squid bodies with the mixture and close them with a toothpick so the filling won't come out during cooking. § Heat the oil in a heavy-bottomed pan (or an earthenware pot), add the filled squid, and cook slowly over medium-low heat. Turn them often so they won't stick to the bottom. § After about 15 minutes, add the white wine and continue cooking until the liquid has evaporated. § Serve hot.

■ INGREDIENTS

- 2 lb/1 kg small squid
- 1 small onion, finely chopped
- 1 cup/5 oz/150 g muscatel raisins/sultanas
- ⅔ cup/2½ oz/75 g pine nuts
- 1¾ cups/3½ oz/100 g bread crumbs
- 2 eggs, beaten to a foam
- salt and freshly ground white pepper
- 2 tablespoons extra-virgin olive oil
- 1 cup/8 fl oz/250 ml white wine

Wine: a dry white (Verdicchio dei Castelli di Jesi)

Spiedini di scampi
Skewered grilled shrimp

This recipe calls for a grill pan to place over the element on a gas or electric stove to cook the shrimp. They are also very good if cooked over a barbecue, from which they will take a delicious smokey flavor.

Serves 6; Preparation: 30 minutes; Cooking: 30 minutes; Level of difficulty: Simple

Shell the shrimp and remove the dark intestinal veins. Chop off the heads and rinse thoroughly in cold running water. § Thread the shrimp onto skewers and sprinkle with the flour. § Melt the butter in a saucepan and pour half of it over the shrimp. Sprinkle with salt and pepper. § Heat the grill pan to very hot and place the skewers in it. Let the shrimp cook on one side before turning to cook on the other. § Lay the skewers on a serving dish, garnish with lemon and parsley, and serve hot. The remaining melted butter should be served separately in a warmed dish.

■ INGREDIENTS

- 2 lb/1 kg giant shrimp
- 4 tablespoons all-purpose/plain flour
- scant ½ cup/3½ oz/100 g fresh butter
- salt and freshly ground black pepper
- 1 lemon and sprigs of parsley, to garnish

Wine: a dry white (Sauvignon del Collio)

Right:
Calamari dolci delicati

Conchiglie di pesce
Scallop shells filled with fish, potato and mayonnaise

This tasty fish appetizer is easy to make and can be prepared ahead of time. Ask your fish vendor for scallop shells or serve the fish mixture in the curved inner leaves of lettuce hearts.

Serves 4; Preparation: 15 minutes; Cooking: 40 minutes; Level of difficulty: Simple

Prepare the mayonnaise. § Chop the boiled fish and mix with the diced potatoes. § Add the parsley, capers, mayonnaise, salt and pepper. Mix carefully. § Spoon the mixture into the scallop shells and set aside in a cool place for 30 minutes before serving. Garnish with slices of lemon and sprigs of parsley.

■ INGREDIENTS

- ½ quantity *Mayonnaise* (see recipe p. 16)
- 14 oz/450 g boiled fish fillets (hake, sea bream, sea bass, or other)
- 3 boiled potatoes, peeled and diced
- 1 tablespoon finely chopped parsley
- 1 tablespoon capers
- salt and black pepper
- lemon and sprigs of parsley, to garnish

Wine: a dry white (Verduzzo Friulano)

Insalata di mare
Seafood salad

Serves 8; Preparation: 1 hour + 30 minutes in refrigerator; Cooking: 30 minutes; Level of difficulty: Medium

Clean the squid and separate the tentacles and head from the body by grasping the head and pulling it apart from the body. Remove the ink sac from the head. Remove the bony part and clean out the insides. § To clean the cuttlefish, cut each one lengthwise and remove the internal bone and the stomach. Discard the internal ink sac. § Place the cuttlefish in a pot with 5 pints (3 liters) of cold water and 1 tablespoon of salt and bring to a boil over high heat. § When the cuttlefish have been simmering for 5 minutes, add the squid and cook for 15 more minutes. § Drain and set aside to cool. § Chop the tentacles in small pieces and then slice the bodies in rings. Transfer to a salad bowl. § Bring 6 cups (2½ pints, 1.5 liters) of water and 1 tablespoon of salt to a boil. Rinse the shrimp thoroughly and add to the pot. Cook for 2 minutes. Drain and set aside to cool. § Shell the shrimp and add them to the salad bowl. § Soak the clams and mussels in a large bowl of water for at least an hour. Pull the beards off the mussels. Scrub well and rinse in abundant cold water. § Place the shellfish in a large skillet (frying pan) with 2 tablespoons of oil and cook over medium heat until they are all open. Discard any that have not opened. § Discard the shells and add the mussels and clams to the salad bowl. § Mix the parsley, garlic, chilies, lemon juice, remaining oil, salt and pepper in a bowl. Pour over the salad and toss well. § Place in the refrigerator for 30 minutes before serving.

■ INGREDIENTS

- 1 lb/500 g squid
- 14 oz/450 g cuttlefish
- salt
- 14 oz/450 g shrimp
- 14 oz/450 g clams in shell
- 14 oz/450 g mussels in shell
- 2 tablespoons finely chopped parsley
- 2 cloves garlic, finely chopped
- 1 teaspoon crushed chilies (optional)
- juice of ½ lemon
- 5 tablespoons extra-virgin olive oil
- freshly ground black pepper

Wine: a dry white (Greco di Tufo)

Right: Insalata di mare

Mousse di tonno
Tuna fish mousse

Serves 4; Preparation: 15 minutes + 6 hours in the refrigerator; Level of difficulty: Simple

Put the tuna fish in the food processor and whizz for 1–2 minutes. § Transfer to a bowl and add the mascarpone. Mix well and add the pickled onions and parsley. Season with salt and pepper. § Lightly butter a mold and line with aluminum foil. Fill with the tuna mixture and place in the refrigerator for 6 hours. § Wash and dry the arugula and arrange on a serving dish. Invert the mousse onto the bed of arugula. § Garnish with the olives and serve.

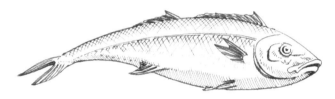

Bignoline di cozze
Mussel dumplings

Serves 4-6; Preparation: 30 minutes+1 hour to soak the mussels; Cooking: 30 minutes; Level of difficulty: Medium

Soak the mussels in a large bowl of water for at least an hour to purge them of sand. Pull off their beards, scrub, and rinse well in abundant cold water. § Put the mussels in a large skillet (frying pan) over high heat, sprinkle with the wine, and cover. § When all the shells are open (discard any that don't open), remove from the skillet. Pick the mussels out of their shells one by one. § Bring the water, butter, and salt to a boil in a small pot, add the flour, and remove from the heat. Beat with a wooden spoon until the mixture is thick and well mixed. § Return to medium heat and stir until the mixture sticks to the sides and bottom of the pot. § Let cool. Transfer to a bowl, stir in the eggs one by one, and add the parsley, parmesan, and mussels. § Heat the oil to very hot. Use a spoon to add small quantities of the mussel batter into the oil. The dumplings will swell and turn golden brown. § Drain on paper towels, sprinkle with salt, and serve hot.

■ INGREDIENTS

• 8 oz/250 g tuna fish in oil
• 8 oz/250 g mascarpone cheese
• 2 oz/60 g pickled onions, well drained and very finely chopped
• 1 tablespoon finely chopped parsley
• salt and freshly ground black pepper
• 1 tablespoon/½ oz/15 g butter
• 1 bunch arugula (rocket)
• 8 black olives, pitted and chopped

Wine: a dry white (Locorotondo)

■ INGREDIENTS

• 1½ lb/750 g mussels in shell
• ½ cup/4 fl oz/125 ml dry white wine
• ¾ cup/6 fl oz/180 ml cold water
• 2 tablespoons/1 oz/30 g butter
• salt
• 3½ oz/100 g all-purpose/plain flour
• 4 eggs
• 2 tablespoons finely chopped parsley
• 4 tablespoons freshly grated parmesan cheese
• 2 cups/16 fl oz/500 ml oil, for frying

Wine: a dry rosato (Teroldego Rotaliano)

Right: *Mousse di tonno*

■ INGREDIENTS

- 12 scallops in shell
- 2 tablespoons finely chopped parsley
- 1 clove garlic, finely chopped
- 3 tablespoons extra-virgin olive oil
- salt and freshly ground black pepper
- juice of 1 lemon

Wine: a dry rosato
(Teroldego Rotaliano)

Cape sante alla veneta
Scallops Venetian-style

Serves 4; Preparation: 10 minutes; Cooking: 10 minutes; Level of difficulty: Simple

Pry open the shells, take out the scallops, and rinse under cold running water. § Sauté the parsley and garlic with the scallops in the oil. Season with salt and pepper. § Cook for 4–5 minutes over high heat, stirring continuously. Remove from the heat and add the lemon juice. § Arrange in four shells and serve.

Cape sante con funghi e besciamella
Scallops with mushrooms and béchamel sauce

Serves 4; Preparation: 15 minutes; Cooking: 40 minutes; Level of difficulty: Medium

Wash the scallops well in cold running water. § Cook over high heat in a skillet (frying pan) until they open. § Remove the meat and simmer for 15–20 minutes in a pot of boiling water. § Boil the shells in a pot of boiling water for a few minutes. Let cool and clean thoroughly. Set aside. § Trim the mushrooms, wash carefully, and pat dry with paper towels. Chop coarsely. § Sauté the onion and garlic in ¼ cup/2 oz/60 g butter. Add the thyme, ham, and mushrooms. Season with salt and pepper and cook for 10 minutes. § Prepare the béchamel sauce. § Use the remaining butter to grease the shells. § Chop the scallop meat coarsely and fill the shells. § Stir the mushroom mixture into the béchamel sauce and spoon over the scallops. § Sprinkle with the parmesan and place on a baking sheet in a preheated oven at 400°F/200°C/gas 6 for 10–15 minutes. § Serve hot.

Torta di gamberi
Shrimp pie

Serves 6; Preparation: 30 minutes; Cooking: 50 minutes; Level of difficulty: Simple

Shell the shrimp and remove the dark intestinal veins. Chop off the heads, and rinse well in cold running water. § Sauté over medium-high heat for 5 minutes in a skillet (frying pan) with the garlic and butter. § Pour in the brandy and cook for 2 minutes more, stirring all the time. Season with salt and pepper and remove from the heat. § Roll out the pastry dough very thinly and line an ovenproof pie dish 8–9 in (20 cm) in diameter. § In a bowl combine the eggs, flour, salt and pepper, and mix until smooth. § Add the parsley, cream, shrimp, and the liquid they produced while cooking. Pour into the pie dish and bake in a preheated oven at 400°F/200°C/gas 6 for 40 minutes. § Serve hot or at room temperature.

■ INGREDIENTS

- 8 fresh scallops
- 10 oz/300 g white mushrooms
- 1 small onion, finely chopped
- 1 clove garlic, finely chopped
- ¼ cup/2 oz/60 g butter
- ½ tablespoon finely chopped fresh thyme
- 2 oz/60 g chopped ham
- salt and freshly ground black pepper
- 1 quantity *Béchamel sauce* (see recipe p. 22)
- 4 tablespoons freshly grated parmesan cheese

Wine: a dry white
(Tocai di Lison)

■ INGREDIENTS

- 1½ lb/750 g shrimp
- 2 cloves garlic, minced
- 3 tablespoons/1½ oz/45 g butter
- 2 tablespoons brandy
- salt and freshly ground black pepper
- 14 oz/450 g plain pastry (store-bought)
- 3 eggs
- 2 tablespoons all-purpose/plain flour
- 4 tablespoons finely chopped parsley
- 7 oz/200 ml fresh cream

Wine: a dry white
(Traminer aromatico)

Right:
Cape sante con funghi e besciamella

Aringhe fresche marinate
Marinated herrings

Serves 6-8; Preparation: 30 minutes + 24 hours; Cooking: 40 minutes; Level of difficulty: Medium

Sauté half the carrots, thyme, bay leaves, and peppercorns in a skillet (frying pan) with the butter for 3–4 minutes. § Add the flour and cook for 2–3 minutes more. § Add the wine, vinegar, salt, sugar, parsley, cinnamon, cilantro, and cloves. Bring to a boil and cook over low heat for about 30 minutes, or until the liquid has reduced by about a third. § Remove from the heat and add the marjoram. § Clean the herrings, cut off the heads, wash and pat dry with paper towels. § Arrange the herrings in a single layer in a large pan and pour the hot marinade over the top. Cover and cook over low heat for 10–12 minutes. § When cool, transfer to a large flat dish and cover with the marinade. Keep in a cool place for at least 24 hours. § Remove from the marinade and arrange on a serving dish. Sprinkle with the remaining carrots, the onion, the lemon juice, and a tablespoon or two of marinade.

■ INGREDIENTS

- 3½ oz/100 g carrots, very finely sliced
- dash each of thyme, cinnamon, marjoram
- 2 bay leaves
- 10 white peppercorns
- 2 tablespoons butter
- 1 tablespoon all-purpose/plain flour
- 2 cups/16 fl oz/500 ml dry white wine
- 1 cup/8 fl oz/250 ml white wine vinegar
- salt
- 1 tablespoon sugar
- 1 tablespoon finely chopped parsley
- 1 teaspoon cilantro
- 4 cloves
- 12 fresh herrings
- 1 onion, finely chopped
- juice of 1 lemon

Wine: a dry rosato (Salice Salentino)

Pompelmi ripieni
Grapefruit filled with shrimp

Serves 4; Preparation: 20 minutes + 30 minutes in the refrigerator; Cooking: 10 minutes; Level of difficulty: Simple

Cut the grapefruit in half and with a sharp knife extract the pulp. Take care not to cut or spoil the grapefruit shells which are used to serve the shrimp. Remove the white membrane and dice the pulp (in a dish or plate so that the juice is conserved). § Put the onion, celery, bay leaves, and shrimp in a small pot of cold water and simmer over medium heat for about 10 minutes, or until the shrimp are cooked. § Prepare the mayonnaise and combine with the mustard. Mix well and stir in the lemon and grapefruit juice. § Remove the shells from the shrimp and cut off the heads. Chop coarsely and add to the mayonnaise sauce. Stir in the diced grapefruit and fill the grapefruit cups with the mixture. § Place in the refrigerator for about 30 minutes before serving.

■ INGREDIENTS

- 2 grapefruit
- 1 small onion
- 1 stalk celery
- 2 bay leaves
- 1 lb/500 g shrimp
- salt
- 1 quantity *Mayonnaise* (see recipe p. 16)
- 2 teaspoons mild mustard
- juice of 1 lemon

Wine: a dry white (Torgiano Bianco)

VARIATIONS
– Sprinkle 2 tablespoons of *bottarga* (roe of tuna fish or gray mullet) over the grapefruit just before serving.
– Spread 1 small can of caviar over the grapefruit just before serving.

Right:
Pompelmi ripieni

Coppini di limoni al tonno
Tuna-fish lemon cups

Serves 4; Preparation: 20 minutes; Level of difficulty: Simple

Cut the lemons in half crosswise. § Using a sharp knife, scoop out the insides without piercing the rind so they can be used as cups. § Put the tuna fish, capers, gherkins, and egg yolks through a food mill several times. § Transfer the mixture to a bowl and add the oil, mayonnaise, and lemon juice. Mix well and fill the lemons. § Arrange on a serving plate on a bed of washed and dried lettuce leaves and garnish with olives and slices of gherkin or bell pepper.

■ INGREDIENTS

- 4 lemons
- 7 oz/200 g tuna fish in olive oil
- 2 tablespoons capers
- 2 tablespoons gherkins
- 2 hard-cooked/hard-boiled egg yolks
- extra-virgin olive oil
- 1 quantity *Mayonnaise* (see recipe p. 16)
- salt
- a few lettuce leaves, olives, slices of gherkin and bell peppers/capsicums, to garnish

Wine: a dry white (Locorotondo)

Fritto di calamari e scampi
Fried squid and shrimp

There are one or two golden rules to remember when preparing fried dishes. First, make sure the oil is hot enough before adding the seafood. Check by adding a tiny piece of bread — if it turns golden brown immediately, the oil is ready. Second, don't put too many squid rings or shrimp in the pan at once. If you completely fill the pan, the squid and shrimp will stick together in an unappetizing lump. You will also lower the temperature of the oil too much and the seafood will not seal immediately against the oil and will take longer to cook. This means it will absorb more oil and the dish will be heavier.

Serves 4-6; Preparation: 30 minutes; Cooking: 30 minutes; Level of difficulty: Simple

Clean the squid following the instructions on p. 266. Cut in ¼-in (6-mm) rings. § Remove the shells and dark intestinal veins from the shrimp, chop off the heads, and rinse thoroughly in cold running water. § Heat the frying oil to very hot in a deep-sided skillet (frying pan). § Place the flour in a bowl and add the squid rings. Take them out a few at a time, shake off excess flour, and plunge them into the hot oil. Each panful will need about 8 minutes to cook. § Repeat the process with the shrimp, which will take about 5 minutes to cook. § Drain on paper towels to eliminate excess oil, sprinkle with salt, and garnish with slices of lemon and sprigs of parsley. § Serve immediately.

■ INGREDIENTS

- 1 lb/500 g small squid
- 8 oz/250 g giant shrimp
- 1 cup/3½ oz/100 g all-purpose/plain flour
- 2 cups/16 fl oz/500 ml oil, for frying
- salt
- 1 lemon and 6–8 sprigs parsley, to garnish

Wine: a dry white (Bianco di Pitigliano)

Right:
Coppini di limoni al tonno

SFORMATI DI GAMBERI
Shrimp molds

■ INGREDIENTS

• 1½ lb/750 g shrimp
• 1¼ cups/10 fl oz/300 ml whole/full cream milk
• 3 eggs
• bunch of chives, finely chopped
• salt and freshly ground black pepper
• 1 tablespoon/½ oz/15 g butter

*Wine: a dry white
(Orvieto Classico)*

Serves 6; Preparation: 40 minutes; Cooking: 30 minutes; Level of difficulty: Medium

Shell the shrimp and remove the dark intestinal veins. Chop off the heads, and rinse thoroughly in cold running water. Dry well and chop into small pieces. § Combine the milk, eggs, chives, salt and pepper in a bowl and beat with a fork until well mixed. § Add the shrimp and pour the mixture into six 4-in (10 cm) buttered molds. § Place a large container filled with water in the oven and heat to 350°F/180°C/gas 4. Place the mold pans in the water and cook *bain-marie* for 30 minutes. § Serve warm or cold.

BRUSCHETTE DI FRUTTI DI MARE
Seafood bruschette

These bruschette *are easy to make and delicious to eat. Be sure to spoon the seafood sauce over the* bruschette *just before serving. To prepare ahead of time, proceed as far as the thickened sauce and set aside. After an hour or two, reheat the sauce, add the seafood, and finish cooking.*

Serves 4; Preparation: 30 minutes+1 hour to soak; Cooking: 20 minutes; Level of difficulty: Medium

Soak the mussels and clams in a large bowl of cold water for at least an hour to purge them of sand. § Pull the beards off the mussels and scrub both clams and mussels well. Rinse thoroughly under cold running water. Drain well. § Sauté 1 tablespoon olive oil, 1 clove garlic, and 1 tablespoon parsley in a large skillet (frying pan) for 2–3 minutes. § Add the mussels and clams and pour in half the wine. § Cover the pan and place over medium-high heat. Shake the pan often, until the shells are all open. § Drain the liquid they have produced into a bowl, strain and set aside. Discard any shells that haven't opened. § Detach the mussels and clams from their shells and set them aside. § To clean the squid, separate the tentacles and head from the body by grasping the head and pulling it apart from the body. Remove the ink sac from the head. Peel off the skin. Remove the bony part and clean out the insides. Rinse well in cold running water. § Shell the shrimp and remove the dark intestinal veins. Chop off the heads, and rinse thoroughly in cold running water. § Carefully wash the bell pepper, cut in half, remove the seeds and core, and dice. § Sauté the scallion in a skillet with the butter and the remaining oil. Add the diced bell pepper and sauté briefly, stirring continuously with a wooden spoon. § Add the remaining wine and continue cooking over high heat. § When the wine has evaporated, add the mussel liquid and the saffron dissolved in lukewarm milk. Season with salt and pepper. § Continue cooking over high heat for a few minutes until the sauce is thick. Add the mussels, clams, shrimp, and squid and cook for 3 minutes more, mixing often. § Sprinkle with the remaining parsley. § Prepare the *bruschette.* § Spoon the seafood sauce over the *bruschette* and serve hot.

■ INGREDIENTS

- 8 oz/250 g mussels in shell
- 8 oz/250 g clams in shell
- 2 tablespoons extra-virgin olive oil
- 2 cloves garlic
- 2 tablespoons finely chopped parsley
- 1 cup/8 fl oz/250 ml dry white wine
- 7 oz/200 g small squid
- 8 oz/250 g shrimp
- 1 red bell pepper/ capsicum
- 1 scallion/shallot, finely chopped
- ½ tablespoon butter
- 1 teaspoon saffron, dissolved in ½ cup/4 fl oz/125 ml lukewarm milk
- salt and freshly ground black pepper
- 8 slices *Bruschetta* (see recipe p. 22)

Wine: a dry white (Nosiola)

Right:
Bruschette di frutti di mare

Cornetti di salmone affumicato con insalata russa
Smoked salmon cones with potato salad

Serves 4; Preparation: 40 minutes; Cooking: 20 minutes; Level of difficulty: Simple

Wash and peel the potatoes and dice. Scrape the carrots and dice. Snap ends off the green beans and cut in small pieces. § Put the vegetables in a pot of salted, boiling water and cook over medium heat for 15–20 minutes. § Drain the vegetables and set aside to cool. § Prepare the mayonnaise. § When cold, put the cooked vegetables in a pot with the peas, capers, gherkin, and pepper. Add the mayonnaise, reserving some for garnish, and mix well. § Arrange the slices of smoked salmon on a serving platter and put a spoonful of potato salad on the center of each slice. § Roll the salmon up around the salad into a cone. § Garnish the plate with the remaining mayonnaise, sliced hard-cooked eggs, and a few sprigs of parsley. § Serve cold.

> VARIATION
> – Cones of prosciutto, or ham, or raw beef (of the type used for *carpaccio*) can also be used instead of the salmon.

■ INGREDIENTS

- 7 oz/200 g potatoes
- 2 oz/60 g carrots
- 2 oz/60 g green beans
- 2 oz/60 g frozen peas
- 1 quantity *Mayonnaise* (see recipe p. 16)
- 2 tablespoons extra-virgin olive oil
- 2 tablespoons capers
- 2 tablespoons diced gherkins
- juice of 1 medium lemon
- salt and freshly ground black pepper
- 8 slices smoked salmon (about 8 oz/250 g)
- 2 hard-cooked/hard-boiled eggs and sprigs of parsley, to garnish

Wine: a dry white (Riesling dell'Alto Adige)

Insalata di polpo
Octopus salad

Serves 6-8; Preparation: 30 minutes + 2 hours to soften; Cooking: 1 hour; Level of difficulty: Medium

Clean the octopus by removing the sac and beak. § Beat with the handle of a large knife to soften the flesh. § Place the octopus in a large pot of cold water with the vinegar, carrot, celery, onion, garlic, parsley, and salt. § Cover and bring to a boil over high heat. Lower the heat and simmer for an hour. § Remove from the heat and leave to cool in the cooking water. This will take at least 2 hours. This cooling process is very important because it makes the octopus meat tender. § Skin the octopus (it will come away easily together with the suckers—a few of the latter can be added to the salad). Cut the sac in rings and the tentacles in small pieces. § Transfer to a serving dish and season with oil, lemon juice, salt, pepper, and chilies. § Toss well and serve.

■ INGREDIENTS

- 2 lb/1 kg octopus
- 1 cup/8 fl oz/250 ml white wine vinegar
- 1 carrot
- 1 stalk celery
- 1 small onion
- 1 clove garlic
- 5 sprigs parsley
- salt and black pepper
- 4 tablespoons extra-virgin olive oil
- juice of 1 lemon
- ½ teaspoon dried chilies

Wine: a dry white (Cirò bianco)

Right: *Cornetti di salmone affumicato con insalata russa*

Piccoli spiedini alla salsiccia
Mixed sausage, chicken, and vegetable skewers

Serves 4; Preparation: 20 minutes + 1 hour to marinate; Cooking: 15 minutes; Level of difficulty: Simple

Wash and dry the zucchini. Trim the ends and chop into ½-in (1-cm) thick wheels. § Wash and dry the bell pepper. Remove the seeds and cores and chop in squares. § Wash the tomatoes and leave them whole. § Chop the sausages into 1-in (2.5-cm) thick slices. § Chop the chicken into squares of about the same size. § Combine all the ingredients in a bowl with the sage, rosemary, parsley, salt, pepper, and oil and leave to marinate in the refrigerator for 1 hour. § Prepare the skewers, alternating pieces of chicken, sausage, and vegetables. § Heat the grill pan to very

■ INGREDIENTS

- 1 large zucchini/courgette
- 1 red or yellow bell pepper/capsicum
- 12 cherry tomatoes
- 2 Italian pork sausages
- 1 large chicken breast
- 2 tablespoons mixed finely chopped sage, rosemary, and parsley
- salt and freshly ground black pepper
- 2 tablespoons extra-virgin olive oil

Wine: a dry red (Chianti Ruffino)

Salame e fichi freschi
Salami with fresh figs

Figs begin to appear in the markets in Italy in June, but it is not until August that local fig trees begin producing these delicious fruit and the markets are flooded with them. At that point Salame e fichi freschi *make regular appearances as appetizers on many Italian tables. The mixture of the sweet flesh of the fruit with the strong salty taste of the salame is perfect at the end of a long summer day.*

■ INGREDIENTS

- 10 oz/300 g fresh green or black figs
- 7 oz/200 g salame, thinly sliced

Wine: a dry rosé (Salice Salentino - Five Roses)

Serves 4-6; Preparation: 5 minutes; Level of difficulty: Simple

Wash the figs thoroughly and pat dry with paper towels. § Remove the rind from the salame. § Arrange the figs and salame on a serving dish. If you can get them, use fig leaves to garnish the dish.

Right: Salame e fichi freschi

Fagottini di prosciutto dolce ai funghi porcini
Prosciutto rolls filled with porcini mushrooms and fontina cheese

If you can't get fresh porcini mushrooms, use white mushrooms in their place. Serve the rolls straight away; they are particularly tasty while still warm.

Serves 4; Preparation: 20 minutes; Cooking: 15 minutes; Level of difficulty: Simple

Wash the mushrooms carefully under cold running water and pat them dry with paper towels. § Separate the stems and caps and dice them into bite-size pieces. § Sauté the stems in the oil with the garlic, calamint (or thyme), and salt and pepper for about 8–10 minutes. Add a little broth to keep the mixture moist. § Add the caps and cook for 5 minutes more, or until the mushrooms are cooked. § Add the cheese, turn off the heat immediately, and mix well. § Distribute the mixture evenly among the slices of prosciutto, placing it in the middle of each. § Fold the ends of the prosciutto around the mixture and tuck them under the package. Tie each with a chive. § Serve immediately.

■ INGREDIENTS

- 7 oz/200 g porcini mushrooms
- 2 tablespoons extra-virgin olive oil
- 1 clove garlic, minced
- 1 tablespoon finely chopped calamint (or thyme)
- salt and freshly ground black pepper
- ½ cup/4 fl oz/125 ml *Beef broth* (see recipe p. 16)
- 3½ oz/100 g fontina cheese
- 8 oz/250 g prosciutto
- 8 long chives

Wine: a dry red (Colli Piacentini)

Involtini di bresaola
Bresaola rolls filled with robiola cheese

Serves 6-8; Preparation: 20 minutes; Level of difficulty: Simple

Wash and dry the arugula and chop finely. § Combine in a bowl with the robiola, salt and pepper, and mix well. § Arrange on the slices of bresaola and roll them up. § Drizzle with the oil, sprinkle with pepper and serve.

■ INGREDIENTS

- 1 bunch arugula (rocket)
- 7 oz/200 g robiola or other soft, creamy cheese
- salt and freshly ground black pepper
- 7 oz/100 g bresaola
- 2 tablespoons extra-virgin olive oil

Wine: a dry red (Carmignano)

Prosciutto e melone
Prosciutto and canteloupe

Be sure to choose the highest quality Parma prosciutto and the sweetest canteloupe. This dish is best in summer since its outcome depends on the canteloupe being exquisitely fresh.

Serves 4; Preparation: 5 minutes; Level of difficulty: Simple

Wash the canteloupe thoroughly under cold running water and slice into pieces measuring about 1-1½ in (3-4 cm) wide. § Arrange on a serving dish with the ham and serve.

■ INGREDIENTS

- 10 oz/300 g prosciutto, thinly sliced
- 1 canteloupe/rock melon, weighing about 1 lb/500 g

Wine: a dry rosé (Leverano)

Right: *Prosciutto e melone*

■ INGREDIENTS

- 7 oz/200 g gorgonzola cheese
- 4 oz/125 g mascarpone cheese
- 1¼ cups/5 oz/150 g finely chopped walnuts + some whole to garnish
- salt
- 12 oz/350 g ham, cut in 8 thick slices

Wine: a dry red (Gattinara)

CANNOLI DI PROSCIUTTO COTTO E GORGONZOLA
Ham rolls filled with gorgonzola cheese and walnuts

Serves 4; Preparation: 15 minutes; Level of difficulty: Simple

Combine the gorgonzola, mascarpone, walnuts, and a dash of salt in a bowl and mix to a thick cream. § Spread the mixture on the slices of ham and roll them up. § Chop each roll in half. § Arrange on a serving dish. The rolls will look more attractive if served on a bed of fresh salad leaves (whatever you have on hand) and garnished with a few whole walnuts. § Serve cold.

CROSTINI TOSCANI
Tuscan-style liver crostini

Serves 4; Preparation: 15 minutes; Cooking: 50 minutes; Level of difficulty: Medium

Remove the bile and the larger fibres from the chicken livers. Chop coarsely. § Sauté the onion over medium heat with the oil. Add the bay leaf and chicken liver. § Brown the chicken liver for 5 minutes, then add the wine and Marsala. § Remove the skin from the spleen and chop coarsely. § As soon as the liquid has completely evaporated, add the spleen to a skillet (frying pan) together with the capers and anchovies. § Season with salt and pepper and cook for 40 minutes. Add a little hot stock whenever the mixture starts to dry out. § Remove from the heat, discard the bay leaf, and put the mixture through a food mill. § Place the mixture in a heavy-bottomed pan over low heat and stir in the cream and half the butter. Stir continuously until it begins to bubble, then remove from the heat. § Cut the bread in slices or triangles and spread lightly with the remaining butter. Place on a baking sheet and toast lightly in the oven. § Spread with the liver mixture, arrange on a serving dish, and serve.

■ INGREDIENTS

- 3 chicken livers
- ½ onion, finely chopped
- 2 tablespoons extra-virgin olive oil
- 1 bay leaf
- ½ glass dry white wine
- ½ small glass dry Marsala
- 5 oz/150 g veal spleen
- 1 tablespoon capers
- 4 anchovy fillets
- salt and freshly ground black pepper
- ½ cup/4 fl oz/125 ml *Beef broth* (see recipe p. 16)
- scant 1 cup/7 fl oz/200 ml light/single cream
- scant ½ cup/3½ oz/100 g butter
- 4–8 slices dense grain, home-style bread

*Wine: a dry red
(Brunello di Montalcino)*

CROSTINI RUSTICI
Country-style liver crostini

Serves 4; Preparation: 15 minutes; Cooking: 30 minutes; Level of difficulty: Medium

Chop the celery, carrot, onion, and garlic together coarsely. § Add the parsley and sauté in a skillet (frying pan) with the oil over medium heat. § Remove the bile and the larger fibres from the chicken livers. Chop coarsely. § Add the chicken livers to the skillet and sauté for 4–5 minutes. § Add the wine and continue cooking over low heat for 20 minutes. If the mixture drys out too much during cooking add a little broth made with boiling water and bouillon cube. § Add the capers and cook for 2–3 minutes. § Add the anchovies and season with salt and pepper. Remove from the heat. § Toast the bread until light gold. Spread with the liver mixture and serve.

■ INGREDIENTS

- 1 stalk celery, 1 carrot, 1 onion, 1 clove garlic
- 1 tablespoon finely chopped parsley
- 4 tablespoons extra-virgin olive oil
- 3 chicken livers
- ½ cup/4 fl oz/125 ml dry white wine
- 3 tablespoons coarsely chopped capers
- 2 anchovy fillets, chopped
- salt and black pepper
- 4–8 slices dense grain, home-style bread

Right: Crostini toscani

■ INGREDIENTS

- 1 boiled chicken
- 1 cup/3½ oz/100 g shelled almonds
- 2 avocados
- juice of 1 lemon
- 1 lettuce heart
- salt and freshly ground black pepper
- 2 quantities *Mayonnaise* (see recipe p. 16)
- 2 carrots, finely chopped
- 1 celery heart, finely chopped
- 2 tablespoons finely chopped parsley

Wine: a dry white (Frascati)

INSALATA DI POLLO E MANDORLE
Chicken and almond salad

Serves 4-6; Preparation: 20 minutes + 2 hours in the refrigerator; Level of difficulty: Simple

Remove the skin from the chicken and discard sinews and bones. § Cut the meat into small pieces. § Blanch the almonds for 2–3 minutes in boiling water and peel. § Peel the avocados. Chop into cubes and sprinkle with lemon juice so they won't turn black. § Line a salad bowl with the best leaves from the heart of the lettuce. § Arrange the chicken in the center and cover with the avocado and almonds. Season with salt and pepper. § Set aside in the refrigerator for at least 2 hours. § Prepare the mayonnaise. § Add the carrots, celery, and parsley to the mayonnaise. § Just before serving, pour half the mayonnaise over the chicken and mix carefully. Serve the rest of the mayonnaise separately at table.

■ INGREDIENTS

- 1 boiled chicken
- 1 celery heart
- 5 gherkins
- 3½ oz/100 g gruyère cheese
- 3½ oz/100 g ham, in one thick slice
- juice of 1 lemon
- salt and freshly ground black pepper
- 1 quantity *Mayonnaise* (see recipe p. 16)

Wine: a dry white (Pinot Grigio)

INSALATA DI POLLO E SEDANO
Chicken and celery salad

Serves 4-6; Preparation: 15 minutes + 30 minutes in the refrigerator; Level of difficulty: Simple

Remove the skin from the chicken and discard sinews and bones. § Cut the meat into small pieces. § Wash the celery and chop coarsely. § Slice the gherkins and dice the gruyère and ham. § Combine the ingredients in a deep salad bowl and season with lemon juice, salt and pepper. § Prepare the mayonnaise and pour over the salad. Toss carefully. § Set aside in the refrigerator for 30 minutes before serving.

Left
Insalata di pollo e mandorle

Pâté lombardo
Lombard-style pâté

Serves 6; Preparation: 25 minutes; Cooking: 40 minutes; Level of difficulty: Medium

Remove the bile and the larger fibres from the chicken livers and chop coarsely. § Sauté the chicken and calf's liver together in the butter with the garlic and parsley for a few minutes. Season with salt and pepper. § When the liver starts to dry out, add the Marsala and continue cooking for 5–10 minutes, or until the liver is cooked. § Remove the liver and add the bread crumbs to the juices in the pan. Mix well and remove from the heat. § Put liver and breadcrumbs through a food mill. § Combine the eggs and yolks, liver, bread crumbs, and parmesan in a bowl and mix to obtain a fairly stiff mixture. If it is too dry or firm, soften with a tablespoon or two of broth made with boiling water and a bouillon cube. § Butter a medium-sized mold, line with waxed paper, and fill with the mixture. Put the mold in a large pan of boiling water and leave it for at least 30 minutes, so that the pâté will finish cooking *bain-marie*. § Garnish with sprigs of parsley and serve warm or cold with toasted bread and plenty of butter.

■ INGREDIENTS

- 5 chicken livers
- 1 lb/500 g calf's liver, coarsely chopped
- ¼ cup/2 oz/60 g butter
- 1 clove garlic, finely chopped
- 2 tablespoons finely chopped parsley + sprigs to garnish
- salt and freshly ground black pepper
- 1 cup/8 fl oz/250 ml Marsala
- 1½ cups/2½ oz/75 g bread crumbs
- 2 eggs + 2 yolks
- 1 cup/4 oz/125 g freshly grated parmesan cheese

Wine: a dry red (Oltrepò Pavese)

Pâté di fegato
Liver pâté

Serves 6; Preparation: 30 minutes; Cooking: 50 minutes; Level of difficulty: Medium

Sauté the onion in 1 tablespoon of butter over medium heat. § When it begins to turn golden, turn off the heat and add the remaining butter so it will melt without bubbling. § Cut the liver and lard in small pieces and put through a meat grinder, using the disk with small holes. § Transfer the mixture to a large bowl and add the onion, parsley, and tarragon. § Chop finely in a food processor. § Add the flour, eggs, nutmeg, salt, and pepper, and mix thoroughly. § Butter a medium-sized mold, line with waxed paper, and fill with the mixture. Shake the mold to fill up any air pockets. § Cover with a sheet of waxed paper. Fill a large container with boiling water, place the mold in it and cook *bain-marie* in a preheated oven at 350°F/180°C/gas 4 for about 45 minutes. § Invert the pâté on a serving dish. § Serve cold.

■ INGREDIENTS

- 1 onion, finely chopped
- scant ½ cup/3½ oz/100 g butter
- 10 oz/300 g calf's liver
- 1 cup/8 oz/250 g lard
- 1 tablespoon finely chopped parsley and tarragon
- ½ cup/2 oz/60 g all-purpose/plain flour
- 2 eggs
- dash of nutmeg
- salt and freshly ground white pepper

Wine: a dry red (Barolo)

Right: Pâté lombardo

Making Fresh Pasta at Home

Fresh pasta can be made either by hand or using a pasta machine. I strongly advise you not to use the pasta machines that mix the dough as well as cutting the pasta, since the finished product will be heavy and very inferior to handmade pasta. The first step in pasta making is to prepare the dough.

MIXING PLAIN PASTA DOUGH

For 4 generous servings you will need 14 oz/450 g of all-purpose/plain white flour and 3 medium eggs. Place the flour in a mound on a flat work surface and hollow out a well in the center. Break the eggs into the well one by one and beat lightly with a fork for 1–2 minutes. Pull some of the surrounding flour down over the egg mixture and gradually incorporate it. Continue until the mixture is no longer runny. Using your hands now, combine all the flour with the eggs. Work the mixture with your hands until it is smooth and moist, but quite firm.

To test the mixture for the correct consistency, press a clean finger into the dough. If it comes out easily and without any dough sticking to it, it is ready for kneading. If it is too moist, add more flour. If it is too dry, incorporate a little milk. Roll the mixture into a ball shape.

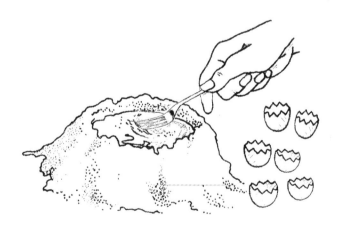

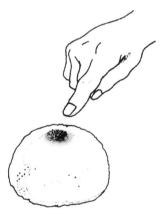

MIXING SPINACH PASTA DOUGH

For 4 generous servings you will need 8 oz/250 g of all-purpose/plain white flour, 5 oz/150 g of fresh spinach (or 3½ oz/100 g thawed frozen spinach) and 2 large eggs. Cook the spinach in a little salted water until tender. Drain well and, when cool, squeeze out any excess moisture. Chop finely with a knife. Proceed as above for plain pasta dough, working the spinach in together with the eggs.

Kneading the dough

Clean the work surface of any excess dough or flour and lightly sprinkle with flour. Push down and forward on the ball of pasta dough with the heel of your palm. Fold the slightly extended piece of dough in half, give it a quarter-turn, and repeat the process. Continue for about 10 minutes or until the dough is very smooth. Place the ball of pasta dough on a plate and cover with an upturned bowl. Leave to rest for at least 15–20 minutes.

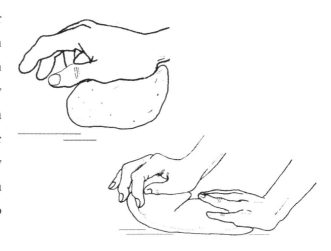

Rolling the dough out by hand

Place the ball of dough on a flat, clean work surface and flatten it a little with your hand. Place the rolling pin on the center of the flattened ball and, applying light but firm pressure, roll the dough away from you. Give the ball a quarter-turn and repeat. When the dough has become a large round about ¼ in (5 mm) thick, curl the far edge over the pin while holding the edge closest to you with your hand. Gently stretch the pasta as you roll it all onto the pin. Unroll, give the dough a quarter-turn, and repeat. Continue rolling and stretching the dough until it is transparent.

Rolling the dough out using the pasta machine

Divide the dough in to several pieces and flatten them slightly with your hands. Set the machine with its rollers at their widest, and run each piece through the machine. Reduce the rollers' width by one notch and repeat, reducing the rollers' width by one notch each time. Continue until all the pieces have gone through the machine at the thinnest roller setting.

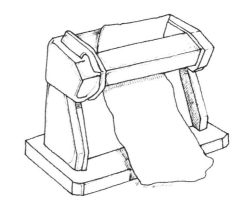

CUTTING THE PASTA BY HAND

For lasagna: cut the rolled out pasta into oblongs sheets measuring about 3 x 12 in (8 x 30 cm).

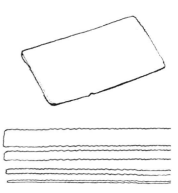

For tagliolini, fettuccine, tagliatelle, and pappardelle: fold the hand-rolled pasta into a loose, flat roll. Using a large sharp knife, cut the roll into ⅛ in (2 mm) slices (for tagliolini), ¼ in (5 mm) slices (for fettuccine), ⅓ in (8 mm) slices (for tagliatelle), or ¾ in (2 cm) slices (for pappardelle). Unravel the pasta and lay it out flat on a clean dish cloth. If you want fluted edges, use the wheel cutter on the pasta laid out flat. You will need a steady hand!

For maltagliati: fold the hand-rolled pasta into a loose, flat roll. Using a large sharp knife cut the pasta into rhomboid shapes. Separate the pieces and lay them out on a clean tea towel.

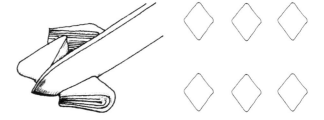

CUTTING THE PASTA BY MACHINE

Cut the pieces of pasta lengthwise so that they are about 12 in (30 cm) long. Attach the cutters to the pasta machine and set the machine at the widths given above for the various types of pasta. Lay the cut pasta out on clean dry dish cloths.

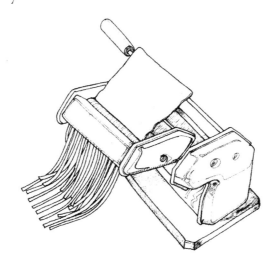

MAKING STUFFED PASTA

Pasta dough for stuffed pasta needs to be fairly moist, so try to work quickly and keep all the dough you are not using on a plate under an upturned dish.

For agnolotti, tortelli, and square-shaped ravioli: these are the easiest filled pasta shapes to make. Using a large sharp knife, cut the rolled out pasta into strips about 4 in (10 cm) wide. Place heaped teaspoonfuls of the filling mixture at intervals of about 2 in (5 cm) down the middle. Slightly moisten the edges of the pasta with your fingertips before folding them over and sealing them. Use a wheel cutter to cut between the stuffing. Run it along the sealed edges to give them a decorative, fluted edge as well.

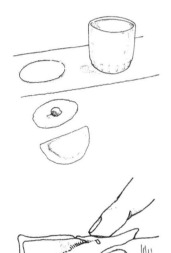

For half-moon shaped ravioli: use a glass or biscuit cutter to cut the rolled out pasta into circular shapes. Place a teaspoonful of the filling at the center, moisten the edges of the pasta with your fingertips and fold it over. Pinch the edges together with your fingers until they are well sealed. For fluted edges, run round each shape with the pastry cutter.

For tortellini: use a glass or biscuit cutter to cut the rolled out pasta into circular shapes. Place ½ teaspoonful of the filling mixture in the middle of each round. Moisten the edges of the pasta with your fingertips and fold the pasta over. Pick the tortellino up and twist it around your index finger until the edges meet. Pinch them together with your fingers and seal them.

For tortelloni: as above, but using a larger glass or a small bowl 3½ in (8–9 cm) in diameter and 1 teaspoonful of the filling mixture.

For cappelletti: using a large sharp knife, cut the rolled out pasta into strips about 2 in (5 cm) wide. Cut each strip into 2 in (5 cm) squares. Place ½ teaspoonfuls of the filling mixture in the center of each. Fold the square diagonally in half to form a triangle. Moisten the edges slightly with your fingertips and seal them together. Pick up the triangle by one corner of its folded over side. Take the other folded over corner and wrap it around your index finger. Pinch the edges together to seal the pasta.

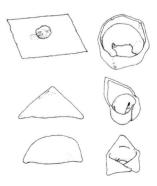

Index